OCEANS AT HOME

Maritime and Domestic Fictions in Nineteenth-Century American Women's Writing

MELISSA GNIADEK

UNIVERSITY OF MASSACHUSETTS PRESS
Amherst and Boston

Printed in the United States of America

ISBN 978-1-62534-572-1 (paper); 573-8 (hardcover)

Designed by Deste Roosa
Set in Univers and Chaparral Pro
Printed and bound by Books International, Inc.

Cover design by Frank Gutbrod
Cover art by K. J. Pargeter/Freepik.com.

Library of Congress Cataloging-in-Publication Data
Names: Gniadek, Melissa, author.
Title: Oceans at home : maritime and domestic fictions in nineteenth-century American women's writing / Melissa Gniadek.
Description: Amherst : University of Massachusetts Press, [2021] | Includes bibliographical references and index.
Identifiers: LCCN 2020053330 (print) | LCCN 2020053331 (ebook) | ISBN 9781625345721 (paperback) | ISBN 9781625345738 (hardcover) | ISBN 9781613768280 (ebook) | ISBN 9781613768297 (ebook)
Subjects: LCSH: Sea in literature. | American fiction—Women authors—History and criticism. | American fiction—19th century—History and criticism. | Domestic fiction, American—History and criticism. | Women and literature—United States—History—19th century.
Classification: LCC PS374.S4 G65 2021 (print) | LCC PS374.S4 (ebook) | DDC 813.009/32162—dc23
LC record available at https://lccn.loc.gov/2020053330
LC ebook record available at https://lccn.loc.gov/2020053331

British Library Cataloguing-in-Publication Data
A catalog record for this book is available from the British Library.

OCEANS AT HOME

Contents

vii *Preface and Acknowledgments*

1 INTRODUCTION
Terraqueous America

19 **PART I**
Lydia Maria Child's Oceanic Pedagogies

21 CHAPTER ONE
Pacific Voices in the *Juvenile Miscellany*

49 CHAPTER TWO
Mary Howard's Mark

75 **PART II**
Continental Territories, Oceanic Plots, and Interior Selves

77 CHAPTER THREE
"Doubting, dreading, fretful guest"
Elizabeth Craw's Diary and Transoceanic Anxiety

100 CHAPTER FOUR
"Outre-mer adventures"
Caroline Kirkland's Frontier and the Maritime World

119 **PART III**
Coastal Gothic and Archipelagic Relations

121 CHAPTER FIVE
"Inwreathed in sand and shells"
Harriet Beecher Stowe's Coastal Gothic

144 CHAPTER SIX
Elizabeth Stoddard and Harriet Prescott Spofford
Amphibious Style and Archipelagic Forms

165 CODA

171 *Notes*

203 *Index*

Preface and Acknowledgments

This book began to take its current form in the summer of 2011, when I picked up one of the American Antiquarian Society's copies of the chapbook *The Little, but Affecting History of Mary Howard* and marveled at the worlds compressed into its small size. It is not unusual for nineteenth-century children's chapbooks to roam across genres or to piece together components of familiar plots into something new(ish). Even so, finding elements of the traditional English ballad–turned–children's tale "The Children in the Wood" together with references to such historical events as the burning of the *Boyd* in New Zealand's Whangaroa Harbor in 1809, all in a brief story about a little tattooed girl, surprised me. How did New Zealand histories make their way into this chapbook printed in New Hampshire in 1836? What might we learn about U.S. literary and cultural engagement with the Pacific—today often associated with immensity, masculinist whale chases, and militarization—by thinking about some of the small, intimate ways that information about the oceanic region circulated in the nineteenth century? How might such an approach help us decontinentalize our vision of the nineteenth-century United States, destabilizing the familiar binary between land and sea as mutually reinforcing yet separate spaces of empire, encounter, and dispossession?

In fact, these questions had been with me long before I picked up that chapbook. Years earlier I had spent time in archives in New Zealand, encountering transpacific histories of empire and settler colonialism that brought Māori, British, and sometimes American or French sailors together on beaches, along coastlines, on ships. I visited many of those sites, looking out over the harbor where the *Boyd* burned and standing on the windblown cliff overlooking the beach where a British woman, Elizabeth Guard, was reportedly captured by Māori and eventually rescued in the first deployment of British troops on New Zealand soil. Guard's story circulated in print, as did others that resonated with concerns about captivity, marking, and interracial relationships. Such stories sometimes made their way through the British empire to the United States, where they provided a lens through which to refract events closer to home. These narratives intersected with the fragile myths of possession and belonging structuring U.S. society, then as now.

In the years since I stood on those beaches and cliffs, American literary studies has become ever more transnational in its scope, acknowledging Atlantic, hemispheric, and, increasingly, Pacific circulations of texts, materials, peoples, and influences. Concomitant with the rise of transnational subject matter has been the introduction of a range of conceptual frameworks to help us attend to these circulations and the perspectives they entail. Paul Gilroy's "Black Atlantic," Epeli Hau'ofa's "sea of islands," and Greg Dening's "beach," for example, have been supplemented and recast through focus on the oceanic and the archipelagic.[1] Hester Blum has encouraged us to think about the "view from the masthead," recognizing the intersection of labor and imagination in the writing of sailors.[2] More recently, Melody Jue has asked us to imagine the conceptual possibilities of encountering media theory underwater, while Tiffany Lethabo King has positioned us offshore to slow or shoal the movement of white settler colonial studies through the intersection of Black and native studies often associated with the mobility of the sea and the supposed fixity of land, respectively.[3] Each of these conceptual orientations offers a different perspective on relationships between water and land—looking toward the horizon from above a ship, looking toward the surface from below, swirling in the sands of a space both watery and landed—and on associated literary and critical traditions.

Oceans at Home looks at the oceanic from the space of the nineteenth-century American home. It takes up a particular vision of "home" through the perspective of white, middle-class femininity, domesticity, and sentiment to consider how the home as a physical and textual space was reconfigured in the 1800s through encounters with the oceanic. In the process, it reveals that distant places such as the Pacific were used to highlight the instability of the home, supplementing more proximal encounters with race, indigeneity, property, and risk to highlight the always already shaky terrain on which nineteenth-century notions of domesticity were constructed. In the texts that I read in this book, the Pacific is not a faraway place on which to displace domestic concerns or project fantasies. Instead, it shows up in chapbooks and diaries, in characters and plotlines, in houses, on beaches, and in mudholes, providing writers with a way to articulate the uncertainties of the domestic—home and nation—while leveraging the popularity of tales of oceanic travel and adventure. Across chapters that focus on the domestic space of childhood reading and education; that most stereotypical of nineteenth-century evolving home spaces, "the West"; and haunted family histories of the New England coast, I trace a female-authored engagement with oceanic spaces that both brings the oceans home and alerts us to less masculinist histories of global empire and settler colonialism than we usually recognize. This is what I felt when I held *The Little, but Affecting History of Mary Howard* in my hand: the small, intimate, material ways in which the Pacific and oceanic circulations were impressed on nineteenth-century home life and the alternative perspectives available to us today if we recognize them.

As will already be clear, this book has evolved over many years and moved through different spaces. Its debts (and mine) are many. Its true origins are in Massachusetts, where my devotion to thinking and writing about the U.S. nineteenth century was established early and nurtured and challenged often. Terry Flynn and Neal Dolan deserve special thanks for this long-ago (and yet miraculously ongoing) support and encouragement.

A Fulbright Graduate Award brought me to Aotearoa-New Zealand for a year, and a University of Auckland Fulbright Grant enabled me to stay for a second year, giving me precious time to learn about New Zealand and Pacific history and literature in the classroom and also to learn through wandering, driving, tramping, reading, and writing. I am eternally grateful to Fulbright New Zealand and to the University of Auckland's Alex Calder, whose support for my interests made this possible. Other members of the Auckland faculty at that time, including Albert Wendt, expanded my worldview tremendously. Devin Castendyk was a co-adventurer on some of my research rambles during this time and facilitated my thinking about water, land, and their intersections; the crew at Cowie Street provided a welcome home far from home.

When I moved to the inland seas of Upstate New York's Finger Lakes, I stood on the shore of Cayuga Lake, lamenting the fact that it was most certainly not the Pacific Ocean. But I soon made a new home above Cayuga's waters. Shirley Samuels provided and continues to provide unparalleled mentorship. She also introduced me to the depths of nineteenth-century U.S. women's writing. Eric Cheyfitz and Mary Pat Brady taught me so much and guided me through a project whose insights seep into this book and everything that I do. Elizabeth DeLoughrey and the members of her graduate course, Islands of Globalization, led me to think about how my interest in the Pacific and in island imaginaries might intersect with my work on American literature in new and unforeseen ways. A trip to Hawaii as part of that course brought me back to the Pacific at a crucial time and served as a reminder that while the Pacific is large, if you're lucky it can also be very small.

At Cornell University, my graduate school colleagues kept me going through vibrant communities of reading, writing, and friendship that have evolved and continue into the present. The members of the Nineteenth-Century Americanist Reading Group (better known as ARG) are proof that academic work can be both rigorous and fun. Alex W. Black, Jillian Spivey Caddell, Brigitte Fielder, Toni Wall Jaudon, and Jonathan Senchyne especially have helped me navigate the daily ups and downs of academic life. A very special thanks to Jill for keeping me writing and for her thoughtful feedback, again and again, and to Jon for always being there with advice and support. Cornell's Historians Are Writers! (HAW!) group has long helped me remember why I write in the first place. And without Karen Bourrier, there would not have been a Global Nineteenth-Century Day.

I could not have asked for a more perfect place to land after Cornell than Rice University and Houston, Texas, more generally. It immediately felt like home, and this book really got under way there. Cary Wolfe, Judith Roof, and the entire Rice English Department offered a supportive environment. Caroline Levander provided a community of Americanists and a model of mentorship that changed the way I envision the possibilities of thinking together. Abby Goode, AnaMaria Seglie Clawson, and Karen Rosenthall are simply the best; they each provided invaluable feedback on aspects of this book. Joe Carson and Rachel Conrad Bracken also offered welcome momentum. My thanks to the Rice undergraduate students who brought my attention to Elizabeth Craw's diary and to the members of my 2012 graduate course, Sea and Land: Unsettling Narratives of Travel and Settlement, who helped me wrestle with early iterations of some of the ideas in this book. I had the good fortune to meet Donna Beth Ellard while at Rice. Her friendship and our ongoing conversations are sustaining. For additional academic comradery and support while we were all in Texas, I thank Kelly Bezio, Tim Cassedy, Lucia Hodgson, Jason Payton, Dan Walden, and Kelly Wisecup.

I stumbled into a wonderful community again when I moved to the University of Toronto, where I discovered a living, breathing definition of collegiality. Thanks especially to Liza Blake, Jacob Gallagher-Ross, Anjuli Raza Kolb, Terry Robinson, Avery Slater, Anna Thomas, and Danny Wright for all kinds of encouragement, advice, and good cheer and to Holger Syme, Dan White, and Alexandra Gillespie for their support and leadership. Thom Dancer, Kara Gaston, Audrey Walton, Kat Williams, and the broader University of Toronto English community provide a much appreciated generous and welcoming environment.

I had the opportunity to present versions of ideas in this book at meetings of the Society of Early Americanists Conference and the Society for the Study of American Women Writers Conference, and at a workshop at University College London made possible by a University of Toronto–University College London Joint Research Projects and Exchange Activities Grant. In London (and Ithaca, Toronto, and Bordeaux), thanks especially to Xine Yao and Hilary Emmett. I am also grateful to Michael Collins, Hannah Murray, Nicholas Spengler, and David Stirrup, as well as Sarah Collier, Chelsea Latremouille, and Stephanie Redekop for their generosity and collegiality at the London workshop. Others who have provided opportunities to share work, offered advice or feedback on everything from nascent ideas to specific details, and inspired me through their own work and goodwill include Hester Blum, Colin Dewey, Sarah Ellenzweig, Mary Eyring, Elizabeth Fenton, Desirée Henderson, Jeffrey Insko, Michael Taylor, Arielle Zibrak, and many additional, helpful colleagues. I am grateful to everyone.

My deep thanks to Brian Halley at the University of Massachusetts Press for his editorial guidance and his patience, to Nancy Raynor for her copyediting expertise, and to the readers for the press for their feedback and generous suggestions. An early version of chapter 2 appeared as "*Mary Howard*'s Mark: Children's Literature and the Scales of Reading the Pacific," *Early American Literature*, 50, no. 3 (Fall 2015): 797–826. A version of chapter 4 appeared as "'Outre-mer adventures': Caroline Kirkland's *A New Home, Who'll Follow?* and the Maritime World," *Legacy: A Journal of American Women Writers* 32, no. 2 (Winter 2015): 196–213. I am grateful to the readers who provided feedback on those essays for the journals and to the University of North Carolina Press and the University of Nebraska Press, respectively, for permission to reproduce this material.

Friends and family members have lived with this project for years by living with me, and I am grateful to them as well. Thanks to Rehana Gubin, Miranda Hochberg (my "oldest" friend), and Beth Marino for their encouragement, friendship, and occasional, necessary tough love. The entire cast of *Trivial* has kept me laughing for years. The fact that I'm not better at trivia is not their fault. Dan Chenoweth has provided everything from welcome cowriting time and computer assistance to steady support, wise council, and great title suggestions. Adam Lyons has helped with the diversions that are actually the foundation of all good things, from good food to projects large and small, to road trips and adventures. I'm very lucky to have all of these people in my life. Thanks also to Ellis for the walks that keep things in perspective.

Finally, I am lucky to have a large and wonderful extended family who have rooted me in place while allowing me to wander. I never take that for granted. A very special, extra-large thank-you to my parents, Robert and Elizabeth, and to my siblings, Kimberly and Gregory. They have been tremendously supportive, despite the long hours and challenges that accompany researching and writing a book. My parents have indulged and enabled my academic interests in every way possible, and my siblings are always there for me. This book is for them.

OCEANS AT HOME

INTRODUCTION
Terraqueous America

In Caroline Kirkland's *A New Home, Who'll Follow? Or, Glimpses of Western Life* (1839), Mary Clavers takes shelter from a rainstorm in a stranger's house on the Michigan frontier. Intrigued by her hostess Mrs. Beckworth's countenance and convinced that "the pensive matron had a story," Mrs. Clavers later asks Mr. Beckworth to relate the details of his wife's past. The story Mr. Beckworth tells is a story of the sea, a tale that spans three chapters in the middle of a book about settling the U.S. West. The sea takes over the narrative through a story of oceanic travel and speculation that moves around the globe before ending back "in the depths of Michigan."[1] Mrs. Beckworth had not herself gone to sea, but her story and her new frontier home are constituted by encounters with oceanic spaces. Despite Mrs. Beckworth's current stability and apparent happiness, Kirkland makes clear that the path to stability was not direct. She also notes that the risks of both oceanic and terrestrial ventures are significant—what's more, they are intertwined. Using the romance and speculation of the sea voyage to highlight the tenuous, fictional stability and romance of new western homes, Kirkland posits a vision of domesticity and settlement that is terraqueous. She shows that terrestrial homes are linked to maritime industry and risk, using maritime plots and imagery to emphasize that the promise of western settlement is unstable and based on a watery, "undulating surface."[2]

This is a book about how authors like Kirkland wrote about the sea and global circulation in nineteenth-century America. Kirkland is an unlikely starting point for a book about oceanic imaginaries. When the popular antebellum magazine writer and editor is discussed at all, it is often in relation to the "pioneer realism" and wit of *A New Home, Who'll Follow?*, which Edgar Allan Poe praised for providing readers with an honest, fresh "acquaintance with the *home* and home-life of the backwoodsman."[3] Kirkland is associated with her sketches of the West and her magazine pieces on a variety of topics written for periodicals like *Godey's Ladies Book*. But as *Oceans at Home* reveals, even Kirkland drew on the contemporary popularity of maritime stories, doing so to depict the complexities of home. This book reads texts by Kirkland as well as other popular female authors such as Lydia Maria Child, Harriet Beecher Stowe, Elizabeth Stoddard, and Harriet Prescott Spofford, writers who are often associated with versions of nineteenth-century domesticity and with cultural critique. It shows how they used maritime stories, culture, and associated histories of global circulation to reflect domestic concerns, advance social commentary, and, in the case of unpublished diarist Elizabeth Craw, to confront personal experiences with settler colonial violence and uncertainty.

We usually associate authors such as Herman Melville with the deployment of oceanic stories and space to advance social commentary in nineteenth-century U.S. literature. Using island topographies in *Typee* and *Omoo* or shipboard spaces in *Moby-Dick* and *Benito Cereno*, Melville famously addressed cultural difference, imperialism, histories of racial violence, labor, and sexuality.[4] Texts by Melville and James Fenimore Cooper, whose sea novels combined history and adventure to foster what was essentially a new genre in the first half of the nineteenth century, have often dominated discussion of the period's U.S. maritime imaginaries for obvious reasons. These authors wrote sweeping epics of the sea. They wrote long books about oceanic and island adventures. And they wrote a lot of them. Their novels have served as reminders that the sea was always another frontier in the U.S. cultural imagination, one that existed in tandem with the terrestrial frontier so often the basis of accounts of U.S. history. As Jason Berger has argued, novels by Melville and Cooper reveal how antebellum maritime narratives served as fantasies with political import in a period of tremendous change.[5] They are not only stories of escape and exploration but also texts that register economic, cultural, and legal shifts and anxieties within the nineteenth-century United States.

The oceanic turn of the last decades developed, in part, to combat what Margaret Cohen calls our "hydrophasia."[6] Attention to labor at sea, to maritime knowledge and "craft," and to the physical and environmental conditions of oceans has reminded us that, in Hester Blum's words, "the sea is not a metaphor," even as we have recognized how maritime narratives provided ways to negotiate changes within nineteenth-century life, as Berger argues.[7] Yet this focus on maritime experience, knowledge, or fantasy has often meant that writing by women is bracketed or absent from discussion because very few women were mariners. When we think about women and the oceanic, we might think of tales of cross-dressing female sailors, the records left by sea captain's wives or missionary wives, or exceptional stories like that of Juana Maria, the Indigenous woman who lived alone on an island off the coast of California in the first half of the nineteenth century. Returning to land with some of the lessons of the oceanic turn in mind, however, allows us to see how even female authors who did not take long trips into the Pacific or spend time on distant islands drew on the maritime world and its circulations of goods and peoples. They did so in ways that sometimes engage metaphor or abstract notions of the sublime but that also register the materiality of the oceanic world and the marks left by its circulations.

Countering a vision of maritime literature that is centered exclusively in oceanic spaces and often focused on male-authored texts, *Oceans at Home* takes seriously details such as the Beckworths' story of global voyaging, embedded in a travelogue about the Michigan frontier. Doing so reveals a use of the oceanic that is quieter than we are used to and whose scale is relatively small. But this focus nevertheless points to the outsized place of sea stories in nineteenth-century America, as well as how female authors who did not themselves labor at sea borrowed and recirculated popular maritime narratives and histories of contact that resulted from oceanic travel to expose fractures in home life. Within children's literature, a personal diary, travelogues, and female bildungsromane, the authors that I read in *Oceans at Home* draw on the oceanic world in ways that reconfigure U.S. geographies of empire and settler colonialism from the space of the continental and domestic. It is precisely because women did not often go to sea as sailors that their writings deploying aspects of the oceanic provide us with new ways to think about terrestrial spaces and relationships between terrestrial spaces and between water and land. Rather than the absence of female voices in the maritime world being a limitation, the profusion of those voices that engage with oceanic realms from home opens up new possibilities.

Such conceptual reorientations are aligned with those recently labeled "archipelagic." To view the Americas as archipelagic is to emphasize "island-ocean-continent relations which have exceeded US-Americanism and have been affiliated with and indeed constitutive of competing notions of the Americas since at least 1492," as Brian Russell Roberts and Michelle Ann Stephens put it.[8] This involves recognizing U.S. imperial relationships to island spaces in the Pacific, Caribbean, and elsewhere. But it also involves acknowledging the culturally constructed nature of continental and island spaces, the insular nature of some geographies usually thought of as purely continental, and relationships between water, land, and coastlines that are shifting and multiple rather than fixed. The result can be, as Paul Giles puts it, "a relative obliteration of geographical distance and a problematization of conventional binary oppositions between center and margin, near and far."[9] In *Oceans at*

Home, I focus on an archive of women's writing from the first half of the nineteenth century that stretches outward across oceans and islands but ultimately resides at home, in the continental and the domestic, raising questions about "near and far" and about the structures and narratives that constitute and uphold the nineteenth-century U.S. home in an era of simultaneous settler colonial expansion and maritime voyaging.

My focus on the first half of the nineteenth century centers a period before the railroad made continental travel more viable, before maritime commercial activities like whaling began to wane with the discovery of crude oil reserves and the development of competitors to whale oil, and before the Civil War disrupted the whaling industry.[10] These were decades when maritime activity brought the United States into sustained contact with the Pacific. By the 1820s and 1830s, narratives of whaling voyages and of state-sponsored expeditions in the Pacific and reports of missionary activities in the Pacific were circulating throughout the U.S. and were deeply embedded in the cultural imaginary. Of course, Euro-American engagement with the Pacific had been established decades earlier through such events as Captain James Cook's three Pacific voyages, which stretched from 1768 until his death in the Hawaiian islands in 1779. The islands of the Pacific subsequently became sites of alluring mystery, sensuality, and violence in the popular imagination, tropes that Herman Melville and other writers would engage and solidify. In 1846, Melville's first novel, *Typee: A Peep at Polynesian Life*, loosely based on his own experiences jumping ship in the Marquesas a few years earlier, would draw on these ideas about the Pacific with great success. *Typee* was popular, published in different editions in both America and England in 1846, making Melville—the bearded sailor-author—famous and paving the way for his subsequent Pacific novels. The first four chapters in *Oceans at Home*, however, focus on texts written before Melville first crossed the Atlantic in 1839 or joined the crew of a whaling ship in 1841. This book thus establishes a female prehistory to now canonical, male-authored depictions of the Pacific like Melville's, while arguing for the importance of the Pacific and the oceanic more generally to an archive of female-authored texts concerned with U.S. domestic matters. I bring the Pacific into conversation with the Atlantic world, which has received more attention in American literary studies, but by beginning with a focus on the Pacific, I contribute to efforts to recognize its place in the early American imaginary.[11]

The writers discussed in *Oceans at Home* read compiled histories of distant places like New Zealand that would later inspire such authors as Melville and Edgar Allan Poe, poems by women with familial links to conflicts in the Pacific, and a range of popular oceanic tales. And they drew on these sources to negotiate the construction of home spaces. The stories and stuff of Pacific voyages, from plots inflected by the long absences and repeated returns of whalers to the material goods brought back from such ventures, enabled women writers to negotiate domestic concerns ranging from violence against Indigenous peoples, imperial anxiety, personal grief, and the speculative nature of frontier settlements. They drew on oceanic and island spaces, sea stories, or ideas about places and peoples circulating in the cultural imaginary as a result of oceanic voyaging. Though they did not labor at sea or travel through the Pacific, women writers took up the sea with their pens.

OCEANIC AND DOMESTIC SPHERES

Connections between gender and the oceanic in nineteenth-century America are often framed by the cross-dressing sailor heroines of the Revolutionary and Early National periods on one end and the solitary, islanded figures of Sarah Orne Jewett's *The Country of the Pointed Firs* on the other. One goal of this book is to reconsider some of the nodes of the story of gender and the oceanic in intervening decades, which, as in earlier periods, is largely one of dispossession and violence. Many of the women who traversed maritime spaces in the centuries before abolition of the transatlantic slave trade were enslaved women who were kidnapped and transported across oceans to labor in the Americas and to reproduce more laboring bodies. Jennifer L. Morgan writes that "notwithstanding the predominant images of captive African men, African women and children together made up the majority of those transported to the Americas during the entirety of the transatlantic slave trade." These are stories often lost to the archive of the ocean, requiring what Christina Sharpe calls "wake work" in her discussion of how the wake of a ship conjures other wakes: processes of mourning those whose bodies are now one with the oceans or whose identities, for example, author Phillis Wheatley, became linked to the very slave ships producing those wakes.[12] Increased attention to fictional texts like the anonymously authored *The Woman of Colour* (1808) and to such autobiographical narratives as *The History of Mary Prince* (1831) and *A Narrative of the Life and Travels of Mrs. Nancy Prince* (1850) has highlighted the stories of Black women moving around the Atlantic world in the nineteenth century, when the legacies of earlier histories of violence and dispossession played out. At the same time, in the eighteenth- and nineteenth-century Pacific, female bodies were often at the forefront of

European and American cross-cultural encounters with Pacific communities. Indigenous women appear in travel and exploration narratives as sexualized objects of fantasy, whereas violence enacted against them is obscured. "If women are absent from the European ships that ventured into and across the Pacific," writes Michelle Burnham, "they are everywhere present on shore, and in fact violent conflicts between Atlantic visitors and Pacific Natives are routinely marked by the sexualization of indigenous women's bodies."[13]

As Burnham indicates, the gender divisions of seafaring labor meant that European and American women were not usually at sea themselves during the eighteenth and nineteenth centuries, though there were exceptions. Oceanic travel was an important method of transportation. Captains' wives would sometimes accompany their husbands on voyages. On rare occasions these women might be called on to nurse the ill or even to navigate in extreme circumstances, but for the most part they would be confined to their cabin or at least limited in their shipboard movements.[14] Women traveled as missionaries and missionaries' wives, spending years in Hawai'i, New Zealand, and other places with an active missionary presence and writing about their experiences.[15] They were sometimes captives caught up in imperial conflict and cross-cultural confusion, even as they were occasionally agents in imperial ventures themselves.[16]

In general, however, it was common for women to stay home and to keep families and households afloat during the long absences of male family members. This division was so fixed that when transcendentalist philosopher Margaret Fuller needed to imagine what women might do if only they were given the opportunity, she turned to the sea. In her controversial manifesto *Woman in the Nineteenth Century* (1845), Fuller imagines being asked what "offices" women may fill; she replies, "Any. I do not care what case you put; let them be sea-captains, if you will. I do not doubt there are women well fitted for such an office." Advocating for "a much greater range of occupation" for women and greater freedom for them more generally, Fuller turns to a figure that embodies authority, skill, and mobility.[17] This has rhetorical effect precisely because a female sea captain would have been practically unheard of. Fuller's imagined female sea captain did have precedent in early accounts of female pirates, including Anne Bonny and Mary Read, that no doubt helped inspire popular ballads and stories about women who went to sea.[18] And there were eighteenth- and nineteenth-century accounts of British and American women who cross-dressed to travel or work on ships. Supposedly on vessels in disguise, these women subverted the social regulations that would have prevented them from being at sea at all or confined them to certain spaces and roles. Such accounts may have inspired popular, fictional narratives about cross-dressing female sailors and soldiers, including the three pamphlets published by Boston printer Nathaniel Coverly Jr. that were gathered together under the title *The Female Marine* in 1816.[19] *The Female Marine*, like the pamphlets that comprised it, sold exceptionally well and inspired other stories about cross-dressing sailors and soldiers in the first decades of the nineteenth century, stories whose recovery has added complexity to our understanding of the Atlantic world and to historical ideas about gender and sexuality.[20]

Certainly, some women went to sea, and certainly, there are stories, fictional and factual, about women's mobility, but *Oceans at Home* shows that we can find the oceanic not only in the exceptional when it comes to women's writing in the American nineteenth century—not only in the experiences of the women who did write about time spent at sea or in fiction about women at sea—but also, notably, in the quotidian. Through its focus on the oceanic world within texts set in continental spaces or associated with such domestic activities as childhood reading, *Oceans at Home* participates in ongoing conversations about the idea and space of the domestic in the nineteenth century. It also engages with scholarship complicating the sentimental genre often associated with the domestic and with separate spheres discourses in nineteenth-century America. A number of historians have shown that the changes brought about by the market revolution of the first half of the nineteenth century resulted in the separation of work and home into male and female realms. Home and the domestic became associated with women in a manner reinforced by popular domestic manuals, mothers' books, and sentimental novels, whereas male labor occurred outside the home. In many ways, Fuller's invocation of the sea captain to critique the limitations placed on nineteenth-century women seems to rely on these distinctions, even as she famously deconstructed the boundaries of masculinity and femininity, writing: "Male and female represent the two sides of the great radical dualism. But, in fact, they are perpetually passing into one another. Fluid hardens to solid, solid rushes to fluid. There is no wholly masculine man, no purely feminine woman."[21] Indeed, nearly as soon as divisions between masculine and feminine spheres were established within scholarship on this period, literary and cultural studies scholars and historians challenged them, noting that the domestic world was never cut off from other realms, that domesticity itself is inextricable from the marketplace, and that male writers, too, were concerned with the sentimental and with domesticity. In other words, we recognize that the notion of "separate spheres"—of a male public realm and a female private realm—is far too simplistic to account for the complexities of both lived experience and historical, cultural production.[22]

While the maritime world might seem an exception to these complications because ships were primarily male spaces, these divisions, too, have been shown to break down. Anita Duneer, for example, has argued for the need to examine the language of domesticity at sea in order to destabilize separate spheres discourses, while Lisa Norling has illuminated various ways in which the sea shaped life onshore for women left behind by seafaring husbands, including influencing the very language they used. Nantucket women did not go to sea or hunt whales themselves, but Norling shows that the world of the whale fishery inflected their language and their worldview.[23] And, of course, the maritime world shaped experiences of waiting, grief, and hardship for those left behind, from Nantucket captains' wives to the Indigenous women who the Pequot Methodist minister William Apess writes are "left alone, children half-starved," in part "because their most sensible and active men are absent at sea."[24] These details find their way into female-authored texts, from personal letters and diaries to narratives such as Harriet Jacobs's *Incidents in the Life of a Slave Girl*, in which Linda Brent's brother, William, and son, Benny, ship out on whaling voyages to support themselves, disappearing from and later reentering the narrative.

The maritime world also provided opportunities for certain types of activism associated with the domestic. Scholars including Duneer and Norling have pointed to antebellum calls for seamen's reform and aid as one place where issues of gender, sentimental traditions, domesticity, and the maritime world intersect. Such well-known writers as Lydia Huntley Sigourney and Sarah Josepha Hale, both of whom were "major architects of the culture of domesticity and active in the direct application of domestic ideals to the New England maritime context," in Norling's words, involved themselves in efforts to aid (even, we might say, to domesticate) sailors whose prolonged absence from home communities and supposedly rowdy behavior during time spent in port cities made them subjects for what amounted to civilizing missions.[25] This aid also arose to help sailors and their families navigate the risks of the maritime world, where profits could be immense for some but where many laborers were poorly paid, left disabled by dangerous work, or killed while at sea, as Mary Eyring points out. In her book *Captains of Charity*, Eyring explores the relationship of "charity to the profits and poverty produced by oceanic experience," focusing her analysis on Atlantic seaports where the wealth and poverty of the maritime world coexisted and on writers such as Sarah Josepha Hale and others whose literary careers were bound up in charitable activity that emerged partly in relation to nautical life and enterprises.[26]

Although writers like Sigourney and Hale wrote about the sea, wrote for sailors, or engaged in work directly related to seamen's reform and charity, the authors and texts appearing in *Oceans at Home* generally have more indirect connections to the maritime world. Oceanic realms sometimes appear rather obliquely in the texts discussed here. Attending to these oblique references emphasizes how these oceanic realms and ideas about them and their inhabitants became so deeply embedded in U.S. culture that they appear in unexpected places—a small chapbook printed in New Hampshire as well as *Moby-Dick*, the Michigan frontier as well as the Eastern Seaboard—where they are put to work for unexpected ends. These are not texts that take on issues such as seamen's aid. Instead, they use elements of the maritime world and oceanic circulations to explore some of the very foundations of U.S. domestic life. Amy Kaplan's canonical essay "Manifest Domesticity" foregrounds related interactions between the foreign and the domestic. Kaplan argues that "part of the cultural work of domesticity might be to unite men and women in a national domain and to generate notions of the foreign against which the nation can be imagined as home."[27] In drawing attention to how the "development of domestic discourse in America is contemporaneous with the discourse of Manifest Destiny," Kaplan both highlighted the centrality of women to empire in this period and advanced the work of breaking down the separate spheres model as she demonstrated the interconnections between imperialism abroad and empire at home.[28] Related ideas have emerged in the work of other scholars attentive to questions of gender, intimacy, domesticity, and empire in global contexts, including Anne McClintock, Ann Laura Stoler, and Lisa Lowe.[29] In different ways, such scholars have shown how race, class, gender, sentiment, affect, and domesticity construct and resist imperial control. In different ways they demonstrate that the domestic, the intimate, and the home and its goods were always already constituted by the foreign and involved in the domestication of the foreign.

Oceans at Home builds on such work as it tells a story about textual circulations that bring the oceanic world into the United States in ways that expose the instabilities of national and home life. These texts do not unite individuals in a national narrative, as Robin Miskolcze argues of figures of women within antebellum sea narratives.[30] Instead, they turn outward to expose fractures within that home, collapsing distances between "near and far" in the process. Children were at the heart of nineteenth-century sentimental domesticity and its efforts to construct the nation, as many have argued, but Lydia Maria Child drew on stories about Pacific Islanders and travel in the Pacific to craft stories for children that critique and complicate U.S. settler colonial violence. Emotions can bind people together across time and space, but the diary of Elizabeth Craw, a woman who traveled from Ohio to Texas and back, shows that they can also reveal how global empires are structured by fracturing anxiety. Maritime voyages and economies can provide the capital that builds new homes, but Caroline Kirkland shows how risky such ventures can be. And Harriet Beecher Stowe, Harriet Prescott Spofford, and Elizabeth Stoddard craft terraqueous literary landscapes, genres, and forms that reflect the violent global circulations that construct homes as they critique nineteenth-century gender restrictions.

Underlying my conception of the home here are nineteenth-century ideas of domesticity that emerge in household manuals and mothers' books, as well as the settler colonial context in which North American settler spaces were constructed as homes for some while displacing others in the nineteenth century. The authors that I discuss were writing during decades when movement into and around the Pacific coincided with ongoing appropriation of Indigenous territory to construct settler homes. My readings of the dynamic relationships between Pacific and continental spaces draw attention to the fact that the Pacific is the oceanic space that connects the major settler colonial nations or dominions of the nineteenth century. If settler colonialism is differentiated from other forms of imperial relationships by the long-term, permanent occupation and use of land already belonging to others, primary settler colonial spaces of the early nineteenth century include the United States as well as Canada, Australia, and New Zealand. As Iyko Day notes, the spread of whiteness and related ideas of liberal freedom in such nations bordering the Pacific in the nineteenth century is tied to the settler colonial work of dispossession through the construction and manipulation of racialization.[31] If we think about the Pacific as increasingly bordered by a rim of white settler nations and dominions in the nineteenth century, how might we think about constructions that uphold or challenge processes of settler colonialism as being forged in or traveling across the space of the Pacific? How might we think about the islands of the Pacific in relation to U.S. settler colonialism well before the 1898 annexation of Hawai'i once thought of as a beginning of U.S. national presence in the Pacific? And how might attention to the Pacific revise our understanding of the Atlantic world and continental space in the same period? While these might seem to be questions better suited to an archive different from one comprised of texts that barely travel outside continental North America, written by middle-class, white women, these texts contain the traces of such issues within them, in part through the circulation and recirculation of print material and ideas about the circulation of bodies and objects. Recognizing this is critical to reconceptualizing representations of the oceanic world within female-authored texts.

PRINT NETWORKS

In recent years we have come to view antebellum reading and writing practices as inseparable from practices of circulation, reprinting, and piracy. Thanks in part to digitization projects and computational approaches to archives, it is easier than ever to recognize the multiple, ever-shifting networks that constituted antebellum print culture, allowing us to decenter overtly literary forms such as the novel and to recognize the dynamism of what Meredith McGill calls the antebellum "culture of reprinting."[32] Decentralized networks of newspapers and periodicals recirculated texts across time and space, sometimes with authorial attribution and often without. The lack of international copyright law facilitated this circulation and reprinting, from unauthorized reprints of books to newspaper articles, and fueled everyday practices that made "circulation . . . a kind of textual repetition with a difference," in Ryan Cordell's words.[33] Private encounters with printed material produced commonplace books or scrapbooks that further reframed public print culture networks for more private purposes.[34]

This context of antebellum print circulation is crucial to the readings within *Oceans at Home* because many of the authors I discuss encountered the oceans primarily through circulated and recirculated print material. In this sense, authors' reading and writing practices are built on the very types of circulation frequently thematized and represented within their writing, constructing transoceanic print networks that demonstrate the imbrication of the local and the global. Caroline Wigginton has recently argued that women's "relational publication"—circulating texts, performance, and objects—was "a counterpoise to republican print" in the early American period. She draws on the intimacy of the concept of the "neighborhood" in early America, showing how "relational publication drew on that intimacy . . . to revise and reimagine the neighborhood" in a way that might have been "geographically localized, but . . . also might have been diffuse, linked in terms of embodied and textual circulation." For Wigginton the circulations of relational publication reveal "bonds [that] were often personal but also transnational."[35] The texts in *Oceans at Home* grow out of authorial engagement with the established print networks of the nineteenth century, but they nevertheless often link the intimate and the local to the transnational and transoceanic in a way that makes clear the ongoing legacies of the colonial encounters that Wigginton describes and that do so in ways that make gender central to the stories that they tell. In the process, they offer a counterpoise to male-authored texts about the oceanic.

Lydia Maria Child, for example, read and repurposed travel narratives and informational texts about the Pacific to craft educational stories for her child readers. These stories arguably contribute to the construction of somewhat coherent imagined communities of child readers, but they also disrupt expectations about what it is to be a "good girl" and related pedagogical projects of nation formation that often rely on the construction of racial difference and ideas about racial purity. Elizabeth Craw wrote a poem in her diary of travel from Ohio to Texas that emerged out of a decades-earlier conflict in the Pacific, crafting a kind of emotional intimacy across time and space that highlights the centrality of anxiety to imperial and settler colonial projects alike. Caroline Kirkland drew on popular plots of oceanic voyaging to describe the uncertainties of settling the western frontier. Harriet Beecher Stowe, Elizabeth Stoddard, and Harriet Prescott Spofford harnessed the materials and marks described within these earlier texts, from pearls and shells to amber and tattoos, to unsettle relationships between characters, families, and even water and land in ways that make oceanic relations generic, stylistic, and formal concerns. Over the course of chapters about these authors and their texts, I move from discussing textual circulation and reprinting in fairly concrete terms (indeed, Child reprints entire passages from George Lillie Craik's *The New Zealanders* in the pages of the *Juvenile Miscellany*) to more abstract notions of circulation, showing how global movements of peoples, goods, and genres become textual circulations within an archive of women's writing. This book's initial geographic orientation toward the Pacific, rather than primarily toward such regions as the Atlantic or the Caribbean that have received significant attention in transnational, oceanic scholarship, further highlights underexplored networks of circulation. The book begins by showing how the Pacific materialized in the Atlantic coastal centers of publishing that we might expect in the nineteenth century but also highlights other geographies, including New Hampshire, Michigan, and the territory that would become Texas. The book's final chapters turn to the more familiar space of the Atlantic world, but do so with the Pacific in mind so as to recast readings of the texts discussed there, theorizing a coastal gothic always informed by global circulations.

Oceans at Home is divided into three parts. The first, "Lydia Maria Child's Oceanic Pedagogies," shows that prolific and popular writer, editor, and reformer Child was reading such texts as George Lillie Craik's *The New Zealanders* and incorporating material from the sources into her children's fiction. As is well established, Herman Melville and other writers drew on such texts, and writers such as Cooper and Melville used ideas about particular Māori men to craft some of their characters. Child incorporated some of the same source material and Pacific figures in her children's stories. Paying attention to how she deploys this material can, as noted in this part's two chapters, invigorate our understanding of how information about the Pacific circulated in the first half of the nineteenth century and shed light on contemporary ideas about indigeneity in the Pacific as they were deployed to both shape and entertain young minds.

The first chapter, "Pacific Voices in the *Juvenile Miscellany*," discusses how Child imports ideas about language, writing, and communication from her Pacific source material into the juvenile periodical that she edited, interweaving Indigenous Pacific characters into her lessons for children. The chapter charts a longer history of missionary tracts about the Pacific and their influence on children's literature, as well as the *Juvenile Miscellany*'s general interest in oceans. It then turns to questions of signification, textuality, and dialogue that show Child engaging global indigeneity and settler colonial violence while teaching her child readers fundamental lessons about kindness and care that we might associate with early nineteenth-century pedagogies. The second chapter, "Mary Howard's Mark," builds on this material to read Child's most sustained use of New Zealand in her children's fiction within the story "Mary Howard," which appeared in *The Little Girl's Own Book* (1831). Unraveling the web of influences within this story and exploring how "Mary Howard" itself traveled as it was reprinted in rural New Hampshire in abridged form as a tiny chapbook, this chapter illuminates how Child used familiar genres such as the female captivity narrative in ways that destabilize our notions of the moral lessons often associated with children's literature. Together, the chapters in this first part set the stage for the book's exploration of female authors' engagements with oceanic realms, and specifically the Pacific, and the implications of those engagements for home spaces, by foregrounding the culturally important but still understudied category of children's literature. These chapters explore how the nineteenth-century's "culture of reprinting" brought Pacific spaces and peoples into homes and into small hands, depicting intersections between settler colonial violence, racialization, and gender in the process.[36]

The book's second part, "Continental Territories, Oceanic Plots, and Interior Selves," turns from Child's use of the Pacific in her children's fiction to texts emerging from U.S. continental expansion into Texas and Michigan. Thus, this part moves from the intimate sphere of child readers and pedagogy to the broader sphere of evolving national space. Yet these chapters still navigate forms of intimacy as they show how two different texts negotiate the personally felt uncertainties and risks of settling continental territory through recourse to oceanic events and plots. Chapter 3, "'Doubting, dreading, fretful guest': Elizabeth Craw's Diary and Transoceanic Anxiety," reads Craw's record of her trip from Ohio to Texas in 1835. It explores how her diary links personal and political anxieties grounded in contemporary tensions in the space that would become Texas to another woman's anxieties about her brother's fate as a result of imperial ventures in the Pacific. Craw's diary, which is also a kind of commonplace book, allows us to consider another way in which the reprinting and recirculation of texts in general, and of texts emerging from encounters with the Pacific in particular, negotiated the evolution of home spaces and uncertainties about those home spaces, in this case in exceedingly personal and individual ways.

Chapter 4, "'Outre-mer adventures': Caroline Kirkland's Frontier and the Maritime World," is the first in this book to focus on the circulation of popular oceanic plots more generally, along with specific stories and historical figures from the Pacific. Here I build on the discussion of territorial tensions and the recirculation of texts in the previous chapter to show how Kirkland's semiautobiographical, semifictional travelogue *A New Home, Who'll Follow?* uses popular oceanic plots to express concerns about the risks of terrestrial settlement on the Michigan frontier. This seeming paradox underscores the interconnections between maritime and terrestrial spaces and endeavors in the nineteenth century; it also emphasizes the terraqueous properties of particular western spaces, highlighting the contingent nature of ideas about land as property at play in Kirkland's text.

Oceans at Home's various threads, from analysis of reading material for children to consideration of anxieties about property and empire, come together in the fiction discussed in the book's final part, "Coastal Gothic and Archipelagic Relations." Chapter 5, "'Inwreathed in sand and shells': Harriet Beecher Stowe's Coastal Gothic," reads two of Stowe's New England novels, *The Minister's Wooing* (1859) and *The Pearl of Orr's Island: A Story of the Coast of Maine* (1862), highlighting Stowe's use of maritime plots and coastal settings to facilitate critiques of gender restrictions and to suggest the absorption of violence, dispossession, and alterity into the domestic scene through what I call "coastal gothic." Certainly, these are domestic, regional tales that end in happy Christian marriages. But recognizing their unsettling elements positioned at the intersection of land and sea puts them in conversation with the texts discussed in the sixth and final chapter, texts by authors whose prose styles and visions of the domestic are very different from Stowe's but who also draw on the coastal gothic to illuminate how oceanic empires constitute the home.

This last chapter, "Elizabeth Stoddard and Harriet Prescott Spofford: Amphibious Style and Archipelagic Forms," focuses on Spofford's "The Amber Gods" (1860) and Stoddard's *The Morgesons* (1862). It posits that Stoddard and Spofford extend the coastal gothic through a style that emphasizes "amphibious" associations and archipelagic connections. Acknowledging engagements with the Pacific and the oceans more generally in Stoddard's *The Morgesons*, chapter 6 moves beyond the economic readings of global empire and the readings of the oceanic sublime that have often characterized discussion of oceans in this text, examining the novel's dissociative, elliptical style in relation to the oceanic. Reading Spofford's long short story in similar terms, this chapter shows that by midcentury, depictions of the oceanic in such female-authored texts had become a way to express the fluid boundaries of the domestic stylistically and to give voice to female characters who push the boundaries of gender conventions, though without going to sea themselves. Although we often think of the texts discussed in this last chapter as peculiarly "modern" and as anticipating the writing of later periods, I argue that understanding them in relation to the oceanic circulations of earlier decades enables us to trace a female-authored oceanic imaginary that recognizes the violence of global empire and settler colonialism within the domestic. The texts discussed in this final part often treat the Pacific as inextricably linked to Atlantic and global circulations of goods and peoples, illustrating how New England homes, stories, and families are constituted by movement between the Pacific and Asia, the Atlantic and the Caribbean, movement that converges in their terraqueous coastal spaces. *Oceans at Home* concludes with a coda that briefly places its readings in the context of current environmental concerns at the intersection of sea and land.

Finally, a note about this book's key terms is in order. Drawing on insights and critical questions opened by transpacific studies, oceanic studies, and the field that has become known as "archipelagic American studies," the analyses in this book emerge at the intersection of these areas and nineteenth-century American literary studies. As a result, *Oceans at Home* does not confine itself to discussion of the oceans, the Pacific, or islands and archipelagoes, though it engages these spaces and associated critical concepts. I use the term "oceanic" to designate the general set of concerns that have become associated with oceanic studies within American literary studies, namely, the spaces of the oceans and maritime activities conducted in oceanic settings in contrast to terrestrial spaces and activities. I use the term "Pacific" to refer to the enormous region of the Pacific Ocean and its islands and archipelagoes. The Pacific as a region defined by an ocean stretches from the Arctic Ocean to the Southern Ocean and Antarctica, covering about one-third of the surface area of the earth. It is immense, and Western conventions have divided this space into a number of subregions. When it focuses on specific geographies within the Pacific, *Oceans at Home* generally emphasizes U.S. involvement with New Zealand and the islands of Polynesia (and even with ideas about Antarctica) rather than with Micronesia, Melanesia, or the Asia-Pacific region, though these areas, too, are sometimes conjured within the texts discussed here. Certainly, important work is being done and remains to be done on literary relationships with these other regions, but *Oceans at Home* seeks to complicate and to deepen existing scholarship on the region often referred to as Polynesia, in part because of the prominence of discussions of authors like Melville and these regions within studies of the nineteenth century. Of course, these regional designations are constructs, sometimes used to craft ideas about racial difference that would uphold settler logics of possession.[37] Movement and mobility across the space of the Pacific is central to the study of its history and present, especially and importantly in the work of Indigenous scholars of the Pacific. As the Tongan-Fijian writer and scholar Epeli Hau'ofa put it in a formulation well-known within scholarship on Oceania, the Pacific is "a sea of islands" rather than "islands in a far sea." The idea of "islands in a far sea" is one imposed by "continental men," Hau'ofa writes, who saw the islands of the Pacific as "tiny, isolated dots in a vast ocean," rather than a dynamic "sea of islands with their inhabitants."[38] In light of Hau'ofa's important point, "Oceania" would be another, in many ways preferable, term for this extensive oceanic space, but I do not employ this word to avoid confusion with my use of "oceanic" as an evolving set of critical questions within American literary studies, even as I want to acknowledge the ideological work that the term "Pacific" and ideas about its subregions do to divide this "sea of islands."[39]

Oceans at Home's later chapters engage ideas associated with archipelagic American studies, which brings some of the critical questions of island studies to bear on the study of the Americas. A focus on the "archipelagic Americas" reorients attention away from the continental United States to see it as part of an evolving imperial archipelago, but "the concept of archipelago" also, to quote Brian Russell Roberts and Michelle Ann Stephens, "serves to mediate the phenomenology of humans' cultural relation to the solid and liquid materiality of geography" in "a push and pull between the metaphoric and the material."[40] Both of these aspects of the archipelagic are at play in *Oceans at Home*, especially in the book's final chapters, as its readings of texts expose U.S. imperial archipelagos and also destabilize the relationship between continental, coastal, and oceanic spaces. More generally, through its inversion of ideas of the domestic that have often shaped American literary study, through its attention to the circulations of print connecting the Pacific, England, New England, Texas, Michigan, and other regions, as well as through its attention to material connections between land and sea, *Oceans at Home* engages the ideas of relationality central to emerging conversations between American studies and island and archipelagic reorientations of the transnational.[41] The authors discussed in this book may not have been sea captains or sailors, but through their writing they engaged some of the ideas, peoples, and narratives emanating from oceanic travel and contact with spaces such as Pacific islands in ways that help us continue to reevaluate our thinking about the boundaries, networks, geographies, and spatial imaginaries of the nineteenth century.

PART I

Lydia Maria Child's Oceanic Pedagogies

CHAPTER ONE
Pacific Voices in the *Juvenile Miscellany*

In the September 1832 issue of the *Juvenile Miscellany*, a popular children's magazine published in Boston, Massachusetts, a brief entry appears between a poem titled "Lines Addressed to My Cousin on His Birth-Day" and a moralizing, fable-like tale titled "The Ant, the Butterfly, & the Lark." This paragraph-long story, itself untitled, reads: "A native of New-Zealand, named Tooi, made a visit to England. The gentleman who had the care of him wrote just such letters to his friends at home as he dictated. In one of these letters the young savage says:—'Tooi learn little hymn—very hard—I do anything with my finger—my head in morning go all away. Tooi no like London—shove me about. Mr. Hall took me see the Tower—see thousand thousand guns: no give me one at all. See lion, elephant, monkey, and cockatoo: the cockatoo he know me very well.' He meant that he had been accustomed to see cockatoos" (figure 1).[1]

This story, brief as it is, reveals something about contemporary contact with the Pacific and its people. It shows that as European and American ships, whalers, sealers, adventurers, and missionaries traveled to the Pacific, so too did travelers move in the other direction. By the 1830s it was not uncommon for Indigenous Pacific Islanders to travel to England, whether as visitors, curiosities, subjects of conversion, or, most likely, a combination of these. Noting that "such figures are mere guesses," James Belich estimates that "it may be that a thousand Maori travelled overseas before 1840."[2] These "agent[s] of contact," in Belich's terms, traveled to Australia and England and shaped English, European, and American conceptions of New Zealand and its people.[3]

In the *Juvenile Miscellany*'s brief story, Tooi is a subject of conversion, exemplified by the fact that he is set about learning a "little hymn." He is also a visitor who is toured about, taken to see the Tower of London and various animals. But the list of animals—"lion, elephant, monkey, and cockatoo"—combined with the statement that "the cockatoo he know me very well," also momentarily positions Tooi among the animals. He is a specimen himself, looked at by others while he looks at the sights of London. And yet the interpretation of Tooi's statement in the story's final sentence ("He meant that he had been accustomed to see cockatoos") separates Tooi from the list of animals once again, indicating that he is not well known to the cockatoo as a fellow creature but is, rather, familiar with such birds. He has knowledge of a world outside London, and according to the narrator, that world includes cockatoos. An image of a bird intended to depict a cockatoo follows the paragraph, ensuring that young readers will also feel familiar with the bird.

The narrator's assertion of Tooi's meaning at the end of this paragraph is the final step in a series of translations and transcriptions of contact between the Pacific, England, and the United States that brought "Tooi," who is based on two different historical figures, to the pages of the *Juvenile Miscellany*. There, in one short paragraph, he serves to educate child readers about the world and about his own knowledge and struggles to learn. By the time Tooi appeared in this periodical, Lydia Maria

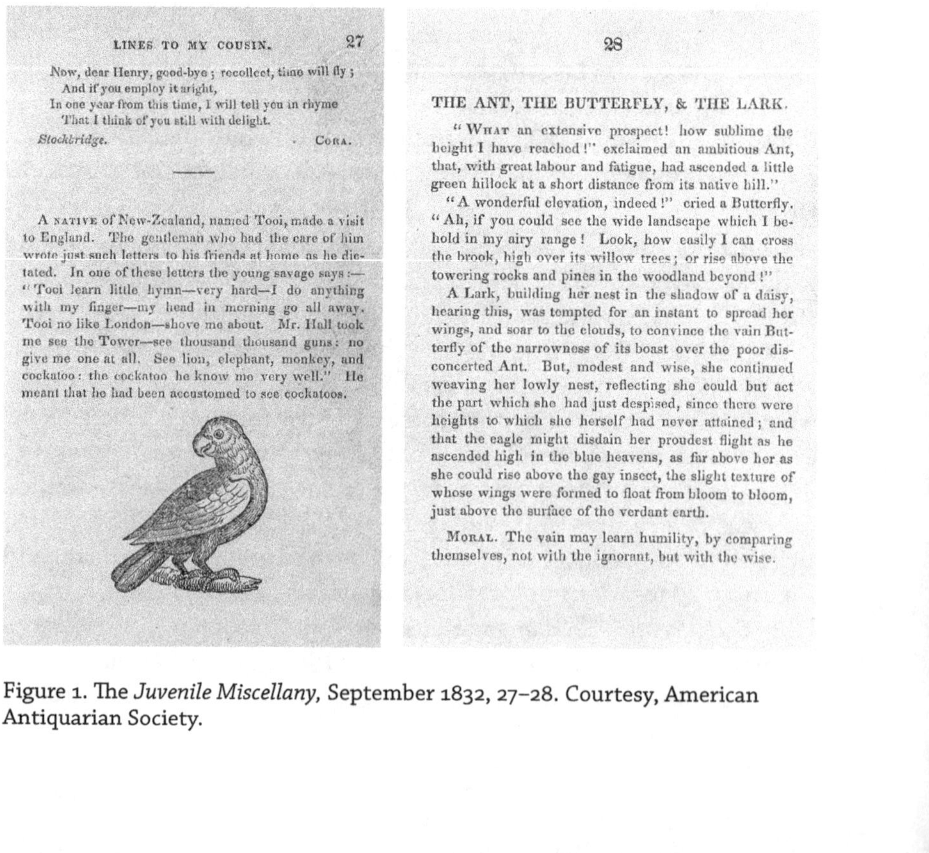

LINES TO MY COUSIN. 27

Now, dear Henry, good-bye ; recollect, time will fly ;
And if you employ it aright,
In one year from this time, I will tell you in rhyme
That I think of you still with delight.

Stockbridge. CORA.

A NATIVE of New-Zealand, named Tooi, made a visit to England. The gentleman who had the care of him wrote just such letters to his friends at home as he dictated. In one of these letters the young savage says :— "Tooi learn little hymn—very hard—I do anything with my finger—my head in morning go all away. Tooi no like London—shove me about. Mr. Hall took me see the Tower—see thousand thousand guns : no give me one at all. See lion, elephant, monkey, and cockatoo : the cockatoo he know me very well." He meant that he had been accustomed to see cockatoos.

28

THE ANT, THE BUTTERFLY, & THE LARK.

"WHAT an extensive prospect! how sublime the height I have reached !" exclaimed an ambitious Ant, that, with great labour and fatigue, had ascended a little green hillock at a short distance from its native hill."

"A wonderful elevation, indeed !" cried a Butterfly. "Ah, if you could see the wide landscape which I behold in my airy range ! Look, how easily I can cross the brook, high over its willow trees ; or rise above the towering rocks and pines in the woodland beyond !"

A Lark, building her nest in the shadow of a daisy, hearing this, was tempted for an instant to spread her wings, and soar to the clouds, to convince the vain Butterfly of the narrowness of its boast over the poor disconcerted Ant. But, modest and wise, she continued weaving her lowly nest, reflecting she could but act the part which she had just despised, since there were heights to which she herself had never attained ; and that the eagle might disdain her proudest flight as he ascended high in the blue heavens, as far above her as she could rise above the gay insect, the slight texture of whose wings were formed to float from bloom to bloom, just above the surface of the verdant earth.

MORAL. The vain may learn humility, by comparing themselves, not with the ignorant, but with the wise.

Figure 1. The *Juvenile Miscellany*, September 1832, 27–28. Courtesy, American Antiquarian Society.

Child, writer, activist, and founder and editor of the magazine, was well on her way to becoming a major force in nineteenth-century American letters and culture.[4] She was also well on her way to becoming a vocal critic of American injustice through her children's fiction and other writings. Her first novel, *Hobomok*, controversial in its time, had been published in 1824 and was an early articulation of her developing politics. A work of historical fiction that ends rather conservatively by shuffling its eponymous Indigenous character off to the west, *Hobomok* nevertheless critiques patriarchy and racism through its interracial marriage plot and revisions of colonial histories. *Hobomok* was quickly followed by other publications, from a collection of writing for children to popular household and child-rearing manuals to a radical, revisionist history of New England. Over the course of a career that spanned much of the nineteenth century, Child would become a household name as she both shaped ideas about domesticity and actively confronted America's failings. Her writings took on histories of racial prejudice and slavery, indigeneity, and women's rights. Her attention to issues surrounding indigeneity is often said to have started during years spent in Maine as a teenager where she visited the few Abenaki and Penobscot families still living nearby. Over the course of the 1820s and 1830s her advocacy on behalf of Indigenous peoples would deepen as she and her husband, David Lee Child, campaigned against Andrew Jackson's Cherokee removal policies and against the ongoing violence of the Seminole Wars. By 1833 she had also established herself as an outspoken abolitionist with the publication of the controversial *An Appeal in Favor of That Class of Americans Called Africans*.

Child's popular children's stories sit at the intersection of her cultivation of ideas about nineteenth-century home life and her activism. The *Juvenile Miscellany* was published during an era when changes to labor and family relations combined with the increasing availability of printed material to produce new notions about children and childhood, in part through the very availability of this printed material. Patricia Crain has argued that, especially "across the nineteenth century, reading and writing became foundational to characteristics we now identify with childhood." Periodicals, chapbooks, and books provided children with the texts that, by the end of the century, would make a cultural fantasy of (white) childhood inseparable from "romantic theories of language and memory" wrapped up in the image of a child curled up in a window seat reading.[5] Children and children's reading became increasingly bound up in ideas of the domestic sphere as well as the schoolroom, while the home became a point of reference, comfort, and retreat in reading for children. But at the same time, children's reading wandered widely in its content, introducing child readers to far-flung places and peoples and using adventure to further pedagogical initiatives. For Child, these pedagogical initiatives often included combatting racial prejudice and cultivating antiracist attitudes through stories about Native American and African American characters. The *Juvenile Miscellany*'s "nonsectarian approach toward forming youthful minds" was, as Carolyn Karcher puts it, "both liberal and innovative for its day."[6]

This chapter expands our understanding of Child's engagement with indigeneity and race in her children's fiction by surveying the *Juvenile Miscellany*'s use of oceanic and Pacific plots and characters. It presents a vision of a more global Lydia Maria Child than we usually recognize, one who was reading and recirculating popular narratives about the Pacific almost as soon as they were published. Child drew on some of the same source texts that Herman Melville would later use to craft his well-known Pacific narratives. Years before *Typee* or *Moby-Dick* were published, readers of Child's stories were introduced to Pacific characters who themselves introduced ideas of global colonialism and cultural relativism. To illustrate these networks of circulation, I will return to Tooi before putting the *Juvenile Miscellany*'s interest in popular tales of global adventure and its use of Pacific stories in a broader context.

The story of Tooi as it appeared in the *Juvenile Miscellany* had its origins in letters dictated by two Māori men, "Tooi" and "Teeterree" (Tuai and Tītere), to Francis Hall.[7] Hall was responsible for the two men while they were traveling in England in 1818 under the auspices of the Church Missionary Society.[8] In the letters combined to form the *Juvenile Miscellany*'s brief story, Tuai and Tītere were corresponding with the Reverend Samuel Marsden in New South Wales to tell him about their travels as they neared the end of their visit to England; they had been living with Marsden in New South Wales and had asked to go to England "to gain more Information," as Marsden put it in a letter to Reverend Josiah Pratt arranging the visit.[9] Essentially, according to Marsden, they wanted to find out about English plans for New Zealand and to develop beneficial relationships with Pākehā (the Māori term for Europeans or foreigners). Marsden, on the other hand, saw this as a prime opportunity to convert the Māori men to Christianity and was generally concerned that they not be "idle" during their time in England. He suggested in the same letter to Pratt that "if you could get any Person to form a Vocabulary of the N. Zealand Language while they remain in London it would be a great advantage to the Mission." "If they cannot be employed in assisting to form a Vocabulary," Marsden continued, "let them be put into a Rope walk and kept close to Labor while they remain in England—A Rope walk will be of more advantage to them than any other work, as they can then find employment when they return to their own Country in working up their own Flax."[10] This letter captures some of the complex motivations behind the travels of Indigenous Pacific Islanders such as Tuai and Tītere to England. On one hand, they hoped that these travels would provide them with knowledge and connections that would help their communities to navigate the shifting terrain of colonial contact. On the other hand, Marsden and others saw opportunities to strengthen the mission's hold on New Zealand through religion, economic ties (teach the men to make rope), and knowledge ("form a Vocabulary").

While in England, Tuai did briefly work with linguist Samuel Lee of Cambridge University in his efforts to record and systemize the Māori language, a project that Tuai had helped missionary Thomas Kendall to begin in Australia and New Zealand.[11] And according to Alison Jones and Kuni Kaa Jenkins, Tuai's and Tītere's trip to England also produced "the first written expression by Māori people in English" in the form of the letters that they dictated, copied, and sent to authorities and acquaintances like Marsden throughout their trip—letters such as the two combined to form the *Juvenile Miscellany*'s story.[12] As Francis Hall recorded, "The words of these Letters are their own. I was their amanuensis, & put them down on a slate, from which they copied them; but they cannot read what they have written."[13] The Māori men are presented as partially successful students at the same time that they are instructors for those working to record their language.

Tuai's and Tītere's English-language letters written with Hall's assistance are marked by simple speech patterns that often seem to represent stereotypes of Indigenous speech. For example, the phrase "thousand thousand guns" in Tītere's letter to Marsden, reproduced in the *Juvenile Miscellany*, uses repetition of a word rather than a more standard expression of plurality in a way that could indicate Tītere's exact speech but is also inflected by contemporary expectations about the simplicity and "naturalness" of Indigenous speech.[14] The meaning of the phrase "I do anything with my finger" in Tuai's letter to Marsden, also reproduced in the same story, is unclear, on the other hand. At the same time, the letters are marked by much more transparent evidence of the teachings of the Church Missionary Society. "I kneel down in my bed room every night and pray to Jesus Christ our Saviour to learn me read the book," writes Tītere to Marsden.[15] The line between Tītere's observations and the influence and desires of the missionaries is unclear.

Not long after they were written, Tuai's and Tītere's letters to Marsden and others became public when they were printed in the *Proceedings of the Church Missionary Society* for 1819. Some of the letters subsequently appeared in various newspapers, including throughout the expanding United States. As products of a missionary endeavor, the letters had never really been private at all. When George Lillie Craik published a compilation of information about New Zealand titled *The New Zealanders* in 1830 for the Library of Entertaining Knowledge, curated by the London-based Society for the Diffusion of Useful Knowledge, he included excerpts from these letters, including the specific sentences reproduced in the *Juvenile Miscellany*, in a section devoted to Tuai and Tītere.[16] *The New Zealanders* sold well in the United States, and Lydia Maria Child seems to have read it not long after it was published.[17] The November 1830 issue of the *Juvenile Miscellany* contains a section on new books that includes an account of *The New Zealanders* comprised largely of excerpts from the book. References to events and historical figures that appear in Craik's book also appear elsewhere in the *Juvenile Miscellany*'s run. Because Child herself wrote between one-quarter to one-third of each issue of the periodical, her authorship of this interconnected material seems likely.[18] Her authorship is reinforced by the fact that related content appears in the story "Mary Howard," published in Child's collection *The Little Girl's Own Book* (1831) and discussed in the next chapter. Child also quoted from Tuai's letter to Marsden in her book *Letters from New-York* (1843), so it seems as though the image of the Māori man who was shoved about by London stayed with her.[19]

Stories about the Pacific were increasingly popular in America in the 1830s as contact with the region increased, so it is not surprising that an author as prolific as Child would engage with the Pacific in some of her writing. That she did so in stories for children also makes sense. Tales of travelers like Tuai provided opportunities to teach about other peoples and parts of the globe while aligning the child reader with the Indigenous traveler who was himself learning about the world. This puts these stories squarely in line with what Anna Mae Duane has identified as the early American production of white childhood in relation to the status of Indigenous and African American people as dependent and vulnerable.[20] Yet while discourses of paternalism and infantilization in early America and into the nineteenth century emphasized dependence, images of childhood also sometimes suggested possibilities for growth, empowerment, and change for both children and the women and racial others with whom they were often aligned. Numerous scholars have noted that Child's desire to honor "certain universal human rights," as Lucy Maddox puts it, relies on evolutionary theories of culture later recognized to be highly problematic.[21] These paternalistic theories align racial others with notions of childhood, and childhood or youth with simplicity and vulnerability, even as Child advocated for universal rights and for possibilities for growth and change. This tension appears both in her writing for children and in other work.

For example, in *An Appeal for the Indians* (1868), Child asks: "How *ought* we to view the peoples who are less advanced than ourselves? Simply as younger members of the same great human family, who need to be protected, instructed and encouraged, till they are capable of appreciating and sharing all our advantages."[22] In this articulation of the evolutionary model of cultural development, as Maddox puts it, "American Indians are figured as the nation's slow-maturing children, to whom the older and stronger members of the 'human family' owe the duty of protection, education, and uplift, offered with patience."[23] In her reading of the familial metaphors within this passage, Laura Mielke argues that Child suggests "missionaries and teachers should draw on American Indians' language and cultural practices to aid their acquisition of English language and culture. Her pedagogy literally makes of all American Indians children to be nurtured and trained by patient and disciplinary (not punitive) parents." As she sought to draw attention to the sufferings and inequities surrounding marginalized groups in a way that was radical for the time, working to "imagine unity through difference," in Mielke's words, Child nevertheless struggled to avoid naturalizing difference.[24] Her recognition of a universal humanity was limited by the frameworks available for her to conceptualize this humanity.

These tensions appear within Child's representation of Pacific Indigenous characters as well. Her oceanic children's stories that reproduce popular tales of travel and adventure sometimes rely on rather flat stereotypes. But in some of these stories, especially those drawn from Craik's *The New Zealanders*, Child uses characters to theorize language difference and acquisition in ways that create dynamic Indigenous characters, remind child readers of practical pedagogical goals, and advance the progressive messages about cultural and historical relativism with which we associate much of her writing. Although stories and articles about the Pacific represent a very small proportion of the writing in the *Miscellany*, their presence is notable for how they engage the popularity of oceanic tales more generally and for how they show Child thinking about race and indigeneity in global contexts as she seeks to educate child readers in geography and history as well as in care and compassion.

The remainder of this chapter first establishes the *Juvenile Miscellany*'s sustained interest in popular tales of global adventure and situates its Pacific stories in a broader context of religiously oriented or educational writing about the Pacific for children at the beginning of the nineteenth century—writing that often emphasizes white benevolence and Christian goodness. Next, I briefly survey a selection of the *Juvenile Miscellany*'s oceanic stories about voyaging or adventure in general, many of them reprinted or adapted from other sources, then turning to specific examples of the magazine's stories of Pacific adventure to consider Child's treatment of Pacific Islanders and her focus on texts and written communication within some of these stories. Child often depicts these figures in the process of learning about the world, about reading, and about writing, while her child readers are learning the same. With this context in mind, I finally turn to "Dialogue, between the Shades of Duaterra, a New Zealand Chief, and Philip of Pokanocket," which appeared in the *Juvenile Miscellany* in 1829, a year before the publication of *The New Zealanders*. Although much of Child's writing about indigeneity for child readers seeks to teach children sympathy for Indigenous people and might align them as active learners, this chapter ends with a dialogue that is distinctive for its imagined navigation of both the connections and the physical and temporal distances between *Indigenous* peoples rather than between Euro- and Native Americans. Momentarily bridging these distances within the pages of her children's magazine, Child stages a didactic conversation between a Māori leader and a New England intertribal leader that begins to give voice to a global history of settler colonialism across time. She articulates connections between nineteenth-century New Zealand and seventeenth-century New England that require readers to reconsider the pasts and presents of colonial violence. Together with the next chapter, which focuses on Child's depiction of New Zealand in her children's story "Mary Howard," this chapter allows us to put Child's campaigns against Indian removal policies and her writings that address questions of Indigenous rights in a global frame. Though she is often considered an author thoroughly grounded in New England contexts and themes, Child sought to introduce her child readers to global histories of colonial violence, often in ways that encourage those readers to revisit histories of spaces closer to home.

SITUATING PEDAGOGIES, FROM WOODS TO ISLANDS

The wide-ranging preoccupations of the *Juvenile Miscellany* are evident from the very beginning of the periodical's publication. For example, the first two stories in the initial installment of the magazine in September 1826 juxtapose adventures in what would become U.S. space and in global spaces while offering clearly articulated lessons about character to the child reader. The first story, "Adventure in the Woods," offers a historical tale of a family traveling from England to settle in colonial Boston. The two children in the family, Benjamin and Rachel, adjust to their new home and everyone seems to enjoy peace and prosperity. "The Indians at this time were at peace with the English Settlers, who were not afraid to let a few of them come into their houses," the story notes. Indeed, when a sick Indigenous woman is found in the settlement, the children's mother offers her food and shelter. Yet Benjamin and Rachel "were very much afraid of them, for they had heard frightful stories about their wickedness and cruelty."[25] A year later when a group of children venture out into the woods to search for fruits and berries, Benjamin and Rachel get lost and are found by the same old Indigenous woman who had been offered kindness by their mother. Remembering that kindness, the woman returns them to the English village, and later in the autumn she returns with woven baskets for presents. After that she returns annually for a visit, and "the children loved her and expected her yearly visit with pleasure."[26]

"Adventure in the Woods," like many of Child's children's stories, appropriates familiar plotlines to convey a lesson about compassion. Laura Mielke notes that the tale "subverts the standard Indian captivity tale through the operations of maternal intermediaries."[27] Through her example, as Karen Kilcup puts it, the mother in the story demonstrates and "argues for kindness and mutual respect among peoples."[28] Yet, as both Kilcup and Mielke also make clear, the Indian woman remains an outsider to the developing Euro-American community. The form of sympathy that Child demonstrates in this tale and teaches her child readers has its limits. The very first story in the *Juvenile Miscellany* exemplifies some of the tensions between Child's emphasis on common humanity and its narrative limitations.

The second story in the magazine, titled "The American Traveller," operates quite differently. It recounts the life of John Ledyard, an American adventurer born in Connecticut in 1751. The story narrates highlights from Ledyard's adventures, from a youthful trip down the Connecticut River in a self-fashioned dugout canoe to his participation in Captain Cook's third and final voyage to the Pacific, concluding with his death in Africa while looking for the source of the River Niger on an expedition that he joined with the help of Sir Joseph Banks. Ledyard's was a life that exemplified late eighteenth-century global travel and speculation.[29] According to "The American Traveller," the moral to be drawn from this short, adventurous life is: "If we cannot like Ledyard, defend Gibralter [*sic*], sail round the world with Captain Cook, project trading voyages to the North-West coast, study Egyptian Hieroglyphics, and traverse the dreary northern zone, on foot; we can at least, learn from him the important lesson of *perseverance*." Using Ledyard's adventures as an occasion to teach children (specifically, in this case, "the boy who perseveringly pores over a hard lesson") to develop the habit of patient struggle, the story also establishes global adventure, including through the Pacific, as one of the themes that will run through the years of the *Juvenile Miscellany*'s publication.[30]

These first stories in the *Miscellany*'s run show Child drawing on two popular contemporary genres—historical fiction and tales of global travel and adventure—both adapted for the child reader, who is intended to learn kindness and tolerance for others, on one hand, and lessons of perseverance, on the other. Considered together, these stories also draw attention to how the *Juvenile Miscellany*, from its inception, put histories of U.S. spaces in global contexts. Benjamin and Rachel's "Adventure in the Woods" relies on the conflicts and potential intimacies of settler colonial relations to stage its moral lesson, whereas "The American Traveller" catalogs the international adventures of a "great" American man to arrive at its moral. But both make their characters' movements into new spaces and the challenges that emerge from those encounters central to their lessons. Lydia Maria Child's magazine for children begins by bringing local histories and global adventures and economies into conversation to advance didactic messages in a way that anticipates her use of Pacific plots and characters later in the *Juvenile Miscellany*'s run. When Tooi enters the periodical's pages, he is not accompanied by an overt lesson similar to that which punctuates "The American Traveller," but his voice is part of this network of travels and travelers throughout the magazine's pages—travels and travelers that both reveal something about and shape ideas of home.

Lydia Maria Child was certainly not the first to bring the Pacific or a character like Tooi into pedagogically oriented literature in the United States. Almost as soon as English missionaries established themselves in such locations as New Zealand, these locations found their way to New England in the form of religiously oriented pamphlets. The Church Missionary Society, responsible for bringing Tuai and Tītere to England in 1818, had set up a station in New Zealand's Bay of Islands in 1814. By 1820, "S. G. Goodrich, at the Hartford Sunday School Repository" in Connecticut, had printed *Memoir of Mowhee, a Young New Zealander*, an English Church Missionary Society tract first published in London.[31]

Memoir of Mowhee reproduces a letter from the Reverend Basil Woodd detailing the life and death of a young Māori man who had been in Woodd's "superintendence and care" in England in 1816.[32] It "discloses an extraordinary series of the interpositions of Divine Providence," and republished as part of a New England Sunday School series alongside books of hymns and catechisms, it brings a Pacific captivity and conversion narrative into early nineteenth-century New England.[33]

S. G. Goodrich, who printed the tract for the Sunday School Repository, was none other than Samuel Griswold Goodrich, who would later write and publish the popular *Peter Parley* children's series, indicating the deep interconnections between global missionary work, religious tracts, and children's literature during this period.[34] As a publisher, bookseller, editor, and author, Goodrich, like Child, had a tremendous impact on nineteenth-century American literature and culture. Books in the *Peter Parley* series were so well known that generations of children could recite lines from them. Starting with *Tales of Peter Parley about America* in 1827 and moving through Parley's tales about Europe (1828), Africa (1830), and Asia (1830), with additional collections of juvenile tales and books of geographic instruction interspersed among those volumes, Goodrich published *Peter Parley's Tales about the Islands in the Pacific Ocean* in 1831. Beginning with a map of the Pacific that highlights the volume's emphasis on geographic knowledge (figure 2) and the introductory chapter "About the Pacific Ocean," the book then follows Peter Parley around the region, offering descriptions of various islands, of the west coast of North America, of New Holland (Australia), and of the inhabitants and customs of these places. Along the way it offers digested histories of European encounters with the Pacific, from the story of Alexander Selkirk to that of the mutineers from the *Bounty* who settled on "Pitcairn's island."

In general, the book teaches geography and history and reinforces global capitalism and the spread of Christianity all at once. Certainly, its didactic revisions of history are anything but subtle. "The Temple of the King was a large building surrounded by monstrous images of wood," Parley reports in a section of the book on the Sandwich Islands. "Some of these images had their mouths stuck full of dogs' teeth. Such was the state of things when I was at the Sandwich islands; but this, you will recollect, was more than twenty years ago. Since that time, great changes have happened. In the year 1819, these people came to the conclusion that their wooden gods were a miserable set of creatures, and so they burnt them up. Soon after, some missionaries who sailed from Boston arrived among them. These missionaries found the people quite ready to listen to them, and so they began to teach them the christian religion."[35] The author crafts a narrative in which Indigenous Hawaiians conveniently decide to abandon their "wooden gods" so that they are empty vessels for the missionaries' teachings. Here the book ignores violence and presents imperial ventures as inevitable.

At other moments, events described in *Peter Parley's Tales about the Islands in the Pacific Ocean* serve to instruct the child reader not in geography, history (fabricated or otherwise), or the supposedly inevitable conversion of Indigenous peoples but rather in their own necessary Christian faith. For example, Parley describes a storm at sea, during which:

> "The superstitious fears of the sailors were . . . excited, by seeing little balls of fire, called corposants, which glided along the ropes and sails of the ship, and sometimes balanced themselves upon the spars and the masts. All sailors believe that these are tokens of coming evil; I need hardly tell my readers, however, that they are only electrical sparks, that may sometimes be seen in stormy weather, as well on the land as on the sea.

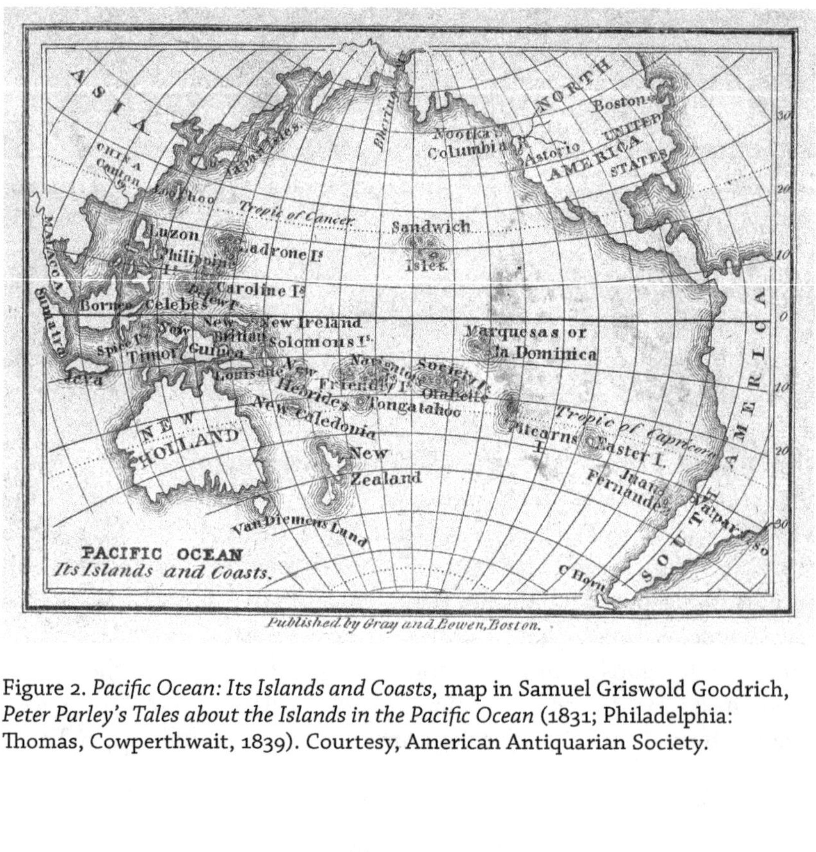

Figure 2. *Pacific Ocean: Its Islands and Coasts,* map in Samuel Griswold Goodrich, *Peter Parley's Tales about the Islands in the Pacific Ocean* (1831; Philadelphia: Thomas, Cowperthwait, 1839). Courtesy, American Antiquarian Society.

> But, in times of danger all strange appearances operate on our fears, and there is no security or peace, but that which is drawn from confidence in God. I hope it may never be the lot of any of my little readers, to be in such peril as awaited us during that night, of which I am telling them the story. But if they experience not such peril, they will all certainly find the time, when they would give all other possessions for the assurance, that God is their friend in life or death."[36]

Harnessing a dramatic episode within the fictional travel narrative, Goodrich reaches out to his "little readers," preparing them to face their own challenges by turning to God. This passage exemplifies the tone of much similar children's literature of the period as it uses adventure and a memorable moment to advance a message about the necessity of Christian faith.

Although similar moments appear throughout the book, some episodes unfold without clear didactic ends, emphasizing the entertainment value of adventure and reinforcing plots that would come to define literary depictions of the Pacific over the first half of the nineteenth century. The chapter of *Peter Parley's Tales about the Islands in the Pacific Ocean* set in New Zealand, for example, focuses on an adventure in which Parley falls over a cliff while on a hunting expedition. Rendered unconscious by his fall, Parley wakes hours later in the darkness of night. Worried that his shipmates have abandoned him, he wanders for a day and night until he encounters a group of "savages" who strip him of his clothing and offer him what he is sure is a cannibal feast. He is eventually taken to a village where he is kept for two days. When he realizes that his ship has returned, he makes a dramatic escape, essentially running a gauntlet of "savages" who throw rocks at him and attempt to prevent him from leaving. This chapter echoes numerous Pacific travel narratives published in the first decades of the nineteenth century in which sailors, whalers, or sealers are lost on and rescued from Pacific islands. In such episodes we see some of the standard scenes of encounters with the Pacific being codified, including the presumed cannibal feast and the dramatic, violent escape from the island. Such episodes would later be fictionalized in popular novels like Melville's *Typee* (1846).

This particular chapter of Parley's adventures also demonstrates prevalent and evolving stereotypes about the Indigenous peoples of the Pacific, in this case "New Zealanders." Goodrich shows Māori as cannibalistic savages, but they are also, according to *Peter Parley's Tales*, "a good deal farther advanced in civilization than [the inhabitants] of some of the other islands," a claim presented both as a result of qualities inherent to Māori and as a result of contact with Europeans.[37] This claim is evidence of what Maile Arvin calls "a logic of possession through whiteness," whereby Polynesian peoples are "positioned as almost white . . . in a way that allows white settlers to claim indigeneity in Polynesia, since, according to this logic, whiteness itself is indigenous to Polynesia."[38] In the nineteenth century, Māori in particular were presented as racially different from and "farther advanced in civilization," to quote Peter Parley, than other Pacific peoples, reinforcing hierarchies of antiblackness while also, as Arvin argues, helping to naturalize white settlement of islands such as New Zealand's.[39] Yet this status was not fixed, and Māori were also persistently othered in the popular imagination. When Parley escapes from the island, he reflects: "If I had been left with these barbarous people, it is probable they would have killed me, and eaten my flesh. There are Missionaries now at New Zealand, and they are teaching the people that it is their duty to be kind, gentle, forgiving, industrious, and charitable. It is very pleasant to know that they listen to the missionaries, and are beginning to see the advantages of being Christians, rather than savages."[40] In a tradition extending back through early narratives of exploration and conquest, as well as through fiction such as Daniel Defoe's *Robinson Crusoe* (1719), Parley's adventure in New Zealand is ultimately framed by the "advantages" of Christianity, even though much of the chapter reads as a narrative of adventure and captivity. Māori are "barbarous," but they are presented as particularly capable of being civilized.

I cite *Peter Parley's Tales about the Islands in the Pacific Ocean* at length because it exemplifies a type of contemporary children's literature that merges religious and imperial messages with geographic education and entertainment. Such children's literature reflects a range of contemporary ideas about the Pacific and its people and was inflected by texts emerging from contact with the Pacific, from religious tracts such as *Memoir of Mowhee* to contemporary travel narratives. Emerging in the very same years, the *Juvenile Miscellany* absorbed much of the same material and often reproduced similar messages about white benevolence or the advantages of Christianity through its Pacific plots. But with Child at the helm, the way Pacific settings, plots, and characters are deployed sometimes looks slightly different, especially when it comes to the periodical's interest in New Zealand.

CHILD'S OCEANS

It is worth noting that stories about the Pacific islands and Indigenous Pacific Islanders within the *Juvenile Miscellany* appear alongside articles featuring oceanic voyaging or an interest in the oceans more generally, reinforcing engagement with the Pacific as part of a more general contemporary interest in the oceanic. These oceanic articles are used to teach history, science, and religious lessons. They include tales about historical figures like the one on John Ledyard in the *Juvenile Miscellany*'s first issue, stories that offer histories of global exploration along with lessons about character for young readers. One article teaches children about the "polar regions," while two dialogues between "James" and "Aunt Maria" (who might be thought of as Child's thinly veiled alter ego) appearing in November 1826 and January 1827 teach about coral reefs, oceans, and fish. At the end of the second dialogue, James asks Aunt Maria, "Where did you learn all these interesting facts?" Aunt Maria replies, "In 'Smellie's Philosophy of Natural History;' a book, which I advise you to read, if you wish for a fund of amusement and instruction."[41] Beginning with the narrative conceit that "Captain Bradford has just arrived in port" giving James a "beautiful coral branch," proceeding to digest information from a book of natural history (published in 1791 and reprinted numerous times throughout the early nineteenth century), and directing readers to that source to learn more, these two articles use the common pedagogical form of dialogue to offer lessons in geography and natural history based in oceanic realms.[42]

Similarly, later *Juvenile Miscellany* articles on "conchology" are filled with Linnaean classifications and in-depth descriptions of shells, along with illustrations. In one of these articles a description of the "pearl oyster" is supplemented by an "account of the labor and pain of diving for them" copied from "Lieutenant Hardy's Travels; the author of that book went out as Commissioner to the Pearl and Coral Fishery Association, of London." Knowledge of nature is put in the context of global travel and commerce, but even these subjects are punctuated with a religious message. Following the description of the pearl oyster and before the transcribed passage from Hardy's *Travels* appears the sentence: "The precious truths of the gospel have been compared to Pearls; and well would it be, if these magnificent treasures of the deep, which we use to ornament our frail bodies, served to remind us of those divine truths."[43] Referencing mention of pearls within the Bible, this sentence reminds readers of the *Juvenile Miscellany* that even when diving beneath the sea for pearls or wearing the ornaments, they should also be looking into other depths. The wonders of nature and its beauty should lead them to the divine.[44]

In addition to historical tales of travel and information about natural history interspersed with the occasional religious message, many of which were likely written by Child, various stories about characters who go to sea that appear within the *Juvenile Miscellany* were adapted from other sources, whether by Child or others who contributed to the magazine. For example, the story "The Fisherman's Family" is a sentimental tale about danger and loyalty that participates in the contemporary enthusiasm for stories of oceanic adventure and was presumably adapted from an earlier story published in *The Amulet, or Christian and Literary Remembrancer*.[45] "Volney Beckner," a horrifically violent story of the risks of oceanic voyaging, appeared in the November 1830 issue of the *Juvenile Miscellany*. It, too, had appeared in a slightly different form in a religious publication not long before its appearance in that issue. And it would be republished in various forms in other publications later in the century, indicating the sustained interest in these children's stories of oceanic adventure and danger.[46]

Not all stories about the perils of the sea in the *Juvenile Miscellany* are adapted from periodicals or explicitly religious sources, however. Other such stories show Child reimagining contemporary travel narratives in her own way. For example, "William Burton; or, the Boy Who Would Be a Sailor" (September 1831) is a shipwreck and captivity narrative in the spirit of some of Peter Parley's adventures as well as Herman Melville's later *Typee*. Like *Typee*, "William Burton" is indebted, as an editorial note at the end of the story asserts, "for many interesting particulars . . . to a very entertaining little book, called Journal of a Cruise among the Islands of the Pacific; by Lieutenant Paulding, of the U.S. Navy."[47] Hiram Paulding's account of "the United States schooner Dolphin" and its Pacific cruise in pursuit of the mutineers involved in the 1824 *Globe* mutiny was published earlier in 1831, so Paulding's "very entertaining little book" was a very recent publication when "William Burton" appeared in the *Juvenile Miscellany*. In Child's hands, the "interesting particulars" of Paulding's narrative motivate a story about a Connecticut farm boy, William Burton, who is "inspired . . . with an earnest desire to become a sailor" as a result of hearing about the adventures at sea of his neighbor Silas Hall and seeing the "shells, and coral, and war-clubs from the Sandwich Islands, and carved boxes, and painted glass from China" that fill the parlor of the Hall family. William "borrowed all the books of voyages he could hear of for miles round, and all his leisure moments were employed in making little imitations of Otaheite canoes, and New-Zealand spears."[48] Ignoring the pleas of his parents and of Silas's sister, Mary, who is like a sister to William as well (and eventually much more), William sets off on a trial voyage to Santa Cruz with Silas, armed with a copy of *Robinson Crusoe* given to him by Mary, in case he is "cast away on a desert island," and a Bible given to him by his mother.[49] He makes two successful voyages, and while home following the second voyage, he and Mary are engaged. Though his mother hopes that the prospect of marriage will encourage William to settle down, he hears of a ship about to sail to the Sandwich Islands and cannot resist the opportunity to "see that famous race of savages, of whome Captain Cooke had given such an interesting account."[50] On this voyage, the crew mutinies, murdering the captain and all the other officers. The story emphasizes that William was unable to do anything to prevent this. When the remaining crew members eventually land in the Mulgrave Islands, William Burton and John Gordon, the friend who had encouraged him to join the voyage in the first place, are good to the people they encounter, but the rest of the wicked crew steal from and fight with the islanders. Only Burton and Gordon survive, having been saved from death by a chief and an old man, whom they then serve. The story turns into a kind of captivity narrative in which the two men do their best to negotiate life on the island and to navigate its peoples' customs.

In Child's story, Burton and Gordon live with the Indigenous chief Lugoma for four years, during which time they are integrated into the community, learning the ways of the islanders as best they can and also teaching them skills such as weaving and gardening. But Burton yearns for home; he yearns for his mother and for Mary. When an American ship arrives, Lugoma hides the men, but Providence intervenes, and Burton's old friend Silas Hall happens to find a mitten that his sister Mary had knit for William Burton, which prompts suspicion that the crew of Burton and Gordon's ship had been murdered on the island. Burton and Gordon eventually negotiate their return. Following an emotional leave-taking and a return voyage filled with delays and repairs to the ship, Burton, Gordon, and Hall return home, where William Burton is reunited with Mary but discovers that his mother has died. He is, of course, plagued with guilt for having left his mother so as to pursue a life of adventure.

This narrative borrows from, and in some ways closely follows, the accounts of two survivors of the *Globe* mutiny, William Lay and Cyrus Hussey, related in Paulding's book. Building on popular tales of adventure in the Pacific, Child adapts such narratives to illustrate morals about love and loyalty to family and about faith similar to those presented in stories such as "The Fisherman's Family" and also to address ideas about Indigenous peoples. In Paulding's source text it is not clear why Lay and Hussey, the models for Burton and Gordon, are saved from death at the hands of the islanders, but it is presumably not because they are good. Lay's account of these events as reported in Paulding's narrative simply expresses the confusion that he must have felt at the time, and Paulding concludes: "There seems to be no doubt, that the natives saved the lives of these young men from no other motive than that of making them slaves, and availing themselves of the advantage of their labour."[51] In Child's story, on the other hand, it is implied that Burton and Gordon are saved because they are not like the rest of the "wicked crew" who would steal the islanders "cocoa-nuts, and refuse to give them anything in return." Those islanders, Child writes, "appeared to be an innocent and amiable set of people; and had all the white men been as good as Burton and Gordon, they might have associated together in safety and peace."[52] Burton and Gordon, it is implied, are saved because they are good, or at least not "wicked," and they then live among the Pacific Islanders recognizing and experiencing a kind of common humanity. But ultimately this same white benevolence enables them to leave the Pacific, reinforcing a separation and hierarchy that continues to define their relationship with their captors or hosts. Child uses the events described in Paulding's narrative to craft a story that emphasizes Burton's and Gordon's goodness in comparison with the violent behavior of their shipmates, as well as the "amiable" nature of the Indigenous peoples they encounter.[53]

This same spirit of white benevolence in the Pacific undergirds an earlier *Miscellany* story that grows out of a source more explicitly connected to missionary activities in the Pacific than is Paulding's narrative. Two of the *Miscellany*'s stories about the Sandwich Islands (Hawaii) appear early in the periodical's run, in the May 1828 issue. "Productions of the Sandwich Islands" is a rather encyclopedic list of various products emerging from Euro-American contact with the islands, namely "taro," "the paper mulberry tree—from which Tappa, or native cloth, is made," the "palm and rush . . . from which the women weave mats," "yams and sweet potatoes," and various trees and flowers.[54] Most of this article is condensed and paraphrased from, but not attributed to, Charles Samuel Stewart's *Journal of a Residence in the Sandwich Islands* published in 1828 (first in London and then in New York), again indicating that Child was digesting material about the Pacific as soon as it was published and passing it on to her child readers. Stewart himself was an American missionary in the "Sandwich Islands" from 1823 to 1825, part of the second company of the American Board of Commissioners for Foreign Missions to arrive in the islands.[55]

Earlier in the same May 1828 installment of the *Juvenile Miscellany*, a short story also inspired by Stewart's narrative appears. "Lealea-Hoku: The Little Sandwich Island Girl" begins by acknowledging the trade of goods emphasized in "Productions of the Sandwich Islands." It begins by mocking the contrast between what "Sandwich Islanders" have as a result of trading relationships (silk dresses and elegant furniture) and what they lack ("judgment and taste"). These people are, according to the story, "only half-civilized." But the story emphasizes that "though they are a rude and ignorant people, they are not destitute of sense; and there is the same difference among them, that there is among better educated nations."[56] Here, Child seems to reinforce notions that pervade her writings, namely, the idea that Indigenous peoples are like Euro-American Christians but are at a different and lesser stage of development. The plot of "Lealea-Hoku" reinforces this message as readers are introduced to the eponymous little girl and her mother "Kaahu-manu," who neglects her daughter at every turn. "It is some excuse for this wicked mother that she was a savage," the story moralizes, "and had never read the Bible, which teaches the law of kindness and love; but this circumstance does not entirely excuse her—for she did not do so well as she knew how. Selfish people, who love dress, and their own ease, always neglect their duties, whether they are civilized, or uncivilized; and had Kaahu-manu been a native of New-England, I have no doubt she would have left a dying mother to go to a ball."[57] With such sentences, Child reinforces the message that Kaahu-manu is both like and unlike Euro-Americans. Selfish people are the same, regardless of who they are, but Kaahu-manu has the extra weakness of being uninformed by Christianity.

At this point in the story, the young Lealea-hoku is sick while on board a ship with her mother going to Oahu to meet with a group of missionaries; another Hawaiian child shows her a small kindness as if to emphasize that not all Hawaiians are like her mother. But Kaahu-manu leaves Lealea-hoku for dead on the hot sand of an Oahu beach, where she is saved by "Capt. W. of Salem," who takes her on board his ship and, eventually, back to Massachusetts, where his wife names her "Charity." The story ends with the hope that Charity will return to the Sandwich Islands to "teach the natives to read, and write, and sew" and the notion that the reader will, no doubt, still think that the islanders "are pitiful little savages, after all."[58] Using Stewart's *Journal of a Residence in the Sandwich Islands*, Child compiles an encyclopedic account of the "productions of the Sandwich Islands" and also crafts a sentimental tale of white benevolence that supports missionary endeavors, a tale that both emphasizes and denies the similarities between "savage" and "civilized." Although such stories may not seem radically different from those within a text such as *Peter Parley's Tales about the Islands in the Pacific Ocean* in that they share a message of Christian uplift and "civilization," the stories within the *Juvenile Miscellany* do more to depict Indigenous characters as individuals, despite their imperial message and vision.

"PUT DOWN ME"

Child's engagement with the Pacific in the *Juvenile Miscellany* relies, to a large extent, on reprinting versions of previously published stories from religiously affiliated magazines and on crafting tales or informational articles inspired by recent narratives of the Pacific such as those by Paulding, Stewart, and Craik. These tales combine contemporary interest in Pacific adventures with moralizing messages of kindness and white benevolence, but they also enact Child's message of universal humanity. So, too, do many of these stories, especially the ones focused on Indigenous New Zealanders such as "Tooi," make issues of writing, print, or communication central to the conflicts that they stage. The stories thus enact both the pedagogical projects of "civilizing" missions and of a magazine like the *Juvenile Miscellany* itself, which helped children practice skills like reading while offering moral instruction. In "William Burton," for example, Child added details to Paulding's original source material that emphasize books, writing, and Christianity together as part of the Euro-American knowledge that Pacific Islanders lack. The "chief" who saves Burton by taking him into captivity is distraught and frightened when he catches Gordon "looking at the pictures in Robinson Crusoe. He had no idea what the book was; but he seemed very much frightened, and snatching it out of his hand, he instantly tore it into a million of pieces." Ultimately this anecdote feeds into a detail about how the chief, Lugoma, is then afraid to touch Burton's Bible because Burton tells "him it would make the Great Spirit very angry if he destroyed it."[59] Here, the wonder and newness of printed books becomes linked to the inscrutability of cultural and religious difference in a way that echoes hundreds of years of accounts of colonial encounter and that also exemplifies how Indigenous peoples are often presented as childlike and in need of training within both Child's writing and writing of the period more generally. In this case, Lugoma is in need of education regarding printed material and alphabetic writing. The sight of the Bible makes him tremble when his daughter dies soon after his mutilation of *Robinson Crusoe* and he thinks that his treatment of the book is to blame for her death. Later in the story, when Burton tears a "blank leaf from his Bible" to write a rescue note to be delivered to the captain of the ship that stops at the island, Lugoma shrinks away from the note when it is held out to him, screaming: "Take it away! Take it away! It will bring the spirits of my fathers to my hut."[60] Child merges the idea of taboo with print and religion, reinforcing notions of difference that remain unbridged in this story. Burton does not stay in the Mulgrave Islands to teach Lugoma to read. Instead, he returns home, leaving Lugoma in a state of potential, but unfulfilled, education regarding alphabetic writing and books.

In other *Miscellany* articles and stories, however, Child explores ideas about Indigenous marking in ways that grant Māori in particular their own forms of signification, highlighting a kind of cultural relativism and awareness of other systems and values.[61] In "New Books," the 1830 *Juvenile Miscellany* article that digests parts of Craik's *The New Zealanders*, Child reproduces a lengthy passage about New Zealand tattooing, itself an account of the experiences of John Rutherford, an English sailor who had received a *moko* (facial tattoo) in New Zealand in 1816.[62] The passage outlines the process of receiving the moko. At the end of the passage about Rutherford lifted from Craik's book, Child digests another part of Craik's consideration of tattooing, noting: "When they [Māori] transact business, they make a picture of the tattooing on their faces, at the bottom of their papers, instead of signing the name, as we do. This is better than the ancient custom among the Russians: they used to daub the whole hand with ink, and then lay it upon the paper, for a signature."[63] Here Child opts to reproduce ideas from Craik's book that recognize a form of signification associated with bodily marking. This passage notably makes the image of the moko an analogue for a written signature, recognizing it as an alternative form of signification without collapsing it into alphabetic script. The comparison raises the idea of a relationship between tattooing and writing without attempting to "read" the tattoo as text.[64]

Questions about forms of signification across cultures are made even more explicit in a March 1832 *Miscellany* article titled "New-Zealand Ideas of Writing." Like the Tooi story published just half a year later that also involves textuality and cross-cultural translation through an account of one of Tooi's letters to "his friends at home," this article is one short paragraph, which reads as follows: "The first time Finou, a New-Zealand Chief, saw any writing, he asked to have something written for him; being asked what he chose, he answered, 'Put down me.' The man accordingly wrote his name, and read it to him. The chief, suspecting it was all a trick, sent for another Englishman, and asked him what was on that paper; when he again heard his name, the ignorant savage was completely astonished and puzzled. He turned the paper round, and looked at the word in all directions: at last, he exclaimed, 'This is not like me, or any body else! Where are my legs? How do you know it to be I?'"[65] As with the story of Tooi and the excerpt on tattoo designs being used as signatures in Child's article about *The New Zealanders*, the paragraph is adapted, nearly word-for-word, from Craik, but Child does make one notable change. This particular episode in *The New Zealanders* is taken from William Mariner's *An Account of the Natives of the Tonga Islands*, first published in 1817. In Craik's text it is clear that "Finow" is a

Tongan "king."[66] In making "Finou" a "New-Zealand Chief," Child builds on ideas in Craik while maintaining some continuity across issues of the *Juvenile Miscellany* in terms of a focus on Māori and reflecting the fact that, as Craik himself put it, "Of all the people constituting the great Polynesian family, the New Zealanders have, at least of late years, attracted the largest portion of public attention."[67] In other words, in imagining Finou a New Zealand chief, Child makes him a slightly more familiar figure than a Tongan "king" would have been, reinforcing the ideas about New Zealand that she elsewhere presents to her readers.

This particular story aligns itself with ideas of tattooing, selfhood, and writing introduced in the "New Zealanders" article, where "a picture of the tattooing on their faces" stands in for a written signature. In the "Finou" paragraph, Child grapples with the difficulty of conceiving of unfamiliar modes of signification, in essence sympathizing with characters such as Finou, and later Tooi, who encounter unfamiliar forms of written communication. Finou struggles to reconcile unfamiliar, nonrepresentational marks with the sound of his own name. But even as this story seems to sympathize with Finou's confusion, he, like Tooi, is presented as quaint and childlike. Such figures within the *Juvenile Miscellany* are in need of education. Of course, this is true in Craik's book as well, as he claims that the New Zealander's "especial distinction, and that which more than anything else keeps him a savage, is his ignorance of letters. This places the community almost in the same situation with a herd of the lower animals, in so far as the accumulation of knowledge, or, in other words, any kind of movement forward is concerned; for it is only by means of the art of writing that the knowledge acquired by the experience of one generation can be properly stored up, so that none of it shall be lost, for the use of all that are to follow."[68]

Craik also occasionally compares New Zealanders not with animals but with other humans, tracing an evolution from drawing pictures to alphabetic writing. He considers New Zealanders' attitudes toward writing alongside Mexican "picture writing," the marks of "the Chinese of the present day," and in a footnote, he advances the notion that "the *quippas*, or lines by which events were recorded amongst the ancient Peruvians, by knots, were something approaching to alphabetic writing." "Alphabetic probably originated in picture writing," he notes, "but it is important to observe that we have here altogether a new principle brought into operation. We have now marks, representative, not of things, but of sounds. The vast advantage of this improvement it is impossible to overrate. Things are innumerable—articulate sounds are very few in number. By twenty or thirty marks for the latter, as much may be accomplished in the art of writing as by a separate mark for every individual in the countless multitude of the former."[69] And Craik then follows these reflections with the account of Finow to illustrate his points.

In privileging alphabetic writing and its supposed efficiency, Craik essentially argues that the New Zealanders' language needs to be a written one so that they can advance toward greater civilization, at the same time as he creates a kind of global comparative linguistic history.[70] In his treatment of language, Craik reinforces evolutionary theories of culture that Child also espoused, and in other places in *The New Zealanders*, it should be noted, he explicitly frames the "savage" as a child in ways that echo Child's view of "less advanced peoples" as "younger members of the same great human family."[71] "What the Child is to us for the study of man as an individual, the Savage is also for the broader but not less difficult study of man as a species," Craik writes in the introduction to *The New Zealanders*. "The peculiarities of each are to be examined with a like degree of patience and candour." He repeats these ideas at the end of the book, writing, "We shall perhaps, indeed, arrive at the truest and most comprehensive estimate of the condition and character of the savage by considering him as a child in intellect, and, at the same time, in physical powers and passions a man."[72] Craik was, as Geoffrey Sanborn notes, "an advocate of British intervention in New Zealand," and his political agenda is infused throughout *The New Zealanders*.[73] Demonstrating that Māori can be brought into "civilization" supports his goals. Lydia Maria Child's goals were different. She drew on Craik's book to craft stories that would help children to practice reading and would teach about global geographies while cultivating awareness, empathy, and sympathy for others, including Indigenous peoples. That the brief passages lifted by Child from Craik's book for inclusion in the *Juvenile Miscellany* often theorize language difference and acquisition while recognizing other forms of signification and expression of identity like moko shows her aligning the child learner with the Indigenous learner in a way that suggests a need for development, while also recognizing difference in a way that is complex rather than reductive. Although Child does not grasp or convey the significance of tattooing within Indigenous cultures in relation to genealogy and oral traditions, she chooses to reproduce passages from *The New Zealanders* that align the child reader with the Indigenous learner in a way that is more active and egalitarian than it is dismissive or judgmental.

DIALOGUES OF GLOBAL INDIGENEITY

Both "New-Zealand Ideas of Writing" and the brief story about Tooi with which this chapter began appeared in the *Juvenile Miscellany* in 1832, seeming to indicate a kind of evolution in Child's writing about the Pacific from the fact-based, stereotypical articles "Productions of the Sandwich Islands" and "Lealea-Hoku" that appeared in 1828 to these slightly later paragraph-long yet complex tales drawn from Craik's text. These later articles feature Māori characters who are very explicitly caught between worlds and who voice an experience of grappling with their encounter with alphabetic writing in a way that aligns them, to a certain extent, with the child reader. But this sense of an evolution within the *Juvenile Miscellany*'s stories is complicated by an earlier article in the July 1829 issue of the magazine that features a Māori voice quite literally put in conversation with other voices. If we assume Child to have authored the article based on content shared with her other writings, we see her already pushing boundaries of space, time, and language through a New Zealand character, even before the publication of Craik's popular book. In "Dialogue, between the Shades of Duaterra, a New Zealand Chief, and Philip of Pokanocket. *By a little girl ten years old*," Child dispenses with problems of written communication and associated ideas of evolutionary stages as she crafts a transtemporal and translingual conversation set in the mythological space of Hades. Most of the dialogues in Child's writing are between a mother or aunt figure and children, a textual enactment of her pedagogical project. In allowing two Indigenous "chiefs" to speak to each other in this particular dialogue, Child repurposes one of her often-used pedagogical formats to allow those individuals to teach each other at the same time as they teach the reader about different histories of colonialism. Child's critiques of colonial violence come through explicitly, though she cannot envision a way forward that does not involve the absorption of Indigenous voices into the English language and into Euro-American futures.

"Shades" in this article's title indicates an inhabitant of Hades, conjuring the idea of a disembodied spirit. In the dialogue, the "Shade" of Duaterra asks Mercury, in his capacity as Roman god of communication, through Charon, the Greek ferryman of Hades, for ten minutes to speak with "the Indian, Philip of Pokanocket." He wants to ask Philip "why he resisted the attempts of the *Packaha*, (white man) to promote civilization."[74] Ruatara (d. 1815) was a Ngāpuhi-aligned (Māori) chief whose name often appears as "Duaterra" in nineteenth-century documents as a result of the transliteration of the sounds of spoken Māori into written English. He traveled to Australia and, briefly, to England in 1809 and worked to facilitate missionary activities in New Zealand's Bay of Islands region. A key "agent of contact," Ruatara gained control over newly introduced ideas about agriculture and commerce and shaped European notions about Māori character and prospects for conversion.[75] Whereas other Māori might have been presented as rebellious savages in contemporary literature and culture, Ruatara was noted to be "dignified and noble . . . not disfigured with the disgusting marks of the tattoo."[76] James Belich notes that men like Samuel Marsden of the Church Missionary Society viewed his death as a "near-martyrdom."[77] "Philip of Pokanocket," on the other hand, refers to King Philip, or Metacom (1638–76), sachem of a confederation of Indigenous peoples in New England, including the Wampanoag and Narragansett, who led the major war of resistance to colonial incursion that became known as "King Philip's War."

In this conversation, Child puts a seventeenth-century New England Indigenous, intertribal leader in dialogue with an early nineteenth-century Māori leader through the intermediaries of Greek and Roman gods. She uses the timelessness of the underworld to stage a conversation between two Indigenous figures who were, in life, separated by unbridgeable distances of time and space. The conversation that emerges is very much in the spirit of Child's book *The First Settlers of New-England, or, Conquest of the Pequods, Narragansets and Pokanokets: As Related by a Mother to Her Children*, also published in 1829. In that book, Child offers a revisionist history of the settlement of New England, emphasizing the injustices done to Indigenous peoples and the double standards they faced when defending their own communities and lands. Following a preface that lays out the goals of the book, among them "to prove, from the most authentic records, that the treatment they [Indigenous peoples] have met with from the usurpers of their soil has been, and continues to be, in direct violation of the religious and civil institutions which we have heretofore so nobly defended, and by which we profess to be governed," *Settlers* takes the form of a conversation between a mother and two daughters.[78] In the course of that conversation the mother mentions having just read Washington Irving's "interesting memoir of Philip of Pokanoket." Noting that Irving's "just and manly defence of the Indian character, and his sympathy for the wrongs which have been heaped upon them, is truly honourable," she goes on to quote extensively from Irving's history of Metacom and the tensions leading up to King Philip's War.[79] Irving's "interesting memoir" was first published in the *Analectic Magazine* (June 1814) and would be added to the second volume of the British version of his *Sketchbook* in July 1820, along with another story offering a sympathetic picture of Native Americans, titled "Traits of Indian Character." As in much of Child's work, in these accounts Irving is sympathetic to the history and the plight of Indigenous peoples, while emphasizing their "primitive" difference and their distance from "civilization."

The dialogue between Duaterra and Philip in the *Juvenile Miscellany* extends Irving's portrayal of Philip as "a patriot attached to his native soil," making him a voice of violent resistance to colonial incursions, downplaying his status as persecuted, and emphasizing his status as "brave, but unfortunate."[80] In the dialogue, Philip accuses Duaterra of betraying "his country to the Yengeese, and even [building] with his own hands, wigwams for their accommodation."[81] What is more, Philip links Duaterra's betrayal to his Māori language when he asserts "I abhor [the language] of the New Zealanders; for I hear daily accounts of chiefs giving up their lands to the pale faces; speak then with the tongue of a Yengeese; my ears are open." While this exchange seeks to provide an explanation for how these two are able to communicate with each other and how readers can comprehend their conversation ("surely you have been long enough in the land of spirits to know that here we can use any language we choose," admonishes Philip), Philip's demand that Duaterra speak English oddly contradicts his militant attitude toward the incursions of the "Yengeese." Philip seems to advocate the very capitulation to the English that he also decries.[82]

Duaterra is presented as the younger, more easily influenced "shade" who wants to know why Philip "did not encourage the attempts of the Packaha, to civilize your countrymen?"[83] Philip explains in reply that the "Yengeese" did not come to civilize but rather to take land, and that they did so in cunning ways. The implication seems to be that their coming to "civilize," presumably through the introduction of Christianity, would have been less problematic, but the "cunning" taking of land and resources without an interest in "civilizing" is the concern. Duaterra (and by extension Māori people in general) is presented as being loyal to colonizers, concerned that he not "betray a trust" such as that of the "Packaha." But Philip insists that violence is the answer to the "Yengeese's" deceptive self-interest. The conversation ends when Mercury interjects, asserting that the allotted ten minutes have passed and reminding Philip "for the future that to 'forgive and forget' as Duaterra has, is a maxim sometimes to be practised [*sic*]; it would have been better for *you*, if you had known *that* long before you came *here*."[84]

This exchange thus stages different potential responses to settler colonialism, presenting Philip as a violent force of resistance to land acquisition and genocide and Duaterra as a collaborator and enabler of colonial change. To some extent this binary is consistent with popular historical accounts of Metacom and Ruatara, respectively, in the sense that there is a war named after King Philip while Ruatara is often remembered as a collaborator between Europeans and Māori.[85] But this conversation ignores wider conflict in the first decades of the nineteenth century in New Zealand, a period when there were complex relationships and tensions between Māori and missionaries, settlers, and sailors and a period known for the Musket Wars, when the arrival of European weapons changed the nature of intertribal conflict, leading to unprecedented violence. Despite this dialogue's elisions and its final message of acquiescence, in putting these men in conversation and associating different Indigenous peoples and geographies with different responses to settler incursions, Child starts to imagine a global history of settler colonialism across time. This dialogue suggests that as different as their times and places may have been, these men were faced with similar problems, namely, those presented by the violent structures of settler colonialism. Child's project here is very different from Craik's comparative treatment of picture writing and alphabetic writing across cultures. Although Craik engages different histories of peoples across time and space, he does so to craft a master narrative of the evolution of language and culture. Child, on the other hand, allows Duaterra and Philip to speak to each other in order to highlight both seventeenth-century Euro-American and nineteenth-century Pākehā violence and injustice, even as she imagines different types of reactions to this injustice and, ultimately, through Mercury, advocates "forgiving and forgetting."

It is also notable that this dialogue is imagined to be written "by a little girl ten years old." Most of the dialogues within the *Juvenile Miscellany* are not attributed to a fictional child character but are presented as accounts of conversations that model learning without being attributed to a fictional author. Related to the question-and-answer format of the catechism but demonstrating a more organic form of interaction, most of Child's dialogues are nevertheless structured by hierarchies of age and learning: for example, an aunt or a mother figure speaks with a child.[86] But in the dialogue between Duaterra and Philip, authority shifts as the two ask questions of each other and as Mercury intervenes with the last word. But in many ways it is the fictional child author who has the last word, demonstrating for the child reader of the *Juvenile Miscellany* the relativism of historical accounts and the need to recognize and give voice to historical injustice. The reader who is encouraged to engage with the New Zealander and his struggles to learn about the world within the pages of the *Miscellany* is offered a model of how a child might not just absorb historical lessons but think dynamically, in written form, about histories of settler colonialism across space and time.

This dynamism does not change the fact that the conversation ends with the notion "that to 'forgive and forget' . . . is a maxim sometimes to be practiced," a maxim that the fictional child author might be imagined to have been taught in other contexts and one that may be intended as a guide for the child reader's behavior. In the context of a message about Indigenous assimilation or erasure, this maxim might remind us of Child's most well-known Indigenous figure, Hobomok, who, upon learning that the Englishman Charles Brown is alive and has returned to New England, sacrifices his life with Mary and their son so that they can live out their lives among the English. Hobomok divorces Mary through a dictated note written by "Edward Winslow. Governor of the jurisdictione [*sic*] of New Plimouth" and signed with his mark (figure 3).

Hobomok's "noble" conduct is sealed with his "marke" as he essentially asks everyone to "forgive and forget." Unable to write in English, he affixes a sign representing himself to a document that releases Mary from her promises to him. Six years after the publication of *Hobomok*, Child encouraged her readers to consider other Indigenous marks in the pages of the *Juvenile Miscellany* when "Finou, a New-Zealand Chief," demanded "Put down me" and when Tooi dictated letters to "his friends at home." In the intervening years, as Child established her successful children's periodical and simultaneously developed her critiques of the dispossession of Indigenous peoples from U.S. space, critiques exemplified in *The First Settlers of New-England*, she also reproduced popular tales about oceanic voyaging and the Pacific that reinforced lessons about Christian goodness and benevolence. But she simultaneously wrestled with the cultural relativism of signification in ways that give voice to Pacific Islanders, however cursorily. And she occasionally encouraged her child readers to think about indigeneity in comparative contexts, recognizing the marks of colonial violence across different historical periods and global geographies—geographies that included the territory that would become the United States and islands in the Pacific such as New Zealand. "Dialogue, between the Shades of Duaterra, a New Zealand Chief, and Philip of Pokanocket" reminds us of the need to recognize these global conversations within the nineteenth-century archive and to consider how stories about distant peoples and places could, in the pages of the *Juvenile Miscellany*, be occasions to think anew about histories and injustices much closer to home.

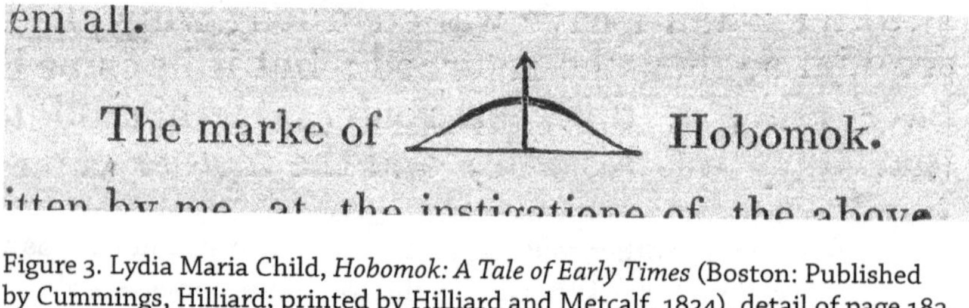

em all.

The marke of Hobomok.

Figure 3. Lydia Maria Child, *Hobomok: A Tale of Early Times* (Boston: Published by Cummings, Hilliard; printed by Hilliard and Metcalf, 1824), detail of page 182. Courtesy, American Antiquarian Society.

CHAPTER TWO
Mary Howard's Mark

Lydia Maria Child's engagement with textual materials emerging from contact with the Pacific, from Hiram Paulding's *Journal of a Cruise* to George Lillie Craik's *The New Zealanders*, produced a range of brief narratives in the *Juvenile Miscellany*. Many of these narratives drew on portions of the source texts, Craik's in particular, that implicitly or explicitly raise questions about relationships between printed material, different forms of textuality, and communication in general, creating sympathy with the New Zealand "savages" who quaintly struggle to comprehend alphabetic writing while claiming that the path to uplift for those Indigenous peoples involves such comprehension. And, in the case of the dialogue between Duaterra and Philip, Child both critiques perceived Māori acquiescence to settler colonialism and suggests that the Christian dictate to "forgive and forget" might be the only available option for living Indigenous peoples and their ancestors, who are now "shades."[1]

At moments within these stories and articles, Child reproduced popular ideas about tattoos being used as markers of identity on paper. She indicates that Māori supposedly view these marks as an equivalent to writing and also as a direct sign of the self, ideas that emerge, as Ngārino Ellis puts it, at "the intersection of Pākehā print literacy with Māori oral literacy."[2] Herman Melville would later draw on similar material from Craik's text as he crafted the most well-known tattooed body in nineteenth-century American literature: that of Queequeg, *Moby-Dick*'s Māori harpooner. As Geoffrey Sanborn has demonstrated, the "principal source" for Melville's Queequeg was Craik's account of Te Pehi Kupe—a Māori chief who boarded a ship and developed a close relationship with its captain.[3] That account includes Te Pehi Kupe's (Tupai Cupa in Craik) own "name" in the form of a drawing of his "Amoco" (*moko*) (figure 4). In *Moby-Dick*, the link between bodily tattoo and written signature is famously probed in chapter 18, "His Mark," when Queequeg enrolls in the *Pequod*'s crew by signing "an exact counterpart of a queer round figure which was tattooed upon his arm," echoing Hobomok's arrow sign (figure 5; for the arrow sign, see figure 3).[4]

A key figure in the famously diverse crew of the *Pequod*, Queequeg is also, as Paul Lyons has pointed out, a figure through which Melville "imagines, for a moment at least, the lives of an Anglo-U.S. citizen and an Oceanian as twinned, through processes that are at once intimate, and nested within larger historical, economic, and political structures." In that moment, Queequeg and Ishmael are "wedded" together by a whaling rope, an image that Lyons harnesses to illustrate the "bound-togetherness" of U.S. and Oceanian history.[5] Nicholas Thomas, a historical anthropologist of the Pacific whose work explores the complexities of exchange and circulation between the Pacific and Europe in the context of colonialism, might use a slightly different term for a similar idea: entanglement.[6] In a sense, this term, too, conjures Melville's whale lines connecting Queequeg and Ishmael—and undulating across the Pacific to the United States.

The last chapter explored such bound-togetherness, such entanglement, largely though Child's use of accounts of Māori men such as Tuai, Tītere, and Ruatara, who, like Te Pehi Kupe, traveled to England and became the subjects of missionary writings that ensured that their bodies and stories continued to travel in textual form. I argued that Child used such figures and their stories to craft her own tales containing messages about the treatment of Indigenous Pacific Islanders that are aligned with many of her arguments about Indigenous North Americans: they are members of the human family and deserve respect, even as they are presented as childlike and separate. In "Dialogue, between the Shades of Duaterra, a New Zealand Chief, and Philip of Pokanocket," Child goes further, however, crafting a conversation that explicitly binds together the experiences of Native Americans and Māori in the face of settler colonialism. In this case, Child brings these two historical figures together not to compare their positions on some kind of imagined cultural ladder but to present both as victims of colonial violence, violence that Child critiqued in texts such as *The First Settlers of New-England*.

Whereas the last chapter offered a survey of stories from the *Juvenile Miscellany* that engage the oceans and the Pacific, sometimes reproducing ideas about white benevolence common in writing that brings Pacific adventure and religiously inflected plots together but at other times giving voice to Indigenous characters in ways aligned with Child's critiques of colonial violence and deception, this chapter focuses on a single story and its entanglements. It reads Child's most extended narrative about New Zealand, the short story "Mary Howard," which first appeared in *The Little Girl's Own Book* (1831). This story brings the female body to the

Tattooing on the face of Tupai Cupa, from a drawing by himself.

Figure 4. "Tattooing on the face of Tupai Cupa, from a drawing by himself," in George Lillie Craik, *The New Zealanders*, 332. Courtesy, American Antiquarian Society.

Quohog.

his ✠ mark.

Figure 5. Herman Melville, *Moby-Dick; or, The Whale* (New York: Harper, 1851), detail of page 100. Courtesy, American Antiquarian Society.

center of a children's story about global travel in ways that complicate the moral lessons we might be inclined to find in much nineteenth-century children's literature and that we do find in many places throughout the *Juvenile Miscellany*. In "Mary Howard," this complication occurs in part through the female body's contact with indigeneity and through related ideas about marking. In "Mary Howard," Child does not preserve a kind of separation between worlds but uses the body of a small girl to emphasize entanglements.

The Little Girl's Own Book, a collection of stories, puzzles, and riddles written by Child, was a natural extension of the success of the *Juvenile Miscellany*. Its publication was, in fact, advertised at the end of the *Juvenile Miscellany* section on "new books" that featured "New Zealanders" in the November 1830 issue of the magazine. Between a paragraph about "The Boston School Atlas" and a short announcement that "Mrs. Sarah J. Hale has written a charming little book of Poems for children," a paragraph announces: "Carter & Hendee are about to publish a New Year's Gift for Children, called The Little Girls' Own Book. It is to contain a description of sixty different games, with directions how to make all manner of baskets, boxes, puzzles, &c. Poetry, Fables, Riddles, Music, and everything that can make a pleasing variety, is to be introduced into this little volume; and all to be illustrated by nearly a hundred engravings. It is written by Mrs. Child."[7]

The Little Girl's Own Book would be reprinted on both sides of the Atlantic numerous times over the following decades, often under the title *The Girl's Own Book*. Inserted alongside practical entries about "active exercises," "bags," and "calisthenics," the story "Mary Howard" stands out for its rather shocking description of travels in the Pacific. Most of the Pacific material in the *Juvenile Miscellany* (with the exception of "Lealea-Hoku") features male travelers and characters, many of whom were actual historical figures who traveled from the Pacific to England. "Mary Howard" shifts attention to female bodies, and specifically to white female bodies who traveled in the other direction, from England or its colonial outposts to the Pacific. In a sense, it is a female version of Child's story "William Burton; or, the Boy Who Would Be a Sailor," also published in 1831. But whereas William Burton longs to go to sea, Mary is taken against her will. And whereas Burton returns home, seemingly breaking off all contact with the Pacific islands where he lived for four years, Mary Howard goes back to England after four years without forgetting or breaking her connection to that distant place. She returns home marked by her experiences. Although this might seem to suggest judgment placed on the female traveler who transgresses boundaries, judgment not placed on the male child, Mary Howard is presented as a good girl to the end.

This chapter first outlines the textual and historical influences on this short story as it appeared in *The Little Girl's Own Book*, tracing its entanglements with events in the Pacific as well as with popular poems and ballads. I argue that "Mary Howard" requires us to consider the place of female captivity narratives within histories of comparative settler colonialism such as that staged by Child's dialogue between "Duaterra" and "Philip of Pokanocket." The chapter then shifts its attention to the circulation of "Mary Howard" in an abridged form as an anonymously authored chapbook titled *The Little, but Affecting History of Mary Howard*, printed in rural New Hampshire a few years after the story's initial publication in *The Little Girl's Own Book*. Highlighting the reprinting and recirculation of this story beyond the pages of Child's New Year's gift book, this part of the chapter illustrates how stories about the Pacific were absorbed by but also spread through Child's writing. It elucidates how deeply and completely narratives about the Pacific moved into U.S. spaces and how even a story as fairy tale–like as "Mary Howard" brings the Pacific home by putting bodies marked by Pacific encounters into small New Hampshire hands. The chapbook extends the story of American entanglement with the Pacific, with New Zealand, and with Māori in the early nineteenth century that I have started to trace in the previous chapter, an entanglement that ultimately breaks down binaries between little hands and big lessons, domestic and "foreign" spaces, and small chapbooks and the large novels and travel narratives often associated with the nineteenth-century Pacific. Tracing these interactions within "Mary Howard" further reorients how we frame historical and literary encounters with the Pacific and raises questions about how we read Child's writing for children, as well as children's literature in general, as a category of fiction notoriously bound together with others.

THE MESSAGE OF "MARY HOWARD"

At first, "Mary Howard" seems like quite a conventional story. It begins in a familiar manner and quickly engages a number of well-known references, from a popular children's song to a folktale. Mary Howard herself is the well-off, well-loved, and well-behaved "daughter of wealthy parents in England." She is generous and sensitive, "the darling of the whole house." She is so "tender-hearted" that when she causes the cat to mew "because she had pulled her fur, she ran and hid her head in her mother's lap, and grieved sadly."[8] In keeping with other antebellum children's literature and with the advice offered in contemporary mothers' books similar to Child's own, Mary's relationship to her pets serves as an index of her goodness.[9] She dresses her pet lamb in flowers every day and, in turn, is tended with as much care as she gives her animals. The image of Mary and her lamb in particular would have been increasingly familiar by 1831. Sarah Josepha Hale's poem "Mary Had a Little Lamb" was first published a year earlier in the *Juvenile Miscellany*, and later that year it appeared in the collection *Poems for Our Children*, advertised just after *The Little Girl's Own Book* in the November 1830 issue of the *Juvenile Miscellany*. In 1831 it was published in Lowell Mason and Elam Ives's popular child's songbook the *Juvenile Lyre*.[10] In Hale's poem, the notion that Mary's lamb loves Mary because Mary loves the lamb reinforces widely held ideas about kindness toward animals as an element of child rearing.

Mary's idyllic life with her parents and animals is soon shattered, however, when her father is thrown from his carriage and killed. She is forced to confront death, but, the narrative tells us, "she was not old enough then to know that when we die, we only go to the home God has provided for us; that the good, who are left on the earth, may grieve, but that the good, who have gone before them, are happy." The sentences following her father's death in the narrative are taken up with Mary's questions: "What made him go, mother? We loved him—why did he not stay with us?"[11] These questions and the mother's narrated response replicate the dialogue form common in primers and religious tracts and, as we have seen, in Child's other writings, from *The First Settlers of New-England* to stories in the *Juvenile Miscellany*. Here the child reader is encouraged to learn the answers to the questions through dialogue with a maternal figure.

Less than a year later, Mary's mother dies of consumption. Mary's only remaining family members are two uncles. Her paternal uncle is appointed to serve as her guardian, but he is "wicked" and wants her father's wealth. "He knew," the narrative continues, "that if she were dead, he should have large houses, and plenty of silver, and gold, and jewels. The more he thought of these things, the more he hated the lovely child, who had been placed under his care by her dying parents; for if we let bad thoughts stay in our minds, they grow stronger and stronger every hour."[12] Here, the evil uncle provides an opportunity for the lesson that follows the semicolon. As the story gets darker, its pedagogical potential remains clear. The child reader is now being taught to let go of "bad thoughts."

These particular aspects of the plot of "Mary Howard" conjure the ballad and story of "The Children in the Wood," sometimes known as

"The Babes in the Wood," which Child also drew on in such stories as "Adventure in the Woods," the first tale published in the *Juvenile Miscellany*. Published as a broadside ballad in England as early as 1595, "The Children in the Wood" tells of an orphaned brother and sister entrusted to the care of their greedy paternal uncle. The uncle hires a pair of ruffians to take the children to the woods and kill them so that he can secure their inheritance. The two ruffians argue, and the one in favor of keeping the children alive kills the other, leaving the children in the woods. He promises to return but does not, and the children eventually die. Their bodies are then covered with leaves by robins. This ballad appeared in other verse forms and in prose form in books and chapbooks throughout the nineteenth century.[13] The trope of the orphan and the greedy paternal uncle would have been familiar to nineteenth-century readers and certainly to readers of Child's previous writing for children. But in "Mary Howard," the plot of "The Children in the Wood" is altered as Mary is taken not into the woods but to sea.

Mary's paternal uncle removes her from her family home, and soon the child's former nurse, the faithful Betty Morris, hears that Mary is lost—that "the gypsies had stolen her, for the sake of an amber necklace."[14] Not believing the story, Betty writes to Mary's maternal uncle in Calcutta, expressing her fears for Mary's safety. In the meantime, the paternal uncle hires a sailor to drown Mary. The sailor, Robert, "had a soft heart; but he had not been taught when young, to remember that the eye of God was upon all of his actions."[15] Although the lure of money initially overpowers any softness, Robert cannot ultimately bring himself to drown Mary. He takes her with him to Wales and then to New Zealand. On board the ship to New Zealand, the two encounter "Duaterra," "the son of a New-Zealand Chief," who is returning home from a visit to London. One day the "savage" is "so very lazy and saucy, that the Captain ordered him to be flogged, in order to teach him better manners." Insulted by his treatment, Duaterra resolves to kill everyone on the ship, except for Robert and Mary: "'I will not kill Robert,' said he to himself, 'because he gave me a Turkish pipe, and always shares his biscuit with me; and as for little mocking-bird Mary, I would not have her killed for all the pipes in the world.' He called her mocking-bird, because she made him laugh, by trying to repeat all the words he spoke to her."[16] Here the issue of language difference and acquisition often theorized in the *Juvenile Miscellany*'s use of stories about New Zealand briefly enters "Mary Howard." Mary is an infantilized and animal-like mimic confronting an unfamiliar language. She is presented as being in the position of Tooi or Finou.

When they reach New Zealand, Duaterra tells his father about his treatment, and the "savages" plot an attack on the English. As promised, Robert's and Mary's lives are spared, but Mary is traumatized by the violence that she witnesses: "For years afterward, it always made her turn pale to speak about it."[17] Despite her supposed friendship with the Māori Duaterra, this violence is attributed to the Māori themselves, who "are savages; very much like what our North American Indians used to be." "The inhabitants of New-Zealand looked so strong and fierce," the narrator continues after the account of the massacre, "that our gentle little Mary was very much afraid of them; and she would often scream in her sleep, when she dreamed of them. They were indeed frightful looking creatures. They had their faces tattooed all over with strange marks; they wore their hair tied very tight on the top of their heads; and had great coarse mats hanging over their shoulders." Yet despite these horrors, the narrative specifies that Mary is not "wretched." In fact, "the savages were all kind to her, and Robert took as good care of her as he could. Then the island was a bright and beautiful island."[18] The next few paragraphs of the story describe the beauty of the island and indicate that as Mary "grew older, she learned to carve in wood and bone, and to do shell-work, and to make baskets of various colored bark; for in all these things the savages were very skillful." Mary is, it seems, becoming something of a "savage" herself. This is also true of Robert: "Robert consented to be tattooed, and put white feathers on the top of his head, and married the Chief's daughter, and became himself a Chief." After a brief description of tattooing and the comment that "savages consider this a great beauty; but it looks very frightful to us," the story notes that "Duaterra wanted to tattoo little Mary's face, but Robert would not consent to it; for in his heart he resolved to send her back to England, the first good chance he could get."[19] Robert has become a "Pākehā-Māori," allowing himself to be tattooed and marrying into Duaterra's family, but Mary's Englishness and purity will be preserved.

The next paragraph, however, abruptly informs readers that "Duaterra did tattoo one side of Mary's forehead, notwithstanding Robert had forbidden it; and when Robert blamed him for it, he said she was going to be his little wife, and he would tattoo her face all over, if he pleased."[20] The tale that began with narrative elements familiar from contemporary children's verses and stories such as "Mary Had a Little Lamb" and "The Children in the Wood" has taken a surprising turn toward forced marking and child marriage. But any narrative suspense about Mary's fate is quickly resolved, as readers are told that about four years after Mary's arrival in New Zealand, when she is eight years old, an English ship carrying one of Robert's old shipmates (who also happens to be the brother of nurse Betty Morris) arrives. John Morris agrees to take Mary back to Betty in England. Because Robert cannot write (a detail that might encourage readers to practice their own ABCs and that momentarily links Robert to Child's Māori characters), he decides to prove Mary's identity to those in England by sending her back with the tattered remains of the black dress she was wearing when she disappeared. Back in England, John Morris and Mary run out of money while waiting for Betty to arrive in London. Mary offers to carve boxes and weave baskets for them to sell in the streets, harnessing skills gained in New Zealand as well as the appeal of her dramatic story to become an economic success.

When Betty Morris arrives in London, she immediately recognizes Mary, despite her tanned skin and "shameful tattooing."[21] The story comes to a close with the revelation that Mary's maternal uncle has returned from Calcutta and is looking for her—he had purchased carved boxes from her and had already invited her to his house without knowing that she was his niece. Mary's fortune is soon restored to her, Betty and John Morris each marry happily, and Robert returns to London after his Māori wife dies. Mary then supports Robert with her wealth. And she quickly sheds the "rude habits she naturally acquired" in New Zealand, becoming an accomplished young lady. Duaterra, we are told, "was very angry when he first found Mary had gone to England; but a year or two after, he married one of his own tribe, and ceased to care about his mocking-bird. Every year Mary sends him hammers, and scissors, and nails, and beads, and such other things as she knows will please his savage fancy." The only remaining mark of her time among the savages, the story concludes, is "Duaterra's tattooing," hidden under a "cluster of curls."[22]

By ending with the image of "Duaterra's tattooing" on Mary's forehead, the story seems to emphasize his creation and possession of the marks and, by extension, his continued possession of Mary herself. Yet the text emphasizes that Mary's marks are not only hidden but also purely physical: "You would not believe she was ever among the savages, unless you raised a cluster of curls, and discovered Duaterra's tattooing."[23] Though Mary is marked by her ordeal, her identity as a good girl and her place in "civilized" society remain stable. Indeed, the implication seems to be that not even a "savage" mark can change Mary's goodness or her tenderheartedness.

PACIFIC ENTANGLEMENTS

"Mary Howard" was undoubtedly intended to entertain its child readers as well as to teach basic geographic knowledge, alerting children to the existence of places such as New Zealand and "savages" like Duaterra who live there. And despite its sensational aspects, the story also contains standard Christian lessons about greed and about fearing and trusting God. "Mortals could not do any thing to help [Mary]; but when I have told you my story," a first-person narrator offers at one point in the tale, "you will see how her Heavenly Father took care of her."[24] This message reinforces the narrative's seeming lack of cause and effect. After all, Mary does not do anything wrong. She is not punished for previous actions. Yet, echoing an American captivity narrative tradition that extends back to Mary Rowlandson, the primary message appears to be, bad things will happen. Trust God. Be good. And if you are good, then good things may happen. You may be redeemed.

"Mary Howard" draws on a number of genres to advance this lesson, including the captivity narrative exemplified by Rowlandson and the type of orphan story exemplified by "The Children in the Wood." The name "Duaterra" also makes clear that "Mary Howard" draws on some of the same sources and historical figures as Child's writings in the *Juvenile Miscellany*. In fact, the New Zealand plotline of "Mary Howard" was almost certainly inspired by George Lillie Craik's account of the 1809 *Boyd* massacre in *The New Zealanders*. The Māori attack on the *Boyd* in Whangaroa Harbor was the result of a complex series of cross-cultural tensions and misunderstandings. The "Burning of the *Boyd*" was a dramatic event that had received a great deal of attention, with accounts circulating in newspapers around the world and inspiring fears about "savage" New Zealanders. Because the 1829 "Dialogue, between the Shades of Duaterra, a New Zealand Chief, and Philip of Pokanocket" in the *Juvenile Miscellany* mentions the *Boyd* and was published before Craik's *The New Zealanders*, Child likely knew of the event from other sources. But one of the excerpts from Craik's book reprinted in the *Miscellany* article "New Zealanders" is about the *Boyd*, so it seems probable that this source also provided fodder for "Mary Howard."

In most accounts of the *Boyd* massacre, including the one offered in Craik's book, the "son of a New Zealand chief" whose shipboard treatment leads to the massacre is Te Ara (whose name is rendered as Tarra or George in Craik). Te Ara was a Māori *rangatira*, or chief, who had traveled and worked on a number of European vessels before his return to New Zealand from Sydney on the *Boyd* in 1809. On that voyage, somewhere between Australia and New Zealand, Te Ara was flogged, perhaps as punishment for a small slight or misunderstanding.[25] Te Pahi, a leader in New Zealand's Bay of Islands region, was blamed for instigating the massacre of the crew of the *Boyd* that followed, apparently as *utu* (revenge) for Te

Ara's mistreatment.[26] This fundamental tension is included in the account of the *Boyd* taken from Craik and reproduced in the *Juvenile Miscellany*'s article "New Zealanders" (and it is specified that the English had given the "young savage . . . the name of George").[27] In "Mary Howard," however, Child makes an alteration to this character by naming him "Duaterra" rather than "George" or "Te Ara," thus effectively creating a composite of two historical Māori figures, Te Ara and Ruatara.[28] While Te Ara and Te Pahi might have appeared rebellious, Ruatara was, as noted in the previous chapter, thought to be "dignified and noble . . . not disfigured with the disgusting marks of the tattoo," and Duaterra in "Mary Howard" combines these ideas of rebellion and nobleness.[29] On one hand, he seems to represent stereotypes of New Zealand savagery. His actions conjure the violence associated with Te Ara and Te Pahi, and his desire for revenge because his *mana*, his honor, has been violated is not presented as itself honorable. Rather, "Mary Howard" asserts that revenge drives Duaterra's actions because he has never "read in the Holy Bible, that men should love and forgive one another."[30] Yet on the other hand, he is kind to Mary and is not presented in an entirely unflattering light. In writing her short story, then, Child draws on the fundamental tensions at stake in the *Boyd* massacre but alters the figure of Duaterra slightly.

The tensions surrounding the mistreatment of the "son of a New Zealand chief" and the resulting massacre are not the only parts of the *Boyd* story to make it from Craik's book to the pages of the *Juvenile Miscellany* and then to influence "Mary Howard." As Child's article "New Zealanders" notes, quoting Craik, "The only individuals who were saved from this cruel [*Boyd*] slaughter were a woman, two children, and the cabin boy." After more quotation from Craik's text, Child summarizes part of the account, noting, "These miserable captives were afterward carried back to England, by the humane exertions of a Scotch captain. One of them was a little girl, only three or four years old." The article then resumes its direct quotation of *The New Zealanders*:

> This child was found to be in the possession of one of the chiefs, and although promised, was not brought to him til after a considerable delay. "This delay," says Mr. Berry, "I afterwards had reason to believe proceeded from the endeavours of the natives to deliver it up in as decent a manner as possible. It was tolerably clean, with its hair dressed and ornamented with white feathers, in the fashion of New Zealand. Its only clothing, however, consisted of a linen shirt, which, from the marks upon it, had belonged to the captain. The poor child was greatly emaciated, and its skin was

> excoriated all over. When brought to the boat, it cried out in a feeble and complaining tone, 'Mamma, my mamma!'" This child was carried to Lima in the City of Edinburgh ship; and it was not till more than two years after leaving New Zealand that she was restored to her father in New South Wales. Although of so tender an age when the destruction of the Boyd took place, she was found, while in South America, to recollect well the dreadful scenes of which she had been witness. "I have more than once been present," says Mr. Berry, "when the cruel but interesting question was put to her, if she recollected what the Zealanders did to her mamma? Her countenance, on such occasions, assumed the appearance of the deepest melancholy; and, without uttering a word, she used to draw her hand across her throat.[31]

In the *Juvenile Miscellany* article about the newly published *New Zealanders*, Child ends her excerpt from Craik here with this dramatic and incongruous image of the small child miming violence, eliminating two final sentences suggesting cannibalism that exist in Craik's text. Other than this change, the only other that Child makes to this account in the *Juvenile Miscellany* is to the child's age. In Craik's account of these events, the little girl is "two or three years of age," while Child makes the girl "three or four years old" in the *Juvenile Miscellany*. In "Mary Howard," Mary is approximately four years old when she arrives in New Zealand and is eight years old when she is found by John Morris and returned to England. While these differences are subtle, Mary Howard is brought slightly closer to adulthood, perhaps to make her interactions with Duaterra somewhat more plausible. The changes also bring the girl's age closer to the potential age of Child's readers, suggesting that Child hoped to craft some kind of identification between readers and characters. Still, the events described would be well outside the experience of those readers, especially because in "Mary Howard" Child adds an additional detail absent from or only vaguely suggested (through the word "excoriated") in Craik's account: the child is tattooed.

When Child mentions tattoos in the *Juvenile Miscellany*, she connects them with Māori characters, but in "Mary Howard" Child engages with the fact that more than the Tahitian word *tātau* was brought back to England by Captain James Cook in 1769. Some of Cook's men returned with their own markings. In the following decades, sailors and soldiers—along with the occasional upper-class traveler—returned from travels in the Pacific with tattoos that needed to be explained and that turned their bodies into sites of spectacle. John Rutherford, whose account of tattooing Craik adopted in *The New Zealanders*, was one of the earliest English visitors to New Zealand to receive a moko—a facial tattoo—in 1816, to dictate his narrative (which claimed that his tattoos were forced on him, though that seems not to have been the case), and to display his body back in England as part of a "travelling caravan of wonders."[32]

Other white tattooed men displayed themselves around Europe, England, and America at the same time as Pacific Islanders traveling overseas displayed their markings. In the years following the 1831 publication of "Mary Howard," there would be a surge of narratives like Rutherford's that accounted for these markings. Irishman James F. O'Connell published *A Residence of Eleven Years in New Holland and the Caroline Islands* in 1836 and then spent two decades displaying his full body tattoo, acquired in the Caroline Islands, around the United States. Editions of Barnet Burns's *A Brief Narrative of the Remarkable History of Barnet Burns* were published in England in 1835 and 1836 and presumably read elsewhere as well. The narrative provides an account of Burns's years living among Māori in New Zealand in the early 1830s and of his tattooing. Like O'Connell, Burns displayed his body and gave lectures, his marks becoming a commodity that allowed him to earn a living and to claim intimate knowledge of another way of life. Other accounts of forcible tattooing in the Pacific also appeared around the same time, including *Narrative of the Shipwreck, Captivity and Sufferings of Horace Holden and Benj. H. Nute* (1836), which may have influenced Melville's account of Marquesan tattooing in *Typee* (1846).[33]

Some European or Euro-American travelers in the Pacific seemed to recognize that tattooing designated a particular social status or gave them power by incorporating them into a particular community or genealogy. But along with this status or power came fears of the threat to identity that Melville's Tommo expresses in *Typee* when he resists the marking of his "face divine." Samuel Otter argues that "the most penetrating assault" in *Typee* "envisions the body not as meat to be sliced and devoured but as a text to be engraved and read." Tommo's fear is not so much that of cannibalism, another misunderstood cultural practice that generated tremendous anxiety for Europeans traveling in the Pacific, but rather that "the body will be consumed by the lines of the tattooist and the eyes of observers." In *Typee*, Otter argues, this fear of tattooing is in large part a fear of racial conversion and of incorporation into the Indigenous system, reinforcing the nineteenth-century American obsession with ethnology and racial purity.[34] Tommo expresses horror "at the bare thought of being rendered hideous for life" and of being "disfigured in such a manner as never more to have the *face* to return to [his] countrymen."[35]

"Mary Howard" grows out of Child's engagement with stories about tattooing reproduced in Craik's *The New Zealanders*, as well as out of these broader historical contexts regarding tattooing, but with notable differences regarding gender and age. Juniper Ellis and others have noted that "historically, most Pacific travelers who bore tattoo beyond the region were men; similarly, most visitors who acquired tattoo and wrote about it were men."[36] Women in Pacific Island communities were tattooed and were central to the process of tattooing, but few accounts of tattooed European female travelers or captives exist. There were, however, some contemporary accounts in circulation that raised issues about gender and cross-cultural contact, if not tattooing in explicit terms. For example, in 1834, Australian-born Elizabeth Guard was captured by local Māori when her husband's ship was wrecked off New Zealand's Taranaki coast. About six months later, Guard, her children, and members of the ship's crew who were captured with her were rescued by British naval forces in the first active deployment of British troops on New Zealand soil. News of the captivity and rescue, and of unsanctioned military violence against Māori, quickly spread to Sydney and then to London.[37] Two years later, a Scottish woman, Eliza Fraser, was shipwrecked off the northeastern coast of Australia on what would become Fraser Island. Her husband was killed and other crew members went missing, but Fraser herself was rescued, becoming something of a celebrity in Australia, Europe, and colonies around the globe. Sensationalized accounts of the shipwreck circulated in newspapers in England and in the United States (see figure 6), and a popular 1838 book about the event, written by a London court reporter who had covered the inquiry into Fraser's captivity, was reprinted in America in 1841.[38]

As might be expected, these accounts negotiated the complexities of cross-cultural contact and settler colonialism by presenting white femininity as threatened by dark "savagery." In rescuing these women, colonial authorities sought to preserve the boundaries between "civilization" and "savagery" at the farthest reaches of the British empire. But published narratives about these captivities did not always successfully maintain those boundaries. Speculation surrounded the nature of each white woman's relationship with her captors. For example, one chronicler of early British encounters with New Zealand asserted that Elizabeth Guard gave birth to dark-skinned twins not long after her return to Sydney.[39] And in some accounts of Guard's captivity there is uncertainty about whether she was really a "captive" at all. Newspaper articles about Eliza Fraser's ordeal described other physical threats: "Being entirely naked, and presenting a contrast in her skin, which the women did not like, she was compelled by them to rub herself all over with gum and herbs, which had the effect of making her nearly as dark as themselves. They likewise tattooed her all over; and having pulled her hair out, covered her head with a sort of gum, and stuck the feathers of parrots and other birds all over it."[40] Fraser's body is described as being marked by her experience in a way that suggests a radical threat to her racial identity, and even to her status as human.

But though the word "tattooed" appears in this article about Eliza Fraser circulating in New England newspapers, Fraser seems not to have actually been tattooed. Most accounts of her ordeal do indicate that she was found naked, her skin darkened with animal fats and dyes, and her hair decorated with feathers and other objects, but not tattooed in any way that was permanent.[41] Later in the nineteenth century, tattooed women appeared in circuses and sideshows, accompanied by stories of captivity and forcible tattooing, and tattooing also became popular among some middle and upper-class women.[42] But "Mary Howard" stands out among texts published in the 1830s for its mention of not only a European female tattooed in the antipodes but also a female child.[43] And whereas newspaper accounts of Eliza Fraser's captivity report that she was marked by *women* who did not like the "contrast in her skin," Mary Howard is tattooed by the son of a "New Zealand Chief."

The racial and sexual implications of this marking are difficult to ignore given the cultural anxieties surrounding tattooing in the early nineteenth century. While Pacific societies certainly did not see tattoos as aberrant, the "penetration" of the tattoo eventually became associated with sexual deviancy in the West. This is more a late nineteenth- and early twentieth-century phenomenon, but tattoos were certainly associated with the promiscuous roving sailor in earlier periods. Indeed, the sexual threat associated with tattoos would seem to be confirmed by accounts of women and children who ran away from James O'Connell on the streets of New York, screaming at his grotesque body. Ministers warned pregnant women to avoid viewing O'Connell, lest his tattoo marks be transferred to their unborn children. As Juniper Ellis puts it, "The fully developed diagnostic tradition suggests that viewing tattoo is tantamount to penetration and incites sexual action; here, the wild transmission of the designs does not even require penetration."[44]

Mary Howard's tattoo, her newly dark skin, her tattered black dress—all appear within the context of sexual transgression implied by later

Miscellany.

From the Salem Gazette.

A PAINFUL NARRATIVE.

Some months ago we copied from an English paper, all that was then known respecting the loss of an East Indiaman, voyaging from Sydney to Singapore—the dreadful sufferings of the crew among the savages—and the rescue of a child, (the son of Major D'Oyley) from the cruelties of his captors. More recently, the widow of the Captain has arrived in England, and gives the following story of her own almost unparalleled sufferings. One cannot read it without a fearful recollection that several American sailors are believed to be yet enduring the horrors of such captivity in the same quarter:

Account of the Crew of the Ship Stirling Castle, and the Conduct of the Savages.

Yesterday, Mrs Eliza Frazer, the widow of Captain Frazer, of the ship Stirling Castle, which was wrecked on a coral reef, on the passage from Sydney to Singapure, in May, 1835, came to the justice room, accompanied by the Captain of the vessel in which she arrived in this country, for the purpose of mentioning the particulars of her dreadful adventures among the inhabitants of the shore to which the crew resorted, as a refuge from the not less appalling dangers of the ocean.

On the 16th of May, 1835, the Stirling Castle left Sydney for Singapore. On the 23d, when they were approaching Torres' Straits, it blew very fresh, and there was a current near the Eliza Coral reefs, which the vessel was unable to resist; she struck on the reefs about nine o'clock at night. There were about eighteen men on board.

after looking about without seeing a creature, she determined to follow some footmarks, and, having proceeded some distance, she saw a crowd of black women approach. These women belonged to the tribe of savages by whom her husband had been taken up the bush on the preceding day, and they set her to work in trailing wood and lighting fires. Being entirely naked, and presenting a contrast in her skin, which the women did not like, she was compelled by them to rub herself all over with gum and herbs, which had the effect of making her nearly as dark as themselves. They likewise tattooed her all over; and having pulled her hair out, covered her head with a sort of gum, and stuck the feathers of parrots and other birds all over it.

One of the women, having two children, obliged her to nurse one of them, notwithstanding the severe labor she had to perform; and if the child was out of temper, the nurse was kicked and scratched and thumped for its peevishness. At the expiration of four days Mrs Frazer saw her husband for the first time since their separation. He was dragging along a tree, and was greatly fatigued. She had begun to inquire how it happened that he did not manage to let her know where he was, to which he was replying that he dared not look for her,—when his tribe suddenly appeared. One of them, having seen them together, made a push at the Captain with a spear, and pierced him through the body, which was a corpse in an instant. Mrs Frazer, ran to her husband, crying out, "Jesus of Nazareth, I can endure this no longer," and pulled the spear

Figure 6. "Account of the Crew of the Ship *Stirling Castle*, and the Conduct of the Savages," *New Hampshire Sentinel* (Keene), October 19, 1837. Courtesy, American Antiquarian Society.

accounts such as that of Betty Guard's "black-skinned twins" and Eliza Fraser's body alterations, compounded by Duaterra's claim that "[Mary] was going to be his little wife, and he would tattoo her face all over, if he pleased."[45] These undercurrents of potential cross-cultural liaisons are, of course, common within female captivity narratives, and a few decades later they would become linked to facial tattooing in the American popular imagination through the 1857 publication of *Life among the Indians*, the story of Olive and Mary Ann Oatman's captivity among Yavapai and then Mohave Indians.[46] The Mohave tattooed the women's faces for reasons that remain unclear or lost in cultural difference, though by some accounts facial tattoos signified marriage for Mohave women (see figure 7). Olive Oatman's "as-told-to" narrative quickly went through three editions, and she became an instant celebrity, the American equivalent of Betty Guard or Eliza Fraser, disruptive to conventions of white femininity not only because of the physical marks of her captivity but also because, according to the (unreliable) narrative of her experience, her return to white society was not voluntary.[47] Like Mary Jemison, a white woman captured during the French and Indian War who spent the rest of her life among her captors, marrying into Indigenous groups and having children, and whose narrative was published in 1824 (the same year that Child's *Hobomok* with its own narrative of interracial marriage appeared), Olive Oatman challenged perceived boundaries between "civilization" and "savagery."

Of course, the interracial relationships often hinted at within such captivity narratives and the historical tensions that they illustrate also appear in other American fiction in the early nineteenth century. As Shirley Samuels notes, historical novels depicting interracial relationships—for example, Child's *Hobomok*, Catharine Maria Sedgwick's *Hope Leslie* (1827), and Cooper's *The Last of the Mohicans* (1826)—were published during a decade of tremendous changes to U.S. policies regarding territory and settlement.[48] Cross-cultural desire, Samuels argues, which is associated with blood and the shedding of blood in these novels, becomes a way to work through contemporary transactions about land. Although "Mary Howard" certainly does not register cross-cultural desire or relationships in the same way that these novels (with their adult characters) do, "Duaterra's tattooing" on Mary's forehead brings the story into conversation with such fiction. The mark on Mary's forehead, like the raised bloody arms in *Hobomok*, *Hope Leslie*, and *The Last of the Mohicans* that Samuels argues produce "an emphatic relation to sexuality and to race," indicates some kind of crossing—of boundaries, of race—and some kind of possession.[49] The circulation and recirculation of Child's "Mary Howard" in the decade following the Indian Removal Act of 1830 and in the national context of the Trail of Tears and conflicts like the Black Hawk War, along with the contemporary circulation of Australasian stories about women such as Betty Guard and Eliza Fraser, requires us to think about not only transpacific exchanges and entanglements but also the place of genres like the female captivity narrative in comparative settler colonialisms.[50] To do so is to acknowledge both "transpacific routes" and, as Paul Giles has written of America and Australia, how former British colonies are bound together historically as settler nations colonized during the same historical era.[51] Child herself made this point in the *Juvenile Miscellany*'s "Dialogue, between the Shades of Duaterra, a New Zealand Chief, and Philip of Pokanocket" as she imagined these two historical figures speaking to each other across space and time. She illustrated that former British colonies are linked across the space of the Pacific, their ideologies shaping settler colonial relationships with the islands of the immense oceanic region, even as, for Child, the Pacific and its peoples provided ways to reengage with continental settler colonial pasts and presents.

Figure 7. Arizona Historical Society–Tucson, Main Photograph Collection, Olive Oatman, no. 1927.

READING THE TATTOOED CHILD

While Lydia Maria Child presumably included "Mary Howard" in *The Little Girl's Own Book* to teach lessons about goodness, kindness, and faith in God, the story also brings the racialized and sexualized violence sometimes found within stories about adult female captives to bear on the body of a young female child. Mary Howard's status as child is further complicated by the agency granted to her on returning to England. As Kathryn Tomasek notes, the story inverts gender roles as Mary becomes the provider for herself and John Morris, drawing on her knowledge and her "exoticism" to make money by selling New Zealand–based crafts back in London.[52] In essence, Mary becomes a version of the tattooed adult male traveler who capitalized on his marks. As Tomasek also observes, such moves suggest "the implication of even little girls in the economies of race, class, colonialism, and sexuality in which the United States and its citizens participated in the first half of the nineteenth century." The story illustrates that "white middle-class girls are always already complicit in the economies of colonial capitalism," but it also emphasizes that "personal knowledge of those economies through entrepreneurialism is in fact the very opposite of deviance."[53] Certainly it seems in keeping with Child's pedagogical goals to suggest that this story is intended to remind child readers to be good and kind as well as industrious and self-sufficient.[54] Yet "Duaterra's tattooing," with all of its implications, remains embedded within the story's depiction of the global economies of colonial capitalism as it is forever hidden beneath Mary Howard's curls. Mary Howard is always marked by New Zealand.

So, too, as we have seen, was antebellum America marked by the Pacific. The depths of New Zealand's reach into the culture and economies of antebellum America becomes even clearer through the chapbook version of "Mary Howard," *The Little, but Affecting History of Mary Howard*, published by the Sandbornton [*sic*] Press in Sanbornton, New Hampshire, in 1836. This sixteen-page chapbook is less than four inches long—a small book for small hands. It condenses the narrative's large geographic scale and multiple generic engagements into a tiny space (see figure 8). This version of "Mary Howard," presumably extracted from *The Little Girl's Own Book* and printed by the small rural press whose other extant publications include an alphabet book, a natural history of beasts, and a book of poems and stories, did not have a large run and probably circulated locally in the years following its printing.[55] That it was being given to young girls in New Hampshire is confirmed by inscriptions in two of the American Antiquarian Society's four copies of the chapbook.[56]

According to those inscriptions, one book belonged to Sarah Spaulding, born in Hillsborough County, New Hampshire, in 1825.[57] The other was "presented to Belinda Colby by her teacher D. Whittemore" (see figure 9). Colby was born in Deering, New Hampshire, in 1839 and was gifted the book presumably sometime in the 1840s or early 1850s.[58] The presentation of the chapbook to a student by a teacher emphasizes the text's pedagogical potential, a potential reinforced by the alphabet that is printed just after the title page. That alphabet appears, perhaps, both as a printer's test page, because it includes not only letters but also punctuation, and as an opportunity for instruction in literacy (see figure 10).

Though the chapbook's small size suggests a personal, solitary reading experience that makes the alphabet redundant (any child reading the story alone would presumably already know her alphabet), as Patricia Crain has shown, the alphabet concerns literacy acquisition, but it is also more generally "the technology with which American culture has long spoken to its children and within which it has symbolically represented and formed them." As such, "alphabetization in the modern period establishes the very possibilities of authorship and readership, permeating the formation of both persons and texts," an observation that might serve as a reminder of George Lillie Craik's discussion of alphabetization and "advanced civilizations" in *The New Zealanders*. The presence of the alphabet at the beginning of this chapbook, even presuming an already literate child reader, reinforces deeply ingrained connections between education, the organization of knowledge, and "discourses of Christian and republican literacy."[59] The alphabet establishes the chapbook's pedagogical function, encouraging us to consider what girls might have been intended to learn from the story that follows, in addition to gaining reading practice.

Much of Child's story is reprinted word for word in the chapbook version, and many of the key moralizing passages remain, but Duaterra's thoughts about why he does not kill Robert and Mary are not reproduced. Numerous paragraphs describing Mary's time in New Zealand and her acquisition of skills are omitted, as is the detail that Robert is tattooed and marries Duaterra's sister. That Duaterra wants Mary to be his "little wife" is gone, as are most specifics about Mary's return to England, including the plotline about selling her New Zealand–inspired wares and sending goods back to Duaterra in New Zealand. Most of the passages removed from the chapbook version appeared toward the end of the story as it appeared in *The Little Girl's Own Book*, suggesting that perhaps whoever was setting the type for the book was editing as he went and found himself running out of space. The result is an exceedingly spare

Figure 8. *The Little, but Affecting History of Mary Howard* (1835; Sanbornton, NH: Sandbornton Press, 1836). Courtesy, American Antiquarian Society.

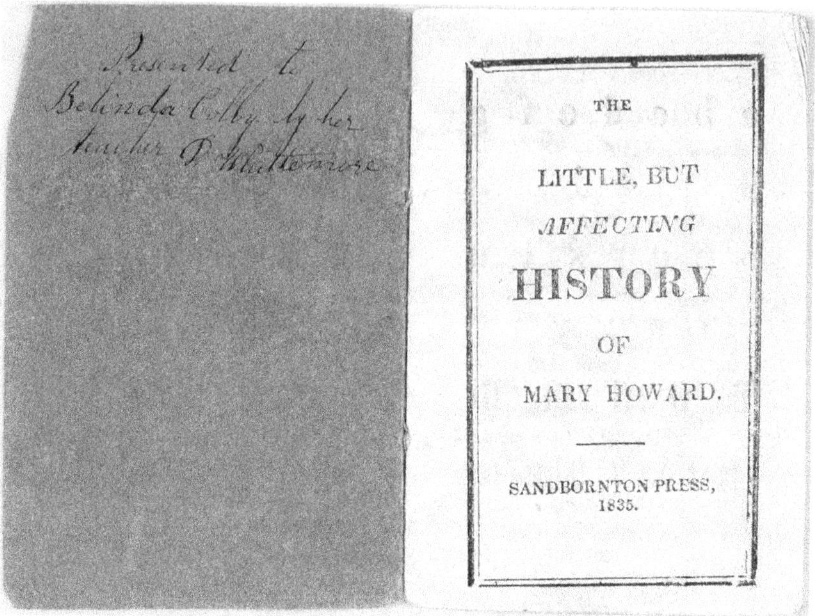

Presented to Belinda Colby by her teacher P. Whittemore

THE

LITTLE, BUT

AFFECTING

HISTORY

OF

MARY HOWARD.

SANDBORNTON PRESS,
1835.

Figure 9. Detail, *The Little, but Affecting History of Mary Howard* (1835; Sanbornton, NH: Sandbornton Press, 1836). Courtesy, American Antiquarian Society.

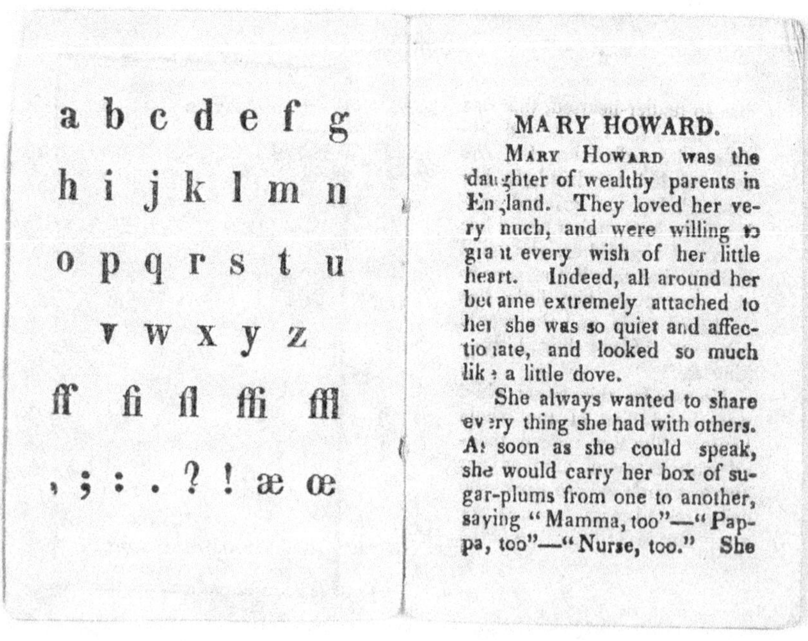

a b c d e f g
h i j k l m n
o p q r s t u
v w x y z
ff fi fl ffi ffl
, ; : . ? ! æ œ

MARY HOWARD.

Mary Howard was the daughter of wealthy parents in England. They loved her very much, and were willing to grant every wish of her little heart. Indeed, all around her became extremely attached to her she was so quiet and affectionate, and looked so much like a little dove.

She always wanted to share every thing she had with others. As soon as she could speak, she would carry her box of sugar-plums from one to another, saying "Mamma, too"—"Pappa, too"—"Nurse, too." She

Figure 10. Detail, *The Little, but Affecting History of Mary Howard* (1835; Sanbornton, NH: Sandbornton Press, 1836). Courtesy, American Antiquarian Society.

story that rushes to a close. In the chapbook Mary is tattooed, then she returns home and loses "the rude habits she naturally acquired," all in the space of two pages. Readers of this version do not receive lessons about economic self-sufficiency or have any sense of Mary's triumph as they do in Child's original tale. Readers are merely told, "You would not believe [Mary] was ever among the savages, unless you raised a cluster of curls, and discovered Duaterra's tattooing." This chapbook version of "Mary Howard" is abridged in a way that makes its moral or message extremely thin.

In its abridged form, the narrative's starkness crystalizes questions about Child's children's fiction that are present within the original story as well, namely, what are we to make of Mary Howard and her mark? Although "Mary Howard" engages didactic forms, from the alphabet that prefaces the chapbook version of the story to the question-and-answer format that enters the text after the death of Mary's father, and while it engages familiar didactic themes, from the need to be kind to animals to the need to trust in God, there is no evangelist here, and Mary Howard is not explicitly an empire builder. She does perform the work of empire by bringing Indigenous knowledge to the metropole and sending goods back to New Zealand, but at the same time her body is incorporated into other systems, and she is then reabsorbed into "civilized" society as her curls cover her markings. She is not recovered entirely intact, but neither does she die, as traditions of cross-cultural encounter and captivity—and the plot of a story like "The Children in the Wood"—might lead us to expect. And she is not "ruined" by the mark that would seem to racialize her.[60] Indeed, in both its original and its abridged form, "Mary Howard" is less clear in its message than we might expect from knowledge of stories such as those within the *Peter Parley* series or even a more liberal publication like the *Juvenile Miscellany*. Whatever ideas about white Christian benevolence appear in some of the stories about the Pacific in the *Juvenile Miscellany* are even more muted here. As such, "Mary Howard" helps us see Child's writing for children at its most provocative and can inspire us to read such children's fiction with an eye toward possibilities that extend beyond didactic aims.

A focus on the morals within stories like "Mary Howard" is predicated on long-standing notions about the child as a model of progress, a model that has been challenged in more recent work on, for example, the child and queer temporalities.[61] We increasingly recognize that the child does not move ever forward into an adulthood equated with a fully formed individual and that even as the child is often associated with the development of the nation or empire in the nineteenth century, that parallel does not always hold.[62] And there were other models and anxieties surrounding childhood in the nineteenth century; for example, Laura Soderberg has recovered the antebellum "incorrigible child," children whose "bodies have been marked unreadable" and whose interior thoughts may not match their outward expression.[63] While Mary Howard is hardly incorrigible, her story and body, with its hidden mark, is somewhat illegible. Her story does not fit a clear pattern of evangelization and successful empire, nor does it fit a clear pattern of refusal of the same as it appeared in *The Little Girl's Own Book* or abridged in chapbook form. Both in its generic engagements and its content, the story seems surprisingly promiscuous.

The very "adult" contexts of Mary Howard's captivity and tattooing might suggest Jacqueline Rose's notion of the "impossibility of children's literature."[64] Rose famously and provocatively argues that children's literature is written to satisfy the needs and desires of adults, rather than to address children's needs. Children's literature, according to Rose, perpetuates adult fantasies about childhood, including notions of purity and innocence and of language as natural and unified. In this sense, the very good Mary Howard and the alphabet that begins the chapbook version of the text register both purity of character and unity of language, of signs. Yet the very threats that images of childhood innocence are intended to repress emerge nevertheless.[65] Little Mary Howard is carried off and marked by "the son of a New Zealand Chief" and, incidentally, marked in a way that is not in keeping with traditional gender patterns. Māori women received a chin tattoo, whereas men received a full facial tattoo, which included the forehead. Mary's forehead marking is, therefore, a kind of tattoo cross-dressing. It is, in a way, doubly subversive. But such a reading inevitably brings us back to the question of intent and of audience, as well as that of how the child reader might have encountered the text. The gendered nature of moko would not have been common knowledge.

Questions about how we read—for "symptom" or "surface"—that have received significant attention are heightened when it comes to children's literature such as "Mary Howard," whose tattoo, carried across cultural boundaries, might provide an analogue for the marks we encounter on the page, carried across temporal boundaries—marks that are not as uniform and legible in their message as they might initially appear given common expectations about the didactic function of nineteenth-century children's literature.[66] While the alphabet that prefaces the chapbook version of the story suggests that children will learn to read the marks, bodies, and lessons contained within it, those bodies and lessons are not always intelligible. These marks, pressed into the fleshy pages of the tiny chapbook printed in New Hampshire and themselves taken from Child's collection of tales and games, draw on a well-known English ballad, a contemporary children's song, and traditions of the captivity narrative at the same time as they bring the distant Pacific into New Hampshire homes and small hands. They advise the child reader to be faithful, but they also titillate and suggest that one can be marked and still be good. What is more, these marks on the page suggest opportunities to engage with U.S.-Pacific entanglements on different scales and through texts characterized by narrative paces that diverge from those of the lengthy travel narratives and novels, exemplified by *Moby-Dick*, that we often associate with nineteenth-century American representations of the Pacific. In so doing, they also provide opportunities to put New Zealand and the United States in conversation as settler nations in which female bodies negotiate problems of cross-cultural contact and belonging. Considering how such stories and bodies appear in nineteenth-century America can help us deepen our readings of the marks of children's literature and of children in American literature, while enabling us to deepen our understanding of the material texts and narratives surrounding Pacific-U.S. entanglements in the years between the first Euro-American encounters with the region and the literary moment when Queequeg and Ishmael are "wedded" by a whaling rope.

In the hands of Lydia Maria Child, ideas and stories about the Pacific circulating in such texts as Craik's *The New Zealanders* become opportunities to subtly revise Christian notions of white benevolence and hierarchies of language propagated in many children's stories about the Pacific. Though stories that reinforce these more conservative ideas appear in the pages of Child's *Juvenile Miscellany*, they appear alongside texts authored by Child that give voice to Indigenous characters and, in the case of "Mary Howard," unsettle stereotypical gender norms through contact with indigeneity. A focus on the Pacific and New Zealand in particular in Child's writing for children reveals her familiarity with contemporary tales about these regions and her awareness of the links between distant imperial and settler colonial spaces, links that she articulated in her stories. These connections are developed in the book's next section, not through children's literature but rather through accounts of travel and settlement in terrestrial North American frontier spaces that negotiate the challenges of making new western homes through recourse to the Pacific and to oceanic plots.

PART II

Continental Territories, Oceanic Plots, and Interior Selves

CHAPTER THREE

"Doubting, dreading, fretful guest"

Elizabeth Craw's Diary and Transoceanic Anxiety

Lydia Maria Child drew on her reading about Pacific islands such as New Zealand to develop pedagogical messages about care and kindness, as well as about historical injustice. She absorbed information from texts like George Lillie Craik's *The New Zealanders* and then sent that information back out to her child readers in new forms. In the next two chapters I shift attention from children's literature and its potential pedagogical work within the nineteenth-century home to texts produced by women actively seeking to construct new settler homes in the North American south and west, in the territory that would become Texas and in Michigan. These texts, a diary recording travel and a fictionalized travelogue, are defined by their recirculation of verse and of narrative plots that reveal the challenges of constructing new homes. Difficulties are articulated in part through recourse to oceanic stories and texts produced by events in the Pacific. This chapter focuses on a diary in which the Pacific is far less explicitly present than it is within Child's New Zealand stories. In this diary, the Pacific is not used to facilitate the instruction of others; instead, within the diary a text emerging from events in the Pacific is used to negotiate intimate, emotional anxieties within the self. But those intimate anxieties are nevertheless situated within, and partially caused by, the broader workings of empire, revealing networks and histories that cross the Pacific and highlight expressions of personal affect in the midst of imperial conflict.

At the center of this chapter is a poem titled "Anxiety," written by twenty-four-year-old Nessy Heywood on September 10, 1792. At that time Heywood was with her family on the Isle of Man between England and Ireland waiting to hear of her younger brother's fate. That brother, Peter Heywood, was being held aboard the HMS *Hector* in Portsmouth Harbor in advance of his court martial for alleged participation in the 1789 mutiny aboard the HMS *Bounty* in the Pacific. Approximately forty-four years later, this poem, composed on a British island in response to events on Pacific islands, was carefully written into the pages of a diary belonging to Elizabeth Craw, an Ohio woman who had traveled to Texas to begin a new life. Little is known about Craw beyond what can be gleaned from the diary, but Craw's reappropriation of Heywood's poem in her diary, alongside fragments of poetry and prose taken from popular printed material, brings late eighteenth-century events in the Pacific into the contested territory of Texas. In this chapter, I read the shifting form of Craw's diary and its intertextual borrowings in order to examine how Craw harnesses another's words about an intensely personal but also public crisis to express her own anxiety during her trip and the unsettled times of the Texas Revolution, into which she was unwittingly headed. Craw's diary and the emotions it records are my starting place for an investigation of affective reverberations that bring the terrestrial imperial tensions of the expanding United States in the 1830s into contact with the late eighteenth-century Pacific. In the previous chapter I focused on the place of female captivity narratives in comparative settler colonialisms. In this chapter, I highlight personal emotions embedded in imperial and geopolitical conflicts as revealed in archival material, further illuminating entanglements between the Pacific and continental territory that would become part of the United States. Elizabeth Craw was far from Tahiti and the Isle of Man, but these island spaces enter her diary through Nessy Heywood's poem, creating an alternative emotional geography of empire.

"WE HAVE GOT LOST"

Sometime in mid-November of 1835, Elizabeth Craw and her traveling companions wandered lost among the bayous between Cheneyville, Louisiana, and San Augustine, Texas. Craw had started her journey in Cleveland, Ohio, and she presumably intended to end it in Texas, though she does not make her destination explicit in the diary in which she records her trip. In the diary's first pages, Craw rather systematically records her travels in the form of an orderly chronicle, beginning on October 10, 1835, but she does not specify the purpose of her travels. She notes the friends she visited as she traveled from Cleveland to Cincinnati, as well as the family members and acquaintances she saw as she lingered in Cincinnati waiting to board a boat down the Mississippi. Some of those acquaintances urged Craw to stay in Cincinnati. On October 22, Craw writes:

> *Mr. and Mrs. M are anxious for*
> *me to spend a year with them*

O that I had the advice of my
Parents but I shall proceed on my
Journey thinking it to my [illegible word].[1]

While the final word of this entry is illegible, Craw's resolution to move on comes through clearly. Her last day in Cincinnati—a Sunday—was spent attending church, where she heard Harriet Beecher's (soon to be Harriet Beecher Stowe) father Lyman Beecher preach ("Dr. Beecher preached an exelent [*sic*] sermon," she briefly noted) and where she dined at the Pearl Street House, one of Cincinnati's oldest hotels.[2] Departing from Cincinnati on Monday, October 26, Craw notes the group of friends who assembled to wave "a farewell," and she seems in good spirits the following day, which "is beautiful the / Water still and company agreable [*sic*]."[3]

All of this—the visits, the dining, the still water and agreeable company—must have seemed a distant memory by the time Craw wrote "we have got lost" in faint pencil at the top of a diary page during weeks spent navigating the Louisiana bayous after heading west from the Mississippi River at the mouth of the Red River.[4] In this part of the diary, the orderly dating and record keeping of the first stages of the journey falls apart. At one point Craw writes: "I have lost the day of the month." A few pages later she again writes:

"it
is called Sunday but I
cannot find a person to
tell me the day of the month."[5]

That most basic of diary structures, the dated entry, has been lost among the gamblers, cotton fields, alligators, and rain that overwhelm the pages.

After Craw's time in the bayous, in the general region where Harriet Beecher Stowe would situate Simon Legree's plantation in *Uncle Tom's Cabin* and where Solomon Northup, a free Black man kidnapped from Upstate New York, would be enslaved in the 1840s, her diary never regains its original orderly, dated coherence. Instead, it evolves into a kind of commonplace book comprised of excerpts from poetry and prose and the occasional record of Craw's life in Texas. The physical manuscript that is today preserved in Rice University's Woodson Research Center seems an intimate manifestation of Craw's personal experiences of orderly beginnings (orderly beginnings that were nevertheless sometimes challenging; "I am quite unhappy" is the extent of Craw's entry on Monday, October 19, while still in Cincinnati).[6] And it is an intimate manifestation of emotions caused by the chaotic events that followed those beginnings, emotions negotiated through publicly circulating language.

The page of Craw's diary that begins "we have got lost" is nearly the end of the first section of the diary, the portion in which Craw rather coherently describes her travels from Ohio to Louisiana between October 10 and mid-November 1835. Here, her orderly record begins to fall apart. In full, the page reads:

we have got lost
O Dear Dear it is noon
And we are still lost
to ourselves and I fear
to another tomorrow [illegible word]
night has come upon
us and we are still
wandering
we believe we ar [sic] not
in the right [two illegible words][7]

The pencil marks on this page are now so faint that the words are difficult to read. Some are illegible. But Craw's worry comes through in reflections that sound almost poetic. The line breaks of her prose, although dictated by the width of the notebook, reinforce the unsettled melancholy of her sentiments. The word "wandering," for example, sits alone on its own line, giving a sense of unhinged loss. To be physically lost is to be absolutely lost—to be lost to the self.

Following this page there is one that is blank front and back, the first page of the diary left entirely empty, seemingly reinforcing the loss, confusion, and wandering emptiness conveyed on the page that proclaims "we have got lost." Craw's sense of being physically lost results in stalled progression in the forward trajectory of the diary. Then, following that blank page is one containing lines that do not merely sound like verse but are clearly verse. A poem titled "Anxiety" fills a page of the diary (figure 11):

Doubting, dreading, fretful guest
Quit oh! Quit this mortal breast
Why wilt thou my peace invade,
And each brighter prospect shade,[8]

Now the forward movement of travel recounted in the first pages of the diary stalls in lines of poetry about an emotion itself characterized by suspension and uncertainty. "We are still / wandering," Craw writes, and after turning a blank page a reader of her diary encounters the word "Anxiety" and is invited to associate that word, and the poem, with Craw's rather frantic account of her wanderings through Louisiana bayous. But the poem is written in ink rather than in the pencil that marks the confusion of the bayous. It was presumably written at another time, when rain was not pouring down and rising into tents and beds, when alligators were not taking "possession of the log [the travelers] used / for a table."[9] Perhaps it was written sometime after Craw reached San Augustine, Texas, which seems to have been sometime before November 30. A few pages further along in the diary a page dated "San Augustine 30 Nov 1835" proclaims:

> *Miss Addiline E. Craw*
> *will open a school in*
> *the room formerly occupied*
> *by Mr. Parker of this place*
> *in which will be taught*
> *reading, writing English*
> *Grammer & arrithmatic [sic].*[10]

Craw had, it seems, emerged from the swamps of Louisiana ready to restore order to her life through the orderly instruction of others. The school will open, this announcement notes, as soon as sufficient scholars are subscribed. The page includes a list of subscribed pupils, and an entry on the facing page dated over a year later (January 1837) indicates that Craw has, in fact, finally "commenced / school in [her] own house."[11]

The pages between the poem "Anxiety" and those containing details about Craw's plans for a school in San Augustine are dated after November 30, 1835 (the date of the school announcement), so it is clear that Craw did not always write in the diary pages sequentially, though there is an overall forward temporal movement to the diary's dated entries from the beginning to the end of the manuscript. Even when Craw does "find" the day of the month after her time lost in the bayous, those days are no longer placed in a linear temporal sequence. But whether or not Craw wrote the page titled "Anxiety" sometime between the days when she was lost in Louisiana in mid-November 1835 and the next date in the diary, March 19, 1836, the poem's placement suggests this time frame. Its placement invites association with the events that both precede and follow its appearance in the manuscript, events that include rain and mud, on the one hand, and war, on the other.

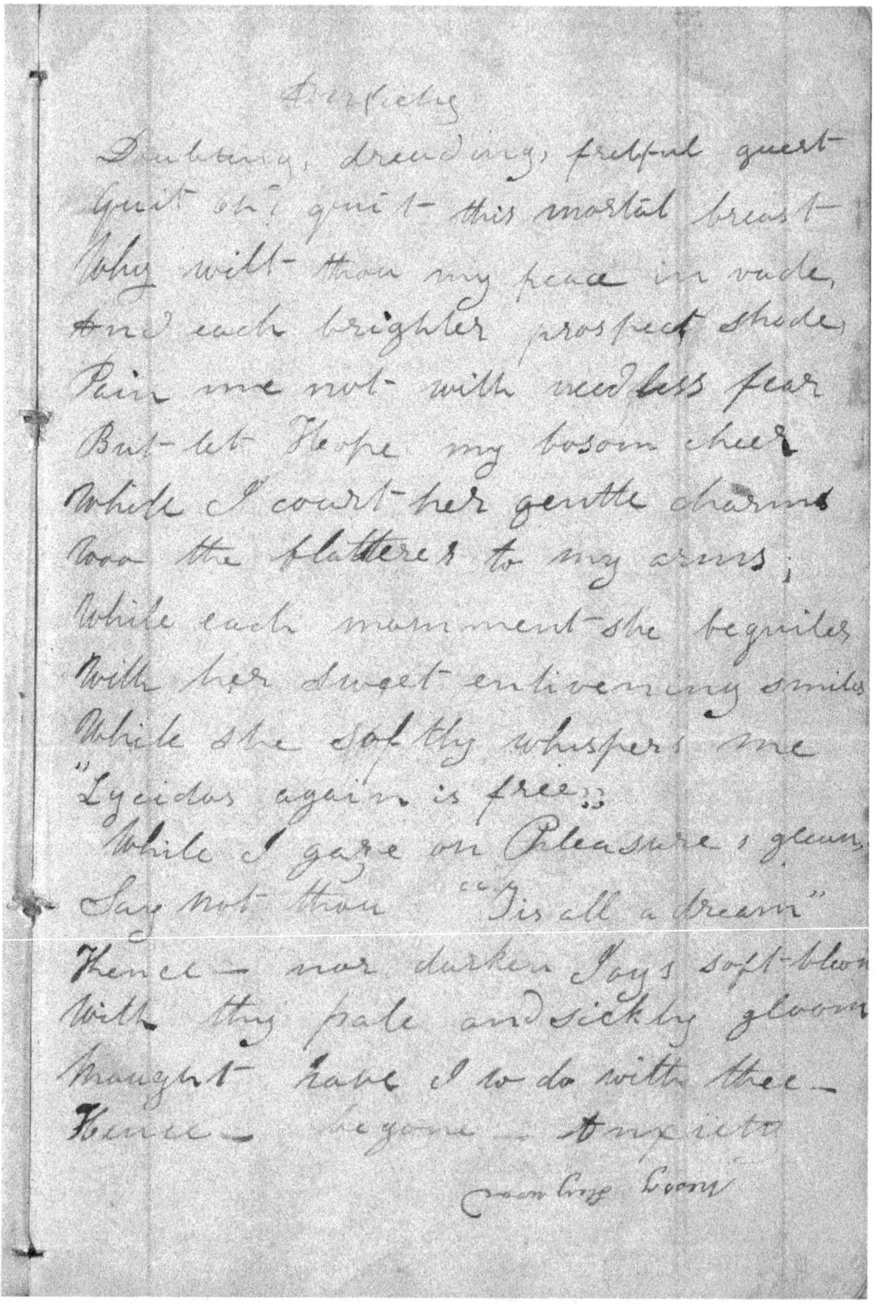
[illegible]

Doubting, dreading, fretful guest
Quit oh! quit this mortal breast
Why wilt thou my peace invade,
And each brighter prospect shade,
Pain me not with needless fear
But let Hope my bosom cheer
While I court her gentle charms
Woo the flatterer to my arms;
While each moment she beguiles
With her sweet enlivening smiles
While she softly whispers me
"Lycidas again is free";
While I gaze on Pleasure's gleam,
Say not thou "'Tis all a dream"
Hence — nor darken Joys soft bloom
With thy pale and sickly gloom
Naught have I to do with thee —
Hence — begone — Anxiety

[illegible]

Figure 11. Elizabeth Craw diary, 1833–1841, MS 386, Woodson Research Center, Fondren Library, Rice University, Houston, TX.

Indeed, there was plenty to be anxious about during these months. The Battle of the Alamo took place from February 23 to March 6, 1836, a fact recorded in Craw's diary in an entry dated March 20, just pages after the poem "Anxiety" but before the announcement of her plans for a school:

> *20 March 1836 San Augustus*
> *this is a dark and lousy day*
> *very cold and dreary we are in*
> *daily expectation of an attack*
> *from the Indians San Anton*
> *has been retaken by the Span.*
> *Samuel Evans was massacred.*[12]

If Craw and her companions found their way out of the Louisiana bayous and arrived in San Augustine, about three hundred miles northeast of San Antonio, sometime in late November 1835, they arrived at a particularly fraught moment. When Craw left Cleveland on October 10, 1835, she was probably aware of ongoing tensions between U.S./Anglo settlers in Texas and Mexican authorities. News of these tensions circulated throughout the United States, including in Craw's home state. A June 27, 1835, article from "a Brazoria [Texas] Gazette" reprinted in the *Scioto Gazette* of Chillicothe, Ohio, on September 2 reported, "The political condition of the Texonians appears to be approaching a crisis—a storm is brewing which may agitate the political elements violently."[13] By early November, Ohio newspapers were publishing information about the "war in Texas" taken from "an extra of the Red River Herald [Natchitoches, Louisiana]," including a letter from General Houston dated "San Agustine [*sic*], Texas, Oct. 5," in which he promised armed volunteers "liberal bounties of Land" in exchange for their efforts "in defense of our rights, our oaths, and our constitution . . . in Texas."[14] But when Craw left Cleveland on October 10, when she passed through Chillicothe on October 15, and when she departed Cincinnati on October 26, she probably had not heard about the skirmish at Gonzales on October 2 that would come to mark the beginning of the Texas Revolution. She likely had not heard that one day after she left Cleveland, on October 11, Stephen F. Austin was elected to lead the volunteer army of Texians who would fight at the Alamo. Craw's travels south were bringing her directly into the emerging crisis that would result in the formation of the Republic of Texas on March 2, 1836, and, eventually, to the annexation of Texas by the United States (1845) and to the U.S.-Mexican War (1846–48).

The first acknowledgment of these tense Texas-Mexico relations that does appear within Craw's diary enters the manuscript during her time in Louisiana, right after she notes that

it
is called Sunday but I
cannot find a person to
tell me the day of the month.[15]

Having emerged from days in the "swamp," Craw and her companions arrive in "Chenyville" (Cheneyville, Louisiana), and she writes:

there is all kind of gambling
carried on here And big storys [sic]
are here told of the Mexicans
and Texans going to war one
company of volunteers have
left this state . . .[16]

It seems, then, that anxieties about the imperial conflict into which Craw was moving might have been inseparable from anxieties about the rain, rising waters, alligators, and horse stealing "Indians" that characterize the diary pages leading up to the poem "Anxiety" after all.

The diary also suggests that the unsettled geopolitical situation into which Craw was moving developed a very personal face with the stark sentence that appears in her March 20, 1836, entry: "Samuel Evans was massacred" (figure 12). Samuel Evans, it has been conjectured, was Craw's fiancé, though definitive evidence is hard to find.[17] The Samuel Evans who was killed at the Alamo had moved to Texas a year earlier from New York State with his widowed father and his siblings, acquiring land in Bastrop County.[18] Craw was, perhaps, traveling to Texas to join him, though there is no such mention in the diary. Whoever Samuel Evans was to Craw, he mattered enough to be mentioned by name, and after this entry much of the diary takes on a tone of mourning, of suffering. If Craw was "quite unhappy" on one of her days in Cincinnati, she seems almost perpetually so in the remainder of the diary. Further down the same page that contains Craw's entry of March 20, for example, is one dated April 13, which begins "my head alike my heart / ache," an entry exemplifying the tone of much of what follows. Between these entries, written in a slightly different color ink and in smaller handwriting, as if inserted in the gap between entries at a later date, are the following lines:

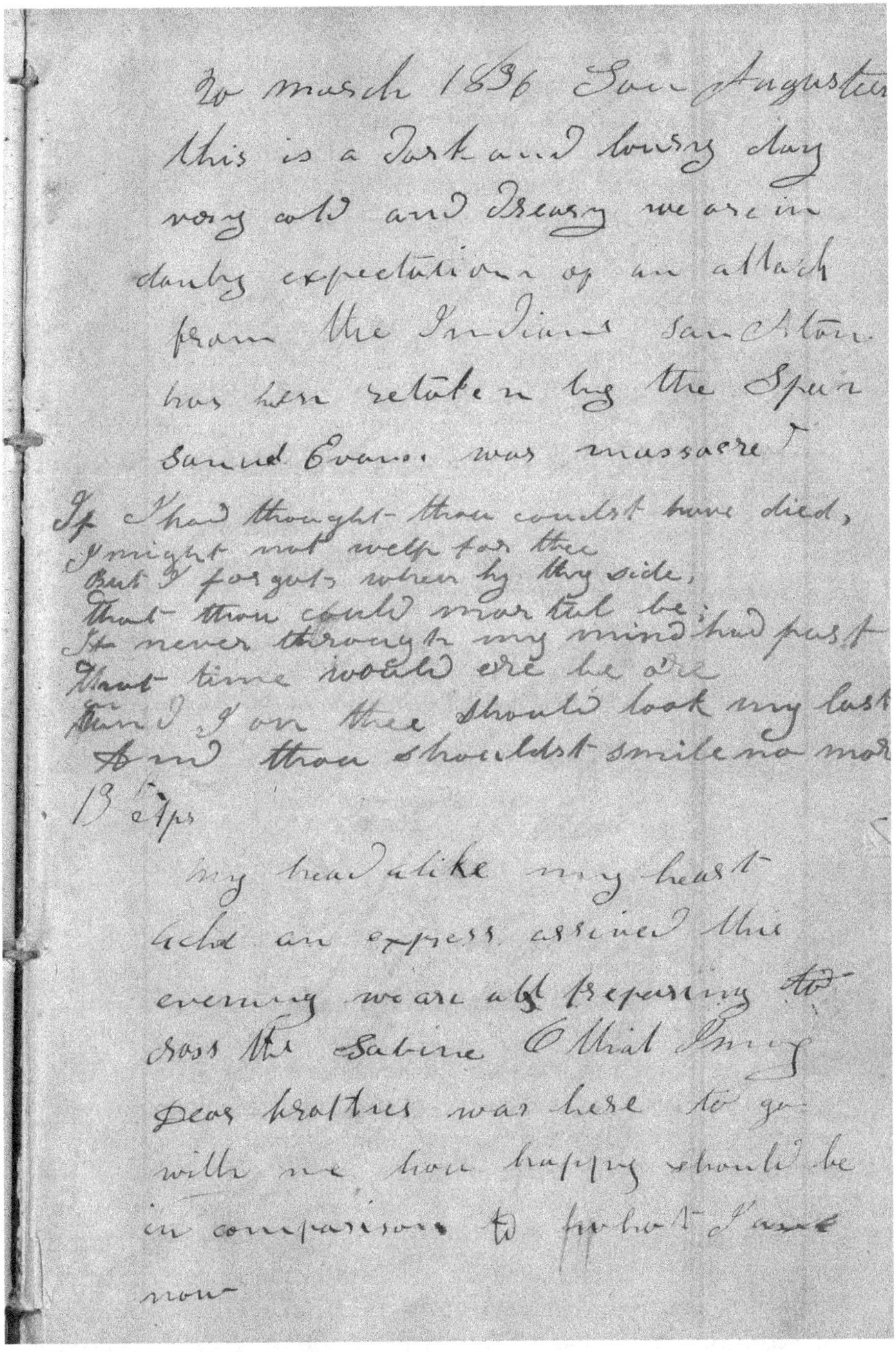

20 march 1836 San Augustine
this is a dark and lowring day
very cold and dreary we are in
dayly expectation of an attack
from the Indians San Anton
has been retaken by the Span
Samuel Evans was massacred

If I had thought thou couldst have died,
I might not weep for thee
But I forgot when by thy side,
That thou could not but be;
It never through my mind had past
That time would ere be o'er
And I on thee should look my last
And thou shouldst smile no more

13 Apr

my head alike my heart
ached an express arrived this
evening we are all preparing to
cross the Sabine O that my
dear brother was here to go
with me how happy should I be
in comparison to what I am
now

Figure 12. Elizabeth Craw diary, 1833–1841, MS 386, Woodson Research Center, Fondren Library, Rice University, Houston, TX.

If I had thought thou coudst have died,
I might not weep for thee
But I forgot, when by thy side,
That thou could mortal be;
It never through my mind had past
That time would ere be ore
And I on thee should look my last
And thou shouldst smile no more[19]

These lines are unattributed, but given they immediately follow the stark sentence "Samuel Evans was massacred," they seem like they could be personal reflections on the emotions associated with this event. But these are not Craw's words but rather the lines of the first stanza of Irish poet Charles Wolfe's (1791–1823) elegiac poem "To Mary," reprinted in various books and magazines throughout the nineteenth century. A few pages later, after Craw's announcements about her school, a full page of the diary written in the same color ink as the first stanza of "To Mary" is devoted to that poem's final stanza:

I do not think, where e're thou art
Thou hast forgotten me,
And I perhaps may sooth this heart
In thinking too of thee
Yet there was round thee such a dawn
Of Light ne're seen before,
As fancy never could have drawn
And never can restore![20]

While not explicitly connected to the sentence "Samuel Evans was massacred," this stanza, too, seems to extend from and reflect back on that moment in the diary, offering a meditation on loss and grief that pervades the rest of the manuscript. The remainder of the diary contains reflective, melancholy lines of poetry and prose that are only occasionally punctuated by small records of everyday life: a list of clothing, drafts of invitations to the burial of a couple's infant son.

The diary that began as a linear, orderly record of travel turns into a kind of nonlinear commonplace book when loss and grief erupt. It is not surprising, given what we know of nineteenth-century print circulation and reading practices, that many of the mournful, reflective entries in this second half of the diary are verses, like Wolfe's, that Craw has taken from various popular printed sources.[21] In this sense, of course, Craw's reading and writing practices remind us of Lydia Maria Child's as she composed the *Juvenile Miscellany* and "Mary Howard," drawing on numerous sources in the process. They remind us of processes of borrowing and recirculation that characterize nineteenth-century writing. The lines in this second half of Craw's diary range from the excerpts from Wolfe's poem to verses that appear in an 1814 novel titled *Duty* by Margaret Roberts ("O time suspend thy rapid flight . . . Ah if thou wilt not pause for love / What can thy rapid flight restrain").[22] Many of these verses focus on the loss of love or on the loss of *a* love. In other places Craw seems to weave lines from published sources into her own reflections as she vacillates between despair and hope, as when she ends a page with lines from an 1839 song titled "The Dream Is Past" ("the dream is / Past and with it fled / The hopes that once my bosom fed"), only to begin the next page with what appears to be her voice:

> *I said the dream was past but*
> ~~*still it is pleasant to reflect to*~~
> *to dream abut* [sic] *memory is a faith*
> *full chronicler of the past.*[23]

Toward the end of the diary an entry headed "December 1841, Cleveland," appears to indicate that Craw has returned to Ohio. The content of this entry is appropriately taken from a poem titled "The Wanderer Come Home; or, The Old Apple Tree" by a Mrs. Crawford. Many of the excerpts after this entry reflect on issues of memory and return (though others after the entry are written from San Augustine, a reminder of Craw's nonsequential use of the diary). For example, a passage from *Tales of Field and Flood, with Sketches of Life at Home* (1829) by John Malcolm begins

> *"Let not those who has [sic] sojourned*
> *in a distant land, give way to a long-*
> *-ing to revisit the scenes of his childhood*
> *and retrace the walks of his youth,—"*[24]

As difficult as was Craw's time in Texas, she apparently found her return to Ohio challenging as well, for she discovered that she could not return to the same home she had left. Nor could she return as the same person. An entry on the facing page reads

> *And shall I go back to my first loved home*
> *To find how all is changed*

Alone, o're those altered scenes to roam
From my early self estranged,
Shall I bend me over the glassy brook,
No more on the face of a child to look.[25]

These lines are from a poem titled "Recollections" by Hannah Flagg Gould (a sometime contributor to the *Juvenile Miscellany*), a poem frequently republished in part or whole in magazines like the *Ladies' Magazine* and *Godey's Lady's Book*.[26]

With the exception of a few lines from *A Midsummer Night's Dream* and several pages where musings appear to be Craw's own ("my life is one long / sad dream," she writes), the pages in the second half of the diary are entirely comprised of unattributed lines taken from popular poems and the occasional prose work, many of which were published or republished in magazines and in gift books like *The Token* at various points in the 1830s and early 1840s.[27] Occasionally lines are slightly misquoted or two lines are reversed, perhaps indicating that Craw wrote them from memory. The result is a record of grief and of intimate self-reflection that exemplifies the simultaneously private and public nature of the diary form as Craw weaves her personal meditations from relatively popular published sources.[28] At once a record of personal grief and confusion amid—and to some extent caused by—struggles over the territory that is now Texas and a record of a woman's struggles with personal change as she leaves and returns to Ohio, faces adversity, and grows ever further from her previous self, this diary contains language made available to Craw through the circulations of nineteenth-century print culture.

"BEGONE—ANXIETY"

Although much of the second half of the diary comprises these fragments, the poem titled "Anxiety" stands out from the rest. It is not only the first poem to appear in the diary but also the only poem that obviously appears in the diary in full, carefully and neatly written on one page. "Anxiety" is also distinct for another reason: it does not seem to have appeared in the magazines and gift books from which most of Craw's other verses are taken. Yet even these lines are not Craw's own, as is clear from the name "Nessy Heywood" written beneath the poem (upside down). The poem emerged as a personal reflection generated out of another imperial context. The now famous *Bounty* voyage to Tahiti began in late 1787, motivated largely by Sir Joseph Banks and his interest in exploration and botanical discovery. The expedition was intended to finally complete a task that had been preoccupying merchants, planters, and colonial powers for years. Breadfruit trees from the islands of the Pacific would be transplanted to the West Indies, where, it was hoped, the trees would flourish. The breadfruit would feed island populations, most notably the enslaved persons whose labor fueled island plantations. This voyage exemplified nineteenth-century global imperialism.

Order and control deteriorated not long after the *Bounty*'s departure from England, exacerbated, perhaps, by a five-month stop in Tahiti, where crew members supposedly had a taste of freedom difficult to reconcile with the discipline of shipboard life. Not long after leaving Tahiti, in April 1789, Acting Lieutenant Fletcher Christian led members of the *Bounty*'s crew as they took control of the ship from its captain, William Bligh. They set Bligh and crew members loyal to him adrift in the ship's launch while they themselves settled on Tahiti and Pitcairn Island. In later reports of these events, it was difficult to ascertain who played what role in the mutiny and to determine whether everyone who remained on the *Bounty* was actually disloyal to the captain. Perhaps men were left behind in the confusion of the moment; perhaps there was not room in the launch for all those who did not want to be associated with Bligh's overthrow. But everyone not set adrift with Bligh was deemed a mutineer, and when Bligh miraculously made his way back to England and arranged for the Admiralty to pursue the mutineers, all crewmen who had remained in the Pacific were subject to trial.[29]

Peter Heywood was among those left on the *Bounty* after the mutiny; he and thirteen other *Bounty* fugitives were picked up by the search ship HMS *Pandora* in Tahiti in late March 1791. After an unsuccessful search for the *Bounty* itself and for the remaining missing mutineers, the *Pandora* ran aground on the outer Great Barrier Reef while en route to the Dutch East Indies. The ship eventually sank, and ninety-nine survivors, including ten prisoners from the *Bounty*, undertook a journey just as harrowing as Bligh's return to England. They made their way to Batavia (present-day Jakarta), where the *Bounty* prisoners were held for nearly two months before being transferred to a Dutch ship and taken to Cape Town. In Cape Town they were transferred to a British warship for the final leg of the journey to England, where they arrived in June 1792.

Nessy Heywood began an active correspondence with her brother Peter that June upon his arrival back in England, a correspondence that continued through the tense days of the court martial, which began on September 12, just two days after Nessy wrote the poem "Anxiety." During these months, Nessy and other members of the well-connected Heywood family were active advocates on Peter's behalf. Yet, of course, the family's advocacy did not necessarily secure Peter's future—his life was in the hands of the twelve naval captains who would serve as judges in the court martial proceedings and in their interpretation of the various accounts of what happened in the early morning hours on a ship in the Pacific three years earlier. (Peter Heywood was one of three men eventually recommended mercy and pardoned by the king, but that was not a foregone conclusion when the court martial started. Four other *Bounty* survivors were acquitted; three others were hanged.)

The much-publicized mutiny and its aftermath—an event centered around a crisis of authority and power at sea in the Pacific that became a crisis of memory and narrative back in the imperial center and a personal crisis of life or death uncertainty for the Heywoods and other families—was the motivation for Nessy Heywood's poem, which Craw wrote into her diary decades later and oceans away as follows:

Anxiety

Doubting, dreading, fretful guest
Quit oh! Quit this mortal breast
Why wilt thou my peace invade,
And each brighter prospect shade,
Pain me not with needless fear
But let Hope my bosom cheer
While I count her gentle charms
Woo the flatterer to my arms;
While each moment she beguiles
With her sweet enlivening smiles
While she softly whispers me
"Lycidas again is free"
While I gaze on Pleasures gleam,
Say not thou "Tis all a dream"
Hence—nor darken Joys soft-bloom
With thy pale and sickly gloom
Nought have I to do with thee—
Hence—begone—Anxiety[30]

In eighteen lines arranged into rhyming couplets, Nessy wishes away anxiety and issues an invitation to hope as she waits to find out whether her brother, only recently discovered to be alive, will be sentenced to death or allowed to live. The poem's personification of "Hope" notably invokes Milton's well-known pastoral elegy "Lycidas" through her whisper to the poem's speaker, a detail that highlights the extent to which Nessy's own emotions are being negotiated and expressed through established poetic traditions. Milton's "Lycidas" memorializes Edward King, who drowned when his ship sank off the coast of Wales in 1637. In the poem, the "uncouth swain" (line 186) remembers his friend Lycidas and mourns his untimely death:

For Lycidas is dead, dead ere his prime,
Young Lycidas, and hath not left his peer.
Who would not sing for Lycidas? He knew
Himself to sing, and build the lofty rhyme.
He must not float upon his wat'ry bier
Unwept, and welter to the parching wind,
Without the meed of some melodious tear.[31]

When Nessy Heywood's "Hope" whispers "Lycidas again is free," she offers the possibility of freedom from death, yet again, for the recently returned Peter Heywood. This line substitutes Peter Heywood for Milton's friend Edward King, one body lost forever at sea, the other still living but long lost to the speaker and author of "Anxiety." After all, by September 1792 Nessy had not seen her brother for over five years. And he soon might be lost again forever, depending on the outcome of the court martial. For "Lycidas" to again be free would certainly be a kind of resurrection.

"Anxiety" is just one of numerous poems that Nessy Heywood wrote during this time of personal and familial crisis. Many of those other poems have titles that announce their occasional nature more explicitly than does "Anxiety," among them "On the Arrival of my dearly-beloved Brother, Peter Heywood, in England, written while a Prisoner, and waiting the Event of his Trial on board his Majesty's Ship 'Hector'" (August 5, 1792) and "On receiving certain Intelligence that my most amiable and beloved Brother, Peter Heywood, would soon be restored to Freedom" (London, October 15, 1792, midnight).[32] Throughout these poems the amateur poet relies heavily on neoclassical poetic traditions—invocations of the Muses, apostrophe, and regular rhyme and meter—as she channels extreme anxiety, uncertainty, and lack of control into conventional poetic forms. And each of these poems uses Lycidas as a figure for the absent Peter. But despite these formulaic moves, Nessy's lines still quiver with the tension of the moment.

Many of these poems, along with a few written by Peter himself and correspondence between members of the Heywood family regarding the court martial, were published in Sir John Barrow's 1831 book *The*

Eventful History of the Mutiny and Piratical Seizure of H.M.S. Bounty*: Its Cause and Consequences*. That book, published in London, was reprinted the following year in New York under the title *A Description of Pitcairn's Island and Its Inhabitants: With an Authentic Account of the Mutiny of the Ship* Bounty*, and of the Subsequent Fortunes of the Mutineers*. Both titles were reprinted numerous times on both sides of the Atlantic throughout the 1830s. In this book Barrow, who was a close friend of the Heywood family and second secretary to the Admiralty, offered a comprehensive account of the *Bounty* dramas, but one heavily focused on the Heywood family and intent on presenting them in the best light possible in the wake of Peter's death earlier in 1831. Peter and Nessy's mother provided Barrow with family papers and letters, which he reproduced throughout his account. Nessy Heywood's letters and poems appear in Barrow's book as part of its project of positive memorialization, presented for their high "tone of feeling for [Peter's] honour, and confidence in his innocence." By this point Nessy, too, was being memorialized, though only incidentally in Barrow's book. Nessy had died in 1793, less than a year after Peter's pardon, a fact that Barrow attributes to her "excess of sensibility, which acted too powerfully on her bodily frame." "This impassioned and most affectionate of sisters," Barrow writes, was seized with "consumption" following Peter's release, her death marked by "several elegiac stanzas" in the style of those she herself wrote for her brother and others.[33] Anxiety and its aftermath had, according to Barrow, killed Nessy.

We cannot know where or when Elizabeth Craw came across Nessy Heywood's poem "Anxiety." Perhaps she read John Barrow's book about the *Bounty*, which was certainly circulating in the early 1830s; perhaps someone else read Barrow's book and copied down Nessy's poem, and Craw took it from that other source. Or perhaps "Anxiety" was reproduced in a magazine or gift book that Craw encountered, dissociated from the context of Nessy's anxiety about the results of the *Bounty* court martial. Craw may have encountered the poem entirely divorced from its Pacific, imperial context. But however these lines written by another woman forty-four years before the Battle of the Alamo ended up in the middle of Craw's diary, their presence in that diary provides an opportunity to consider personal expressions of anxiety and anticipation in the midst of different kinds of imperial conflict and geographies. If we take this poem's presence in Craw's diary seriously, it allows us not only to consider the place of publicly circulating language and formal control or release within personal reflections in the late eighteenth and early nineteenth centuries but also to think through the relationship between the anxious writer and a larger context of imperial anxiety and crisis. It allows us to think through the forms and structures that regulate or fail to regulate emotions and empires. And it allows us to further consider some of the intimate ways that the Pacific, in particular, circulated in nineteenth-century America, in this case through private expressions of anxiety made public in print and then reinscribed into the pages of Elizabeth Craw's diary.

ANXIETIES OF EMPIRE

The cause of Nessy Heywood's anxiety seems clear. Her brother's fate was in the hands of twelve naval captains. The occasion of Elizabeth Craw's anxiety is somewhat more diffuse: her fiancé's death, rain, war. But both women (Craw through Heywood) turn to the word "anxiety" to express the emotional state of a moment or a period of their lives, a word with a complex history in relation to bodies, gender, and empire. "In colloquial English by the early nineteenth century," writes Justine Murison, "'anxiety' did not display the somatic richness of the classical period or the psychological complexity it would achieve after Freud, and yet its history contained both." Etymologically rooted in both Middle French and Latin terms for worry, disquiet, or distress, the word's Latin root also suggests discomfort in the chest or, as Murison puts it, "the hysterical symptom of a ball rising in the throat."[34] Historically, anxiety was grounded in the body, a sense of the word suggested in Heywood's poem through the lines "Quit this mortal breast" and "But let Hope my bosom cheer." Anxiety resides in the chest, and hope has the potential to dislodge it. These subtle somatic resonances of anxiety within Heywood's poem are coexistent with proto-psychological ones, evident in such lines as "Doubting, dreading, fretful guest," and the idea that anxiety darkens "Joys soft-bloom / With [its] pale and sickly gloom." But here the effects of anxiety on "Joys soft-bloom" are still described in physical terms: "pale and sickly." Anxiety is not itself "pale and sickly," but the gloom that it casts is. It causes those it touches to be "pale and sickly." In Heywood's poem, anxiety is something that resides in and manifests on the body as it also disturbs the mind. In this sense, the poem itself prefigures John Barrow's claim that the stress of the *Bounty* court martial led to Nessy Heywood's death, though Barrow's language (an "excess of sensibility . . . acted too powerfully on her bodily frame") reveals gendered assumptions reinforced by long-standing notions of female hysteria that would be codified and medicalized over the course of the nineteenth century.[35] Heywood's poem itself does not rely on these gendered assumptions, expressing a personal yet also generalizable experience of waiting and of worry, yet it is difficult to entirely separate the poem from these assumptions given that Heywood is anxious about the potential loss of a close male figure.

But in both Heywood's and Craw's cases, personal waiting and worry is also situated within broader workings of empire and of revolution. The "anxiety" felt in these individual minds and bodies, even if occasioned by the loss or potential loss of a fiancé or brother, is inseparable from encroachment into the Pacific, on the one hand, and into what is now Texas, on the other hand. The individual, intimate emotions being expressed exist within broader imperial contexts of concerns about stability and control. The *Bounty* voyage, for example, was motivated by ongoing curiosity about the Pacific, a search for knowledge, and concern about the British empire's ability to sustain itself without taking steps to ensure that it could feed its enslaved and laboring populations. This expedition also occurred after decades of European and Euro-American contact with the Pacific and with Tahiti in particular. That contact shaped expectations about the region's potential and its dangers. Sir Joseph Banks's own previous experiences in Tahiti as part of James Cook's first voyage to the Pacific (1768–71) had drawn attention to cultural fascinations such as tattooing, as discussed in the previous chapters, and had helped circulate ideas about the beauty and availability of distant islands, their resources, and their women. Cook's voyages produced narratives and visual representations of the Pacific that reinforced romantic notions of exotic locales. But the *Bounty* expedition also started out a mere nine years after James Cook's death at Kealakekua Bay, Hawai'i, in 1779 and in the wake of ongoing questions about the nature of that event. William Bligh, who would command the *Bounty* voyage, had been present when Cook died, and as Caroline Alexander puts it, "the command of Sir Joseph Banks's prestigious breadfruit journey implied more than a return to naval service [for Bligh] . . . it put Bligh squarely in Cook's footsteps."[36] In other words, the Pacific—its trees, its women—was waiting to be used and enjoyed in the Euro-American imperial imaginary, but the Pacific could also be a threat, through seductive promises or through fatal misunderstandings or mistakes. Although no one could have predicted the mutiny that took place on the *Bounty*, it was part of this crisis of tensions embedded in expectations, encounter, and imperial control or lack of control. And as Michelle Burnham has argued, the mutiny was part of ongoing cycles of revolutionary violence moving back and forth across the Atlantic and the Pacific in the late eighteenth century. "The Pacific," Burnham writes, "seemed sometimes to reflect the political instability and upheaval of the Atlantic and at other times to offer a commercial solution to its problems."[37] Such events as the *Bounty* mutiny reflect the tensions between global forces of revolution and empire and local particularities of European encounters with the Pacific and its peoples.

This is evident in that what followed the mutiny for individuals like Peter Heywood was also part of ongoing instability surrounding European encounters with the region. After the mutiny and before being discovered living on Tahiti by the crew of the *Pandora*, Peter Heywood and other alleged mutineers had immersed themselves in life on the island in the ways common to European "beachcombers." Some of them were living with Tahitian women. Some were tattooed. In a letter written while being held in a ship prison before the court martial, Heywood assured his mother that he was "tattooed like them [Tahitians] in the most curious manner . . . not to gratify my own desire, but theirs; for it was my constant endeavor to acquiesce in any little custom which I thought would be agreeable to them, though painful in the process, provided I gained by it their friendship and esteem, which you may suppose is no inconsiderable object in an island where the natives are so numerous."[38] Like many men tattooed in the Pacific, he insisted that his markings were necessary and strategic rather than desirable. But they still suggested immersion in another way of life and the potential of Peter's "own desire." Peter Heywood had also learned the Tahitian language during his time in the Pacific; he spent some of the time before his court martial writing out a Tahitian vocabulary. Though the court martial itself focused on what individuals did or did not do during the mutiny, the broader context of the mutiny involved deep cross-cultural encounter with the Pacific that grew out of global political and economic forces and resulted in anxieties of a more personal nature. Nessy Heywood's "anxiety" was that of a sister concerned for her brother's fate. But anxiety also lies behind concern about Heywood's behavior on the part of his family and behind broader public concern about numerous aspects of the mutiny and its aftermath. Where did the lack of authority and order at stake in the mutiny itself end? In what ways might the mutiny signal other kinds of upheaval? What kind of desires for other ways of life or manifestations of violence did the mutiny mask?

By the 1830s, the cultural anxieties surrounding conflicts over the territory that would become Texas also had a long history. From the U.S. perspective, those anxieties had everything to do with histories of colonial violence and impulses for ongoing territorial expansion. In the article "War in Texas" published in the *Scioto Gazette* on November 4, 1835, for example, the reprinted letter from General Houston mentioned earlier includes the exclamation, "Our war cry is *liberty or death!* Our principles are to support the Constitution and down with the Usurper."[39] Events in Texas are framed in terms of revolution and independence that here echo the language attributed to Patrick Henry during his speech to the Second Virginia Convention in March 1775. The issue of control of Texas is framed as one about "the rights of free and republican government." "The difference between the Mexican Government and Texas," the article continues, "ostensibly rises out of a change in the Constitution of 1824, made as is alleged, without the consent of the People of Texas. They have refused to conform to it, and this armed force is sent to compel them. But, in truth, the People of Texas wish to separate from Mexico, and become part and parcel of the American Union."[40] The Constitution of 1824 had created the United Mexican States as a federal republic severed from Spanish control. Texas was combined with another province and given one seat in the new state legislature, prompting outrage at a loss of political autonomy. At the same time, the sparsely populated region was vulnerable to incursions. Hoping that settlers would stabilize matters, the Mexican government loosened immigration policies in the late 1820s, and an influx of settlers from the United States, many of whom were slave-owning southerners, moved into the Texas region. These settlers began to outnumber Tejanos (Mexican-born residents of Texas) as Mexico abolished slavery in 1829, leading to further tensions. By the mid-1830s the situation had come to a head.

The same "War in Texas" article reprinted a "recent number of the New Orleans Bee" that outlined the situation, lumping "Mexicans" and "Indians" together against "American colonists":

> The Mexicans appear resolved to keep the Texonians with their hands full. Not only have large bodies of troops been sent to that state—but, Mexican agents have excited the neighboring Indians to attack the American colonists. The Commanches [*sic*] and Cherokees have already made several incursions; so that ex-governor Houston and other gentlemen have been obliged to write to Washington to entreat the interference of the National Government.
>
> Americans to the Rescue! Remember the condition of our revolutionary ancestors, when the Indians were excited against them! Shall we suffer our colonial friends to be masacreed [*sic*] by Indians hired by the Mexicans, and have them driven from the colonies which they have honorably purchased and laboriously improved?[41]

Casting the tensions over the territory of Texas in terms of colonial valor, revolutionary history, and American industriousness as it vilifies

Indigenous peoples, this newspaper article highlights the ways in which conflicts over land and U.S. national expansion, which were also conflicts over the institution of slavery and where it would be allowed, were negotiated in terms of national and perceived racial difference. Such articles highlight how anxieties about difference were harnessed to justify imperial moves, while imperial moves involved constructing and negotiating anxieties about difference.[42]

The anxiety expressed by Craw and Heywood, historical figures seemingly peripheral to yet tightly bound to the workings of empire, provides an occasion to connect expressions of personal affect to our critical engagements with colonialism and imperialism across oceans.[43] In the past decades, readings of colonialist discourse that emphasize confidence, enthusiasm, and success have been supplanted with various forms of postcolonial inquiry that instead highlight the ambivalence—the anxieties—of colonial discourse as represented in the above accounts of the *Bounty* mutiny and incursions into Texas. Scholars have recognized the uncertainties that comprise the imperial record, whether in the form of concerns about racial and national miscegenation, anxieties about the metropole's ability to establish and maintain power and control over distant lands, or thinly veiled disquiet about the fundamental (il)logic and violence of imperialism. More recently, discussions of settler colonialism as a structure of elimination focused on the appropriation of land and of the paradoxes underlying settler claims of belonging have allowed scholars to trace new patterns across geographic and temporal borders. The economic, legal, and ideological processes that undergird settler colonialism have been shown to be operative in both Pacific contexts (such as New Zealand and Hawai'i) as well as continental spaces (such as the United States and Australia).[44]

Anxiety as a reading practice much discussed in recent years, one that focuses on what a text does not or cannot say explicitly given its broader ideological commitments, might allow us to read Heywood's poem in the context of broader imperial and settler colonial anxieties raised by the *Bounty* mutiny and even by Peter Heywood's behavior in the wake of the mutiny as he lived on Tahiti and immersed himself in the life of the island. Anxiety as a reading practice might enable us to read Craw's use of Heywood's poem in similar terms, given the tensions inherent in her time in Texas. But the immediacy of anxiety as affect in both Heywood's poem and Craw's diary means that instead of only theorizing or reflecting anxiety, it is felt through these texts as well. It is present as a somatic expression; it is present as something residing in a "mortal breast." And it is embedded in the material form of Craw's diary, which emphasizes the embodied anxious writer as it moves from orderly travel narrative to emotional commonplace book, with the poem "Anxiety" as a turning point. Nessy Heywood's poem carefully written into Elizabeth Craw's diary lets us configure distant imperial and settler colonial ventures around bodies and writers not always part of these stories, in this case women whose lives were bound up in these structures even as they were not themselves participants in the mutiny on the *Bounty* or present at the Battle of the Alamo.

Of course, these women's writings still obscure the bodies and experiences of many others bound up in the "intimacies" of empire, to adapt Lisa Lowe's formulation, including the "Indians" and "Mexicans" only mentioned in Craw's journal and the Indigenous inhabitants of Tahiti, including those kidnapped and brought to Pitcairn Island by the Bounty mutineers who settled there in the type of acts of violence foundational to global empire. Lowe develops a "'political economy' of intimacies" that unsettles "the meaning of intimacy as the privileged sign of liberal interiority or domesticity, by situating this more familiar meaning in relation to the global processes and colonial connections that are the conditions of its production." She discusses various intimacies among enslaved peoples, Indigenous peoples, and colonized laborers, unsettling historical methods and conventional geographies as she explores the formation of modern liberalism. In many ways she exposes the intimacies that allow Heywood's and Craw's relatively privileged "anxieties" to exist.[45] The affective reverberations within and between Craw's and Heywood's texts might reinforce "intimacy as the privileged sign of liberal interiority or domesticity," yet the reverberations that connect Heywood to Craw, Pacific to Texas, might also expose ideological operations of imperial and settler colonial forms across geographies. This, in turn, can help us recognize a kind of affective relationship embedded within textual circulations, here a relationship that yokes the Pacific and Texas, the islands of Polynesia and the watery bayous of the Red River region through which Craw traveled. This resonance between British activities in the Pacific in the late eighteenth century and disputes over the territory that would become the U.S. state of Texas in the 1830s expressed through the language of personal emotion is significant because it reminds us of the transoceanic dynamics of imperial and settler colonial forms. The Pacific was not the end point of a linear story associated with ideas of U.S. Manifest Destiny. It was a space in which upheavals, claims, power structures, and the anxieties they produce were occurring simultaneously with, and occasionally well before, some conflicts such as the U.S.-Mexican War that are most associated with U.S. territorial expansion and settler colonial violence. This geographic reorientation of approaching U.S.-Mexico tensions via the Pacific and its imperial histories of violence and power struggles, suggested here through emotive language connecting individual bodies and spaces of empire, produces archipelagic relations configured around those bodies and spaces. In the next chapter, such connections will be both narrative and material as I show how maritime plots are deployed in terrestrial realms at the same time as the "new homes" of nineteenth-century U.S. continental empire are shown to themselves be built on watery foundations.

CHAPTER FOUR
"Outre-mer adventures"
Caroline Kirkland's Frontier and the Maritime World

Caroline Kirkland's *A New Home, Who'll Follow? or, Glimpses of Western Life* is set in the wilds of Michigan. A genre-defying collection of sketches that combines qualities of the travelogue, traditions of orality and gossip, and biting social satire, *A New Home, Who'll Follow?* is often read as a warning to those considering moving west—a text that counters and parodies contemporary booster literature intended to lure settlers to new territories with the promise of productive land and quick money. Kirkland herself had moved from Upstate New York to Michigan with her husband and children in 1835, the same year that Elizabeth Craw left Ohio for Texas. Writing witty letters about the trials of frontier life to her friends in the East supposedly prompted Kirkland to pen *A New Home*, which was published in New York in 1839. In the book, houses are raised and populations multiply, but financial speculation fails, banks collapse, and interpersonal relationships within new communities are fraught. Furthermore, narrative expectations of success, of progress, of adventure ("I have never seen a cougar—nor been bitten by a rattlesnake," the narrator tells us in the first chapter) are repeatedly undermined.[1] Whatever romantic notions you have about life in the West, Kirkland reminds her readers, they are not aligned with the actual experience of constructing a new home there.

Kirkland's critiques of the expectations surrounding settlement are heightened through *A New Home*'s literary borrowing. In keeping with what Meredith McGill has termed the "culture of reprinting" explored throughout the previous chapters' discussions of Lydia Maria Child and Elizabeth Craw, Kirkland "culls from many sources, including stories by or about settlers other than herself, references to literary sources (both cited and uncited, prose and poetry), and her own personal experience," as Rachel Azima has noted.[2] She draws on writings about the West by authors such as James Hall and Charles Fenno Hoffman as well as on her readers' familiarity with a range of poetic and narrative traditions in the course of emphasizing that the West settlers imagine—one of opportunity and advancement, productive land and certain wealth—is just that: imagined. Mrs. Mary Clavers, the narrator, emphasizes that the plots of settlement—whether maps of planned towns or the narratives told about them—are akin to familiar fictions, complete with a "climax," "circulated" in print.[3]

While discussions of *A New Home* have often focused on Kirkland's literary borrowing and on the text's wide-ranging generic engagements, the role of stories about the sea within the text have gone unexamined. Tales of maritime adventure appear throughout *A New Home*. For example, Mrs. Clavers quips, "Robinson Crusoe would have been the most rational purchase" for a young couple's frontier reading material, suggesting that a tale of settlement and economic development set within maritime contexts would best suit their needs.[4] At other moments, entire oceanic plots appear within Kirkland's text, as with the story of Mr. and Mrs. Beckworth, whose inevitable marriage is delayed by Mr. Beckworth's years at sea. These maritime references and plots seem incongruous in a narrative about the Michigan frontier. But in what follows, I show how stories about the sea are an integral part of Kirkland's story about the Michigan "peninsula."[5] We might expect these oceanic narratives to reinforce the notion of home as a clearly defined space or concept that stands in opposition to maritime spaces and tales, but Kirkland's sea stories do not do this work. Rather, they serve to reinforce the question mark in Kirkland's title, one that asks "Who'll Follow?," while also unsettling the very concept of "home." Homes, whether in the form of planned but still unrealized towns or rustic frontier houses, remain persistently speculative in *A New Home*. The romance and speculation involved in plots of sea voyages, I argue, becomes another way to reinforce the romance and speculative nature of the West as a fiction. Whereas the anxiety produced by the chaos of the Pacific sea voyage draw together Heywood's and Craw's imperial moments and their individual responses to those moments through Heywood's poem written into Craw's diary, Kirkland draws on the speculation and chance of maritime travel and the narratives produced by that travel so as to unsettle other territories being brought under U.S. control in the 1830s.

Of course, while sea stories might initially seem out of place in a narrative set in Michigan, scholars of nineteenth-century American literature and culture have long recognized links between western and oceanic frontiers in texts of that era. In his 1961 study of James Fenimore Cooper's sea fiction, for example, Thomas Philbrick notes that Cooper "habitually uses marine metaphors and analogies in drawing his pictures of the woods and the woodsman's life." In Francis Parkman's *The Oregon Trail*, the prairie is "like a turbulent ocean, suddenly congealed when its waves were at the highest." James Hall, popular historian of the West and western fiction writer, often described landscapes in similar terms. "The interminable plain extended further than the vision reached, spreading out a landscape which was bounded only by the dim sea-like horizon," he writes in "The New Moon: A Tradition of the Omawhaws." "As the smaller prairies resembled a series of larger and lesser lakes, so these boundless plains remind one of the ocean waste. Here and there a solitary tree, torn by the wind, stood alone like a dismantled mast in the ocean," he writes in his story "The Indian Hater." More generally, wagons traveling westward were sometimes referred to as "prairie ships," "schooners," or "clippers."[6] Such metaphors and references figure western settings as ocean-like; they bring the oceanic frontier into the western frontier.

Although these metaphors make the western frontier like the oceanic frontier as they draw on maritime references to describe unfamiliar terrestrial spaces, some have argued that, historically, the national project of territorial empire building was not simply inextricable from but was supplanted by the (inter)national project of maritime exploration and trade in a way that puts territorial and oceanic frontiers in opposition. As Philbrick puts it in an often-quoted argument: "Viewed as a body, the hundreds of nautical novels and short stories that were produced in this country during the first half of the nineteenth century . . . suggest that before 1850 the American frontier was primarily a maritime one, that the sea rather than the continental wilderness was the principal focus of the yearnings and imaginings of the American dream."[7] Here, Philbrick paints a picture of a nation focused outward to the sea. More recently, Jason Berger has reoriented this maritime vision of the period back toward economic and social transitions within the nation as they engage global economies and movements, examining "how maritime narratives operated in the political landscape of nineteenth-century America."[8] Berger argues that considering maritime narratives in relation to "the social function of fantasy" allows us to think differently about how these narratives negotiate dramatic changes in antebellum economic and social life in an era of increasing globalization. "Maritime fantasies have significant political import in [the antebellum] era," he writes, "for they emerge (or reemerge) to organize, condition, and respond to experiences in which social, political, and economic antagonisms often occurred or came to a head—many of which opened up irreconcilable fissures in existing symbolic coordinates."[9] As part of the oceanic turn in literary scholarship, Berger helps us to reencounter the relationship between oceanic and terrestrial realms in nineteenth-century America by considering not maritime metaphors but maritime fantasies.

But although Berger illuminates antebellum U.S. political, social, and economic concerns, he focuses on texts that are, for the most part, set in global maritime spaces rather than in continental spaces and texts written by familiar, canonical figures such as Cooper and Melville.[10] In attending to how Kirkland imports tales of oceanic voyaging into her "wandering sketches" about a new home on the Michigan frontier, I shift attention from how maritime narratives reflect political and economic concerns through narratives set at sea or how they might be evidence of an antebellum world oriented more toward the sea than toward the "continental wilderness" in Philbrick's older formulation. Instead, I show how, in Kirkland's case, maritime narratives are part of constituting and questioning the plots told about home within a female-authored text.[11] If, in Amy Kaplan's well-known formulation, the domestic "can expand or contract the boundaries of home and nation" in nineteenth-century women's writing, from domestic manuals to popular fiction, reaching outward into the "foreign" and regulating those included in "expanding national boundaries," Kirkland's home is constituted and yet unsettled by the speculation at the heart of *A New Home*'s engagement with oceanic spaces and tales.[12] Kirkland's sea stories might be set in global or even fantasy realms, but these stories reinforce the questions the narrative asks about the speculative nature of home.

THE SEA AND SPECULATION

In contrast to writers such as Cooper, Hall, and Parkman who scatter maritime metaphors throughout their descriptions of frontier landscapes, in *A New Home, Who'll Follow?* Kirkland incorporates entire tales of oceanic adventure into her account of settling Michigan. For example, when Mrs. Clavers and her friend Mrs. Rivers (a name that explicitly conjures watery realms) are caught in a rainstorm following an excursion to the still unrealized town of Tinkerville (which turns out to pose little immediate threat to Mr. Clavers's proposed settlement—the women pass through Tinkerville without realizing that they are actually in the town), they take refuge in "a farm-house—not a Michigan farm-house, but a great, noble, yankee 'palace of pine-boards,' looking like a cantle of Massachusetts or Western New-York dropped *par hazard* in these remote wilds." The scene is one of "*Eastern* enchantment" for Mrs. Clavers, who admits that she has been "troubled with a sort of home calenture at times since we removed westward."[13] The word "calenture" conjures a fever or sickness in general terms but, more specifically, suggests a fever believed to affect sailors in the tropics, one supposedly characterized by delirium in which the affected individual imagines the sea to be green fields and wants to leap overboard. Momentarily figuring Mrs. Clavers as a delirious, homesick sailor who wants to sink into a part of the East seemingly transplanted into the West, this word hints at the maritime tale to come.

The "yankee 'palace of pine-boards,'" it turns out, belongs to Mr. and Mrs. Beckworth, the former "a hearty, cheerful-looking, middle-aged man," the latter a lady with a "mild, intelligent, and very pleasing" appearance. "A slight depression of the outer extremity of the eye-lid, and of the delicately-pencilled arch above it, seemed to tell of sorrow and meek endurance," Mrs. Clavers remembers. Sure that, "like so many western settlers, the fair and pensive matron had a story," Mrs. Clavers begins to try to draw Mrs. Beckworth's story from Mr. Beckworth. All that she discovers is that Mrs. Beckworth has been "thrice married."[14] Eventually, however, as he accompanies the travelers on their homeward journey, Mr. Beckworth gratifies the narrator's curiosity about his wife by relating his own story, which Mrs. Clavers, in turn, relates to the reader over the course of the next three chapters.

Mr. Beckworth's tale is one that would have been generically familiar to readers, at least in outline. The eldest son of a Massachusetts farmer, Beckworth was in love with his cousin, Agnes, who was tasked with caring for her ill mother. Unable to support Agnes after her father's trusting nature causes him to fail in business (a detail that intersects with *A New Home*'s focus on speculation and trust more generally), Beckworth decides to go to sea to make his fortune, hoping to marry Agnes upon his return.[15] He heads to the seaport and only then sends Agnes a letter telling her of his plan and instructing her to collect his wages while he is away. Returning after a long East India voyage, he finds his money untouched and Agnes married to another man. Beckworth's courier, the ironically named Job Jephson, had, of course, failed to deliver the fateful letter. Job explains that on his way home from the seaport with Beckworth's letter he had been distracted by an opportunity to speculate: "there was a chance turned up to spekilate a little, and arter that I went down South to trade away some notions." When he finally returned home, the weather was cold so he put his best coat away with the letter still in the pocket. By the time he came across the letter again, Agnes was about to be married, and Job decided not to deliver it. A humorous character whom Beckworth has already identified as the speculator behind the town of Tinkerville, Job is associated with various speculative endeavors throughout Beckworth's tale, from "cock-fighting" to "steam doctorin'."[16] A jack-of-all-trades who is always looking for a quick way to a fortune, Job is even now, Beckworth explains, "at least as poor as ever."[17] Job's schemes highlight the potentially foolhardy nature of speculation and the risk involved, even as they contribute to the delay in the Beckworth's union.

After Job tells him about Agnes's marriage, Beckworth returns to sea, heartbroken. "His *outre-mer* adventures are of no importance to my story," states Mrs. Clavers, yet she goes on to relate "how, as he stood with two or three messmates, staring, like a true Yankee, at the Tower of London, a press-gang seized them all, and rowed them to a vessel which lay off the Traitors' Gate, the Americans protesting themselves such, and the John Bulls laughing at them;—how, when they got on board the man o' war, they showed their protections, and the officer of his Majesty's recruiting service said he could do nothing in the case till the ship returned from her cruize—and how the ship did not return from her cruize, but after cruizing about for some three years or more, was taken by a French first-rate and carried into Brest. All this is but little to the purpose. But when Henry was thrown into a French prison, his American certificate procured his release through the consul's good offices, and he shipped at once for New-York, somewhat weary of a sea life."[18] Narrating years of adventures that are supposedly unimportant to her story, but that are related anyway, Mrs. Clavers finally tells of Beckworth's return home. He discovers that Agnes is widowed but about to take up with a wealthy colonel.

To avoid disrupting her impending second marriage, Beckworth decides to turn to the sea once again. Job "commended much his prudent course, and recommended a long voyage; an attempt to discover the North-West Passage, or to ascertain the truth of Capt. Symmes' theory; to take the nonsense out of him and make a little money." "For five long years did Henry Beckworth box the compass," continues Mrs. Clavers, "five years of whaling voyages and all their attendant hardships—and when at the end of that time he retouched his native shore, richer than he had ever been before in his life, he heard, as the reader will no doubt anticipate, that Agnes Boon was again unmated." Indeed, the tale's conclusion has already been anticipated by the fact that Agnes Boon is now Mrs. Beckworth, living happily in the Michigan woods. But even if the conclusion had not already been revealed to the reader, Mrs. Clavers suggests that the conventional plot would allow the reader to "anticipate" the ending.[19] Combining initial surprise ("Mrs. Beckworth thrice married! impossible!") with a generically familiar explanation involving thwarted love, sea adventure, wealth, and love realized, Kirkland, through her narrator, engages familiar plots of oceanic travel, risk, and reward.[20]

Indeed, the relatively simple overarching plot (sick mother, fated love, cycles of three voyages) has fairy tale–like qualities complicated by both the generic familiarity and specific details of Mr. Beckworth's maritime adventures (and in this sense the Beckworths' tale might remind us of Lydia Maria Child's "Mary Howard" with its generically familiar qualities and very specific Pacific adventures). In the middle of recounting Mr. Beckworth's "*outre-mer* adventures," Mrs. Clavers comments, "All this is but little to the purpose." Yet "all this"—all the maritime details—seem to be very much part of "the purpose."[21] Popular plots of maritime adventure like the details of Mr. Beckworth's second voyage, which resemble a pared-down version of one of Cooper's sea novels complete with impressment and prison, are part of what constitute *Mrs. Beckworth*'s story. After all, this episode begins with Mrs. Clavers's interest in Mrs. Beckworth—with Mrs. Clavers's sense that she can "claim . . . the character of a physiognomist" who can read a story of "sorrow and meek endurance" in the lines of Mrs. Beckworth's face. There is, then, a sense in which Mr. Beckworth's adventures and the story of his "constancy," his Job-like patience, seem not to stand in for his wife's story but to *be* his wife's story.[22] The lines on Mrs. Beckworth's face are the result of years of waiting, although at the time she did not know she was waiting. And the story of how Mrs. Beckworth came to be "thrice married" is one that moves through the East Indies, confronts transatlantic conflicts, and embarks on "five years of whaling voyages," presumably into the Pacific.[23] Although Agnes stays at home, her story does not.

Not only does Agnes Beckworth's story travel through her future husband, but her tale also makes the speculation and chance of oceanic voyaging part of the story of Michigan: the Beckworths' union and the wealth that undergirds it is a story of the sea. Their home on the Michigan frontier is a structure presumably built with Mr. Beckworth's maritime profits—with the proceeds of his whaling adventures—and with the wealth left to Agnes by her second husband, whom she married when Mr. Beckworth went back to sea to seek his fortune.[24] Like other maritime endeavors, whaling was, of course, an incredibly risky venture in the nineteenth century. The work was dangerous. The length of a voyage was unpredictable but averaged approximately four years. And after all that time, years of "box[ing] the compass" might result in very little profit for individual sailors.[25] Eric Jay Dolin notes, "Even if a ship returned full [of whale oil], financial happiness was far from assured." Once operating costs and the owners' profits were deducted, "the net result was that many of the crewmen on whaleships made little if any money, averaging only about twenty cents per day, and a significant number of them returned in debt." While overall profits were often substantial, individual crewmen were not likely to make anything approaching a fortune.[26]

The idea that Mr. Beckworth returns from five years of whaling "richer than he had ever been before in his life" advances a romantic vision of the whaling industry that Dolin notes competed with contemporary awareness of the harshness of whaling. In the nineteenth century, Dolin writes, "there were those who saw [whaling] as an exciting and even romantic enterprise, most often because they were considering it from the safety of their own homes and had neither experienced the rigors of whaling, nor knew anyone who had. Then there were others who had a decidedly darker image of the profession."[27] The purely romantic notion of Mr. Beckworth's whaling fortune is undermined, however, by Job's character and his advice to Beckworth. Indeed, the tremendous risk and speculative nature of maritime endeavors, from whaling to exploration, is satirized in Job's impractical suggestion that Beckworth should take "a long voyage; an attempt to discover the North-West Passage, or to ascertain the truth of Capt. Symmes' theory; to take the nonsense out of him and make a little money."[28] Here, "nonsense" implies Beckworth's romantic love for Agnes, but the notion that Beckworth should replace that type of "nonsense" with global exploration as a more practical and profitable option is amusing, given the precariousness of such ventures.

Job's reference to the Northwest Passage conjures a centuries-long search for a viable trade route connecting the Atlantic and Pacific Oceans along the northern coast of North America, a search that ended only in the first years of the twentieth century when Norwegian polar explorer Roald Amundsen successfully traversed the passage over the course of a three-year-long expedition. A number of expeditions had set out to explore parts of the passage in the first half of the nineteenth century, and Sir John Franklin's famously unsuccessful expedition would attempt to chart the passage in 1845, never returning to England. When Kirkland mentions the search for the Northwest Passage in her 1839 narrative, it is, then, representative of the dangerous pursuit of something perpetually enigmatic—hardly a sure way to remove "nonsense" or to make money.

The reference to ascertaining "the truth of Capt. Symmes' theory" makes the pursuit of the enigmatic, of the speculative, even more explicit.[29] John Cleves Symmes Jr.'s hollow earth theory was popularized by his 1818 manifesto, *Light Gives Light, to Light Discover—"Ad Infinitum,"* which Symmes circulated to major institutions of learning and in newspapers throughout the United States in an effort to gain support for his ideas. In subsequent writings and lectures, Symmes posited that temperatures grew warmer as one approached the poles, where there were chasms providing access to the center of the earth. As bizarre as this idea now sounds, Symmes's theory indirectly helped inspire actual maritime expeditions. For example, Jeremiah Reynolds was for a time among Symmes's strongest supporters. An advocate for polar exploration and for the United States Exploring Expedition, or "U.S. Ex. Ex.," a scientific expedition through the Pacific region authorized by Congress in 1836 that took place from 1838 to 1842, Reynolds eventually distanced himself from Symmes's theories, but the idea that the United States should work to make known the unknown continued to unite the two men.[30] Symmes's ideas about the hollow earth also inspired fictional narratives, notably the novel *Symzonia* (1820), which purports to be the true tale of an expedition into the earth through the southern polar hole.[31] Inside the earth, the expedition's crew finds a utopian civilization where the United States' capitalist and expansionist impulses are seen as great evils.

Symmes's hollow earth theories, Reynolds, the U.S. Exploring Expedition, and *Symzonia* all influenced Edgar Allan Poe's *The Narrative of Arthur Gordon Pym of Nantucket*, published in 1838, just one year before *A New Home, Who'll Follow?* Poe's novel, it is often argued, looks outward to fantastic global spaces to create an allegory of home, specifically an allegory of the American South and U.S. race relations.[32] It also draws on oceanic travel narratives and the records of scientific expeditions in the Pacific to destabilize the knowledge emerging from such expeditions. By the end of Poe's generically heterogeneous novel, everything seems speculative. Kirkland's narrative, on the other hand, draws on maritime narratives and fanciful tales of global exploration to destabilize territorial homes-in-progress. *A New Home* references external realms to advance its questions about the stability and future of the domestic. Job's suggestion that Beckworth ascertain "the truth of Capt. Symmes' theory" in order to take "the nonsense out of him" invites readers to merge these notions in an ironic commentary.[33] Kirkland's tongue is firmly in cheek here, as it is throughout *A New Home*. The search for Symmes Hole seems as dreamlike as Job's later plans for the town of Tinkerville. And the fact that Mr. Beckworth's maritime ventures met with success, these references seem to remind us, was pure chance and, narratively, a requirement of bringing the tale of the Beckworths' union to its desired and expected close. The Beckworths' "yankee" house in Michigan is built on the profits of risky ventures. Economic and adventurous speculation in the Pacific is similar to, and here also enables, the speculation involved in creating a new territorial home. Putting faith in one is as questionable as putting faith in the other. Acknowledging these maritime references and plots within *A New Home*'s sketches—from the idea of Symmes Hole to the contemporary context of whaling—allows us to resituate Kirkland's text, putting it in dialogue not only with women's writings about the frontier or with male-authored frontier adventure novels like those by Cooper but also alongside of contemporary texts about global adventures set in such noncontinental spaces as the Pacific or even in entirely fanciful spaces.

"THIS UNDULATING SURFACE"

Kirkland's reference to Symmes indicates familiarity with his theories in general and also with the fictional narrative *Symzonia* in particular when, later in the narrative, another reference to Symmes appears. Toward the end of *A New Home*, readers are offered the story of Cora Mansfield, one of Mrs. Clavers's longtime friends, who, we learn, now lives with her dashing husband, Everard, and their daughter in a cottage in the Michigan woods. Cora is, Mrs. Clavers quips, "at least the dozenth old acquaintance I have met accidentally since we came to the new world," portraying the "new world" of the Michigan woods as uncharted space oddly populated with familiar figures who seem to conjure the familiar stories that also populate this "new world," stories like the Beckworths' tale of maritime adventure and romance.[34]

Cora and Everard, well-off cousins from New York, had modeled their young lives after the romances that had filled their heads with "fantastic notions."[35] Barely out of their teens, they had run away in the middle of the night, eloped, and traveled up the Hudson River to Albany, then, presumably, along the Erie Canal into the frontier of southwestern New York. There they found "a spot, so wild and mountainous and woody, as to be considered entirely impracticable by any common-sense settler, so that it seemed just the very place for a forest-home for a pair who had set out to live on other people's thoughts." The "spot" was a "deep dell enough to make one think of listening to the talkers in Captain Symmes' world; and this Cora declared to be the very home of her dreams."[36] "The talkers in Captain Symmes' world" seems to be a reference to the "Internals" in *Symzonia*, the inhabitants of that novel's utopian civilization inside the earth, who speak an unintelligible language. Cora's "deep dell"—her idealized home in the wilderness—is compared to a fantasy world that was, in turn, loosely linked to the initial motivations behind the U.S. Exploring

Expedition into the Pacific. Fantasies about what might exist in uncharted global spaces become linked to fantasies about new frontier homes.

Eventually, after being reunited with their families and learning of the decline of the family fortunes (a detail that links Cora and Everard's romance to the economic uncertainty of the 1830s, including speculative lending practices in developing western spaces), the couple and their daughter moved on to Michigan, where they now reside, apparently quite happily. The reference to "Captain Symmes' world" is not the only moment in their romance that conjures other realms and global adventure, however.[37] The description of Cora and Everard's initial flight west through New York contains another reference to an earlier, iconic maritime adventure. The pair, we are told, stopped in Utica to buy a few books, because "to live in a wilderness without books, was not to be thought of. Robinson Crusoe would have been the most rational purchase, but I dare say [Everard] did not buy that," Kirkland's narrator offers. "Perhaps Atala, perhaps Gertrude of Wyoming, perhaps—but these are only conjectures. For my own part, I should have recommended Buchan's Domestic Medicine, the Frugal Housewife, the Whole Duty of Man, and the Almanac for 18—."[38] Drawing attention to the gaps between romantic notions about western settlement and the harsh realities of life on the frontier as she does throughout the book, Mrs. Clavers here contrasts narrative plots, genres, and related narrative expectations. She associates popular romances (poetic and novelistic) with the young couple's idealized vision of their future adventures, the familiar plot of *Robinson Crusoe* with a slightly less rosy but still appealing adventure, and the fractured, plotless utility of domestic manuals or almanacs with the challenges and necessities that probably await them.

As familiar as many antebellum Americans were with Symmes and his hollow earth theory, *Robinson Crusoe* was an even more familiar referent. The novel was endlessly reprinted and reinvented, especially in the antebellum period. There were 122 separate American printings of the novel between 1840 and 1860 alone.[39] In addition to its popularity as a sea adventure and shipwreck tale, its story of hard work, ingenuity, self-reliance, and development of an island space made it a frequent reference in stories about settlement. In Willa Cather's *My Ántonia*, for example, Jim Burden reads both *Robinson Crusoe* and *The Swiss Family Robinson*, suggesting that such tales were popular among young boys and also relevant to Cather's Nebraska setting. And in instances of "female Robinsonade" throughout the eighteenth and nineteenth centuries, from *The Female American; or, the Adventures of Unca Eliza Winkfield* (1767) to the *New York Times* article "A Female

Robinson Crusoe" (1859), which tells the story of a woman stranded on an island in Lake Superior, the well-known Crusoe plot provides opportunities to blur boundaries between masculine adventure and traditionally female domestic worlds.[40]

Certainly, *Robinson Crusoe*'s status as a fable of *homo economicus*, one sometimes adapted to raise questions about gender and domestic spheres, makes it a fitting reference within the story of Cora and Everard's settler fantasies. And reference to Defoe's attention to acquisition also appears elsewhere in *A New Home*: "Robinson Crusoe exulted not more warmly in his successive acquisitions than did Alice in 'a kitchen, a real kitchen!'" comments Mrs. Clavers when explaining that the family's new house "was finished, or as nearly finished as anything in Michigan."[41] But, as Margaret Cohen has pointed out, readings of *Robinson Crusoe* that focus on Crusoe as consumer and producer are not necessarily incompatible with those that pay more attention to the novel's maritime contexts. Reading Crusoe as "a crafty navigator," Cohen argues, reframes readings that consider risk "a stage on the way to a more rational, moderate form of capitalist behavior modeled by the reformed sinner" and figures him as a character whose enterprises demonstrate that "high-risk activities are endemic to the capitalist pursuit of profit." The problem, Cohen illustrates, is not how to eliminate risk but rather how to undertake high-risk activities "with the best chance of success." In such a reading, the risk and potential reward of maritime endeavors rise to the surface. As Crusoe well knows, Cohen writes, "the ethos of craft contains traits translatable from navigators to speculators."[42] With this in mind, mention of *Robinson Crusoe* within *A New Home* appears not simply as a fable of successful settlement and rational acquisition. It also reinforces the narrative's yoking of sea stories and the speculation and risk driving western settlement. *Robinson Crusoe* becomes not just about developing land or acquiring a kitchen but also about how maritime ventures enable that (perpetually risky) development.

In addition to the Beckworths' story and the mention of *Robinson Crusoe* within Cora and Everard's tale, other maritime references appear within *A New Home* to reinforce hopes surrounding land speculation and settlement. "No word of adventures, no boasting of achievements, not even a breath of the talismanic word 'land,' [was] more interesting to the speculator of 1835–36 than it ever was to the ship-wrecked mariner," we are told when a party of settlers, including the narrator's husband, returns "tired and dirty, cross and hungry," from "a tour with a view to the purchase of one or two cities."[43] "'Luff when it blows,' is a wise and necessary caution," Mrs. Clavers reminds readers when explaining that settlers who venture west "with a determination to live as they have been accustomed to live" are bound to be disappointed. "Those who forget it and attempt to carry all sail set and to keep an unvarying course, blow which way it will, always abuse Michigan, and are abused in their turn."[44] Here, a sailing term provides a reminder of the need to adjust to actual conditions. "To luff" is to spill a strong wind out of a sail by letting the sail out so that the vessel does not tip over. In this reference it is not the romance of the sea voyage or the potential for great wealth that is emphasized but the harsh realities of life on the water, as on the frontier, the unpredictability of it all, and the need to adapt.

Elsewhere in Kirkland's western writings—in *Forest Life* (1842), for example—there are brief moments when references to the sea suggest labor rather than speculation and unpredictability. In *Forest Life* the narrator and other travelers hear "a distant sound of 'Yo heave!' recurring at regular intervals, and transporting one's mind at once to the borders of the well-beloved sea, whose various music was far more familiar to our youthful ears than the murmur of the forest." Reaching the summit of a high bank, the travelers see a "brooklet" in the bottom of a dell, in which "some eighty or perhaps a hundred men were erecting the frame-work of a large mill—an object which seemed almost as much out of place in this primal solitude as would the apparition of a three-decker upon the stocks, which indeed it much resembled." Comparing the mill to a large ship being constructed onshore, Kirkland creates a scene of cooperative labor that explicitly conjures maritime labor: "As the huge mass left the ground, poles and handspikes assisted its ascent, and the 'Yo heave!' was repeated as a signal for every fresh effort, as on shipboard."[45] Here, it is not the economics of the maritime world that undergirds western settlement, as it seems to be in the Beckworths' story, but images of the maritime world that make the economic development of western spaces legible. This comparison of a scene of terrestrial labor to shipboard labor is more akin to moves made by writers like Cooper, Hall, and Parkman who use maritime metaphors to establish that a western scene is *like* a maritime one, whereas in *A New Home*, plots of oceanic adventure are predominant—entire stories that emphasize adventure, speculation, and deferred desire for narrative closure. Yet there are ways in which *A New Home*, too, makes the land of the frontier terraqueous, if not quite rendering it in maritime terms.

For example, the book's depiction of the Michigan landscape furthers Kirkland's project of puncturing expectations about western life. Rather than land waiting to be cleared, cultivated, and thus brought into national space, Mrs. Clavers describes a landscape riddled with mudholes—"characteristic features of the 'West,'" "dark gulf[s]" of "quaking mud."[46] These descriptions provide opportunities for humor—Mrs. Clavers is often stuck in a marsh or swamp—but they also emphasize the unimproved nature of the land and the lack of solidity underlying land speculation. The narrator pities men who stake "their poor means on strips of land which were at that moment a foot under water" and finds that discussions of "the public square, the water lots, the value *per foot* of this undulating surface" is "almost too much for [her] gravity."[47] She relates plans to drain marshes, deepen channels, and create land "on which to found a second New-York." But "although nobody liked to say so," she quips at one point, "the ground seemed *rather* wet for city building."[48]

Even in a spring when there is surprisingly little rain for that season, Mrs. Clavers notes that everything remains damp: "My own private theory is, that when the peninsula [Michigan] was covered with water, as it doubtless was before the Niagara met with such a fall, the porous mass became so thoroughly soaked, that the sun performs the office of rain, by drawing from below to the rich surface, the supplies of moisture which, under ordinary circumstances, are necessarily furnished from aerial reservoirs. Such are my views, which I offer with the diffidence becoming a tyro; but at the same time avowing frankly that I shall not even consider an opposing hypothesis, until my antagonist shall have traversed the entire state, and counted the marshes and cat-holes from which I triumphantly draw my conclusion."[49] Mrs. Clavers presents a humorous vision of land inseparable from its supposed watery past. Water that once covered the land now returns from below, an image that makes the land of the "peninsula" unstable space subject to future change. Indeed, in part because of this watery instability, any vision of the land's future is, Mrs. Clavers makes clear, just that—a vision. And once again here Kirkland incorporates a maritime reference, however veiled. Although the term "cat-hole" no doubt indicates a deep pool, it also has a nautical meaning as the word for one of the two holes at the stern of a ship.

BORROWING FROM THE SEA

Metaphors of fluidity and mobility have become central to oceanic and maritime scholarship, prompting concern that such work might produce, as Jordy Rosenberg puts it, a "hermeneutic that is a bit, if you will, *watery*."[50] Relating *A New Home*'s fluid landscape to oceanic spaces might seem to reproduce a watery hermeneutic. Yet when considered in relation to the maritime references and plots scattered throughout *A New Home*'s sketches—references and plots that bring maritime stories into terrestrial spaces—this watery landscape becomes a way that the text makes material its critique of land speculation, of village plots drawn in chalk on a barroom table, of borrowing on credit—a critique that is continued through rather than absent from its maritime plots. The Beckworths' story, for example, with its series of returns and its expected conclusion, brings a tale of maritime adventure and global speculation into the space of the Michigan woods, highlighting the desire for stable, familiar narrative plots of settlement and the unstable, speculative nature of the narratives actually being told about the territory of the West, with its spatial plots of water lots and catholes.[51] Crossing "perilous half-bridged marshes" and a "causeway of large round logs" over "a slough of despond" along with the narrator during her three-year voyage west, occasionally "anchoring in [a] black swamp," the reader travels geographic spaces that resist physical plotting in a narrative that constantly plays with conventional fictional plots, including plots of global, oceanic travel, so as to emphasize the speculative nature of settlement and the faulty narrative expectations being circulated about the West.[52]

Recognizing these maritime borrowings brings *A New Home* into conversation with popular maritime narratives about the sea that Kirkland engaged in other contexts as they permeated American culture. For example, in the decades following *A New Home*'s publication, reviews of Melville's *Typee*, *Mardi*, and *Redburn* appeared in *Sartain's Union Magazine of Literature and Art*, which Kirkland edited at the time.[53] "We should not be at all surprised to see Polynesia, with its myriad islands and its bewitching climate, becoming to romance what the 'fabled East' has been for more than thirty centuries," begins the magazine's review of *Mardi*. "Magnetism and steam, the railroad and the newspaper, are fast stripping the East of its solemn mystery. Romance, as well as empire, it seems must travel westward. There is indeed no end to the illusions with which an active fancy may invest the vast Continent of Islands that lies outstretched in the great Pacific Ocean."[54] In linking "romance" and "empire," East and West, this review narrates a familiar story about imperialism and its narrative representations. But in *A New Home, Who'll Follow?*, Kirkland destabilizes this narrative as "East" and "West" meet in the North American continent's interior—in Michigan. The "East" in *A New Home* is not the "fabled East" of the *Mardi* review but the "*Eastern* enchantment" of the Beckworths' "great, noble, yankee 'palace of pine-boards'" and the oceanic spaces that have constructed it. And the "West" is both the Michigan frontier and the Pacific whaling grounds and fanciful spaces of Mr. Beckworth's "five long years . . . box[ing] the compass" and of contemporary expeditions such as the U.S. Exploring Expedition.[55] As East and West meet in the space of the Michigan peninsula, Kirkland illustrates the review's point that "there is indeed no end to the illusions with which an active fancy may invest the vast Continent" of mudholes and swampland that forms the basis of new frontier homes.

At the same time, in referring to the Pacific region as a "vast Continent of Islands," the review of *Mardi* published in a magazine under Kirkland's editorship not only makes the North American continent terraqueous but also continentalizes the oceanic. It gives a terrestrial presence to the region in a way that belies a long imperial history of conceiving of the space as "'islands in a far sea,'" to adopt twentieth-century Tongan/Fijian writer and scholar Epeli Hau'ofa's formulation.[56] Of course, this review's phrasing still privileges the continental in that it gives the islands weight and presence by imagining them as connected land masses rather than conceiving of Pacific space as a "sea of islands" as Hau'ofa would over a century later. Hau'ofa emphasizes the ways in which the Pacific as an oceanic region is full rather than empty as Western conceptions might have it, and not only because of land. It is full of peoples, knowledge, and cultural practices not always legible to those who privilege a continental perspective. And yet the phrasing of this review of *Mardi* does continue the reorientation that Kirkland engages in when she makes the North American continent watery. In essence, Kirkland and this review craft a vision of a terraqueous globe in which all land, whether the mudholes of Michigan or the islands of Polynesia, is available to the romance of empire and yet also resistant to that romance. And in so doing, Kirkland articulates a vision of empire that we have come to recognize as "archipelagic," one that emphasizes our "culturally constructed and historically contingent" vision of both continents and oceans while acknowledging the "expansive yet inevitably incomplete set of islands that might be taken to constitute an American archipelago" *and* "recovering the insular and archipelagic status of spaces that have sometimes been casually perceived as easily continental."[57] She demonstrates that the islands of Polynesia are part of the circuits of empire and also that the Michigan peninsula, with its watery landscape and proximity to the inland sea of the Great Lakes, is itself insular—it is terraqueous and interconnected with other terraqueous geographies.

This archipelagic vision emphasizes topography, certainly, as well as the narrative romance that connects distant spaces in an overarching imperial vision. But it also emphasizes the material, economic, and speculative connections illuminated by Kirkland's focus on the finances and goods brought from elsewhere to build frontier homes. Bryan Sinche has shown similar forces at play in poet Lydia Sigourney's collections of poems for and about sailors. Sigourney, a prolific author (who sometimes contributed to publications like Child's the *Juvenile Miscellany*), published poems related to sailors' welfare throughout the 1830s and 1840s, part of her investment in various reform movements.[58] She gathered such poems in numerous editions of poetry for sailors that she published between 1845 and 1857. In these poems, according to Sinche, affective unions between those at sea and those on land strained by distance are replaced "by commercial links between seamen and landsmen . . . The sailor is away at sea, but the goods he transports from distant shores come to rest in middle-class homes in the United States." Sigourney's collections, Sinche writes, do not "ignore the human labor and human suffering that founded a comfortable domestic space." When imagined "maritime laborers tell their stories" in these poems, "readers learn that the hearthstone is not just the preferred alternative to the forecastle but also is a site that depends on sailors' labor, that comfort by one hearthside likely entails want and privation by another."[59]

Kirkland's use of maritime tales within *A New Home, Who'll Follow?*, on the other hand, both shows that comfort by one hearthstone (the Beckworths', for example) is predicated on maritime labor and risk and reinforces the speculative nature of that terrestrial hearthside. Her tales harness oceanic realms in ways that recast visions of the frontier. Oceans become more than metaphors for expansive terrestrial spaces. In *A New Home*, maritime stories reinforce aspects of "the speculating mania" of the era, as references to Symmes Hole and travel and exploration in and around the Pacific become parallels for the dreams that construct new territorial spaces in the era of wildcat banking and unsustainable get-rich-quick schemes. "Cunning magicians," Kirkland writes in *A New Home*, "set themselves about concocting a new species of gramarye, by means of which the millions of acres of wild land which were left on their hands might be turned into *bonâ fide* cash . . . burr-oaks were turned into marble tables, tall tamaracks into draperied bedsteads, lakes into looking-glasses, and huge expanses of wet marsh into velvet couches."[60] The imaginative speculation involved in this process finds a point of reference in maritime romances like the Beckworths' tale and in Cora and Everard's story, with its global references. And these various plots and references show that, to adopt Rachel Azima's formulation, Kirkland's literary speculation as she adapts and reappropriates various tales includes not only "borrowing on credit from the soil" but also borrowing from the sea, encouraging us to rethink conventional boundaries of the domestic and global in terms of both the domestic's reach into the foreign as well as how global realms are used to narrate the uncertain status of the domestic.[61]

The chapters in the final part will show how the various connections between distant spaces such as the Pacific and the domestic space of the United States explored in this book—Lydia Maria Child's pedagogical use of the Pacific, the affective bonds of anxiety linking Nessy Heywood and Elizabeth Craw, and the topographical, material, and speculative narrative links emphasized in Kirkland's text—come together in the coastal gothic bildungsromane of Harriet Beecher Stowe, Elizabeth Stoddard, and Harriet Prescott Spofford. Most of the texts I have discussed so far were written and published in the 1830s, a decade defined by territorial tensions, including the "removal" of Indigenous peoples from their traditional lands in the expanding U.S. nation, increasingly fraught U.S.-Mexico relations, and the financial speculation that Kirkland alludes to, concerns refracted through the oceanic investments of these texts. Moving to the late 1850s and early 1860s, I show how Stowe, Stoddard, and Spofford absorb the oceanic concerns of such predecessors as Child, Craw, and Kirkland, transforming them into New England–based, coastal domestic tales defined by global movements. The presence of the Pacific is muted in the novels discussed in this final part, but reading them with earlier attention to the Pacific in mind helps us think beyond an Atlantic orientation within these texts so as to consider their relationship to other regions and circuits and to put the Atlantic in conversation with the Pacific. Global circulation both produces and affects familial relationships in these novels, ultimately resulting in visions of home and family life marked and unsettled by those circulations. In these texts, oceans come home in ways that build communities but also fracture family relations through loss and death and by revealing the violence of global empire that undergirds New England settler economies and families.

PART III

Coastal Gothic and Archipelagic Relations

CHAPTER FIVE

"Inwreathed in sand and shells"

Harriet Beecher Stowe's Coastal Gothic

Toward the beginning of Harriet Beecher Stowe's novel *The Pearl of Orr's Island: A Story of the Coast of Maine*, Captain Kittridge, his daughter, Sally, and a neighbor child, Mara, wander the cove where he keeps his boat and tar kettle. There had been a storm the night before, and "the sands of the little cove seemed harder and whiter than ever, and were thickly bestrewn with the shells and sea-weed which the upturnings of the night had brought in. There lay what might have been fringes and fragments of sea-gods' vestures,—blue, crimson, purple, and orange sea-weeds, wreathed in tangled ropes of kelp and sea-grass, or lying separately scattered on the sands." The shore is an otherworldly space. "The children," the passage continues, "ran wildly, shouting as they began gathering sea-treasures; and Sally, with the air of an experienced hand in the business, untwisted the coils of rosy sea-weed, from which every moment she disengaged some new treasure, in some rarer shell or smoother pebble."[1] One of these treasures is "a bracelet of hair, fastened by a brilliant clasp of green, sparkling stones," with the letters "D.M." embroidered in seed pearls, a piece of jewelry that immediately suggests an unsettling juxtaposition of bodies, domesticity, the sea, and death through its association with mourning practices.[2]

As Sally excitedly hands the bracelet to Captain Kittridge, he catches sight of another "object partially concealed behind a projecting rock . . . There lay, bedded in sand and sea-weed, a woman with a little boy clasped in her arms! . . . Both were deep sunk in the sand, into which had streamed the woman's long, dark hair, which sparkled with glittering morsels of sand and pebbles, and with those tiny, brilliant, yellow shells which are so numerous on that shore." The woman seems as though she could be one of the sea-gods or mermaids in Captain Kittridge's mythical tales of life on the ocean floor, bedecked with the sea's beauty and one with the beach: "She was all folded and inwreathed in sand and shells and sea-weeds, and a great, weird-looking leaf of kelp, some yards in length, lay twined around her like a shroud."[3] The image of a shroud confirms what the reader has already suspected: the woman is dead. She is described as being "like sculptured marble" with eye-lashes that "had shut down, as a solemn curtain," reproducing conventional images of death and also emphasizing the materiality of her body.[4] The wedding ring on her hand, the bracelet that Sally picks up, the glittering shells, and the woman's body are "folded" together in this scene on the beach.

The boy found clutched in the woman's arms is just barely alive. He is revived and nursed back to health. Mara is immediately devoted to him, first as a childhood playmate and later as a fiancé and spiritual guide. But Mara, the novel's "angel in the house," is too good and too ethereal for an earthly marriage to the worldly boy given the name Moses, who is associated with imperial ambitions and otherness.[5] She sickens while he is away at sea and dies a sentimental death soon after his return, leaving Moses to settle down with Sally when he eventually tires of his maritime wanderings. Moses and Sally build a domestic New England future upon Mara's memory and the profits of Moses' travels.

Serialized in the New York–based Congregationalist weekly the *Independent* in 1861–62 and published as a two-volume novel in England and the United States in 1862, *The Pearl of Orr's Island* is often discussed as a regional tale, grounded in its Maine setting and characters, and as one that explores gender restrictions while reinforcing the messages of Christian faith that we associate with Harriet Beecher Stowe. In this chapter, I argue that these elements combine with moments of the mystical and the circulation of stories, bodies, and objects, like the woman and bracelet found on the beach, to produce what I call "coastal gothic." Stowe infused moments and tones of the gothic into novels such as *Uncle Tom's Cabin*, most famously through the character Cassy, a "madwoman in the attic" figure whose history of abuse and haunting presence aligns her with some of the most recognizable features of the genre.[6] In *The Pearl of Orr's Island* and another of Stowe's New England coastal novels, *The Minister's Wooing* (1859), gothic moments are far quieter and subtle. But taken together they produce an unsettled tone most recognizable when centering the coastal settings and maritime frames of these domestic novels that often focus on home spaces, activities, and relationships. These novels sometimes move female characters, haunting pasts, global empire, and issues surrounding gender from the attic to the beach.

Positioning these novels between Kirkland's use of oceanic ventures to highlight the speculation and risk involved in constructing new frontier homes and Elizabeth Stoddard's and Harriet Prescott Spofford's texts that subvert sentimental and domestic conventions within families haunted by oceanic histories creates a new literary history for Stowe's coastal novels, one that does not lead directly from Stowe's texts to the nostalgic maritime communities of Sarah Orne Jewett's Maine in narratives such as *The Country of the Pointed Firs* (1896).[7] Instead, this alternative history stretches out across the mid-nineteenth-century's maritime investments and highlights Stowe's use of maritime plots and coastal settings to facilitate critiques of gender restrictions and to hint at the absorption of imperial violence, dispossession, and alterity into the domestic scene. The "object partially concealed behind a projecting rock" that turns out to be a woman "inwreathed in sand and shells and sea-weeds" clutching a barely living boy in her arms locates a haunting image on the beach. Eerie stories of objects like a wailing baby cradle that floats ashore and continues to scream even when split up for kindling conjure the lore that binds communities together, as well as the violence and loss that undergirds those communities.

Stowe began sketching *The Pearl of Orr's Island* in the summer of 1852 as *Uncle Tom's Cabin* was becoming a bestseller. *Uncle Tom's Cabin* had been written in Brunswick, Maine, where Stowe's husband had taken up a position at Bowdoin College in 1850, moving Stowe back to the East Coast after eighteen years in Cincinnati (where Elizabeth Craw heard Stowe's father, Lyman Beecher, preach in 1835). Brunswick, near Maine's Casco Bay and its islands, provided the inspiration for Stowe's "Maine story," which, she wrote in a July 29, 1852, letter to her husband, "I am composing . . . every day."[8] Filled with retired sea captains, fishermen, and vigorous New England women in a coastal setting "remarkable for a singular interpenetration of the sea with the land," Stowe turned to a story infused with the maritime world after the publication of the novel that would remain her most famous.[9] But, as Cynthia Alicia Smith has argued, there are traces of the maritime world even within *Uncle Tom's Cabin*, where Stowe occasionally refers to Tom as a "sailor" or a "mariner shipwrecked" and where steamboat trips on U.S. rivers conjure the Atlantic Middle Passage, bringing the violence of the slave ship into continental interiors.[10] Smith reads Stowe's maritime references in relation to the "sentimental sailor" tradition, which figured sailors as men of feeling, capable of saving others and of being saved or reformed themselves. She grounds Stowe's maritime investments partly in the influence of Stowe's sea captain uncle, Samuel Foote, who circulated nautical tales throughout the Beecher household.[11] But, of course, the maritime world was also infused throughout American culture more widely, and this, too, plays out in Stowe's writing. For example, she sometimes sprinkled nautical language infused with religious references into her personal correspondence. Writing to the head of his school in 1864 after her son, Charley, unsuccessfully attempted to run away and become a sailor, Stowe admitted, "Henry and Charles came near to shipwreck in the Boston latin school at this age," and she remembered her father saying "that that period in the life of all his boys was one when he 'cast out the anchors & wished for day.'"[12] Although biblical references involving shipwreck and other maritime imagery are common in early and nineteenth-century American writing, this moment is notable because Stowe is writing about her son's desire to run away to sea. The challenge of raising young boys with maritime aspirations is figured in religiously inflected nautical terms.

In the years between beginning to write her "Maine story," which itself features a young man determined to build a ship and go to sea, and finally publishing it, Stowe's energies would be directed elsewhere. She would continue her explicit involvement with antislavery efforts in *A Key to Uncle Tom's Cabin* (1853) and *Dred* (1856), moving her fictional worlds from Ohio and Louisiana in *Uncle Tom's Cabin* to the resistant spaces of the Great Dismal Swamp in *Dred*. And she would take three trips to Europe. She traveled in England and Scotland as the celebrated author of a bestselling antislavery novel and with family members throughout the European continent. Before finishing *The Pearl of Orr's Island*, Stowe would write *The Minister's Wooing*, serialized in the *Atlantic Monthly* and published as a book in 1859. *The Minister's Wooing* is set in eighteenth-century Newport, Rhode Island, and is embedded in New England history, though it is also sometimes said to bear the influence of Stowe's European trips in its interest in Catholicism. *Agnes of Sorrento* (1862), which appeared in installments in the *Atlantic Monthly* at the same time that *The Pearl of Orr's Island* was appearing in the *Independent*, is more explicit in its European influences: it is set amid religious turmoil in fifteenth-century Italy. Stowe's travels seem to have brought an increasing international dimension into her work over these years, a dimension that might seem lacking in the comparatively staid *The Pearl of Orr's Island*. But, of course, from *Uncle Tom's Cabin* onward, Stowe's novels each demonstrate the nineteenth-century intersection of the domestic and the global in their own way, moving, for example, from kitchen and bedchamber to New Orleans slave auction and Liberia. Stowe's "Maine story" is no exception, though the narrative's focus remains at home.

Certainly, *The Pearl of Orr's Island* and *The Minister's Wooing* are both novels that stay put, narratively. We might liken many of their main characters to Mrs. Beckworth, who stays home and patiently waits for the resolution of her romance plot. And the maritime exploits of these novels' male characters are almost entirely unnarrated. In most cases we do not even get accounts that evoke a Cooper sea novel in miniature as we do through Mr. Beckworth's story in *A New Home, Who'll Follow?* There are no tales of piracy, impressment, or revolutionary daring. Narratively, male characters seem to be sent to sea in these novels to draw out romance plots and to facilitate religious tensions, whereas the narrative focus remains at home. Those plots and tensions are eventually resolved in conclusions that emphasize the Christian home and marriage as ideals to be realized. But we know that domestic and regional fiction can be politically and ethically engaged, just as we know that Stowe's most overt protest novels are still domestic in their settings, concerns, and plotlines.[13] Carolyn Karcher divides Stowe's "literature of social change" into two varieties: "protest literature," exemplified by *Uncle Tom's Cabin*, and "regional" or "sociological fiction, aimed at capturing a changed or changing way of life by portraying the customs, manners, and personalities that typify it." The latter variety, in which Karcher includes *The Minister's Wooing* and *The Pearl of Orr's Island*, is not void of critique; it interweaves "testimony against New Englanders' role in the slave trade, critiques of Calvinist theology, pleas for a liberalized Christianity, and interventions in debates on the 'woman question.'"[14] Between them, *The Minister's Wooing* and *The Pearl of Orr's Island* take up all of these issues, and they do so in part through oceanic plots and coastal settings.

The oceanic and island imaginaries and references within these novels have certainly not gone unnoticed. For example, scholars have drawn attention to how both novels make reference to *The Tempest* in ways that suggest Atlantic world histories of racialization and enslavement, especially in light of twentieth-century criticism on Shakespeare's "America play."[15] This use of the play is also part of a nineteenth-century tradition of references to *The Tempest*'s Miranda in fiction by female authors.[16] Both novels also deploy religious, oceanic imagery like that involving shipwrecks, fishermen, and pearls.[17] In *The Pearl of Orr's Island*, especially, references to the Parable of the Pearl, to visions of Jesus walking along the shore as by the Sea of Galilee, and to associations of shipwreck with Calvinist ideas of divine providence or punishment ensure that the earthly aspects of the oceans' riches and dangers also gesture toward the eternal in a way that we might expect from Stowe. But emphasizing the materiality of coastal settings and oceanic circulations of peoples and objects within these texts, in addition to their use of maritime plots to facilitate romance, reinforce religious faith, and begin to cultivate a kind of nostalgia for a maritime world already changing, helps us read such books differently. Firmly grounded in their New England settings and domestic scenes, these novels create a haunting gothic tone not only through their use of New England histories in ways that align them with the writing of an author like Nathaniel Hawthorne or through their revision of Calvinist providence tales as gothic stories, as Dorothy Z. Baker suggests.[18] They also use objects carried across oceans, carefully arranged in the "best rooms" of homes, or washed up on the beach to bring the mysteries and violence of oceanic activities into domestic worlds.

In what follows, I first show how *The Pearl of Orr's Island* merges sea and land through its setting and domestic scenes, including the sharing of imaginative tales between Captain Kittridge and the novel's child characters. I then discuss how these maritime imaginaries reinforce the novel's gender commentary. Next I turn to *The Minister's Wooing* and its use of objects to illustrate domestic spaces constructed out of the materials of maritime circulation before returning briefly to *The Pearl of Orr's Island* and its character Moses, who comes from the sea and is integrated into the community of Orr's Island. At the intersection of the regional novel, the maritime tale, and the bildungsromane, Stowe reaffirms domestic visions of Christian marriage as redemptive but constructs homes that never forget the dangers of the seas or the products of empire, weaving together visions of uncanny submarine worlds and objects with lives of their own. In these relatively quiet novels, rooted in domestic spaces and local histories and customs, Stowe's politics as well as her religiosity emerge at the intersection of land and sea, in scenes that bring the oceanic onto land and into the home and sometimes create visions of land underwater.

"INTERPENETRATION OF THE SEA WITH THE LAND"

Many of Stowe's novels introduce domestic spaces by describing interiors and the objects within them in ways that illustrate the characters or morals of their inhabitants. This is part of what Lori Merish calls Stowe's creation of a midcentury "home religion" in her domestic manuals and novels, where she crafts a "discourse of sentimental proprietorship . . . which highlights the significance of objects in the emotional culture of persons."[19] Our introduction to the Pennels' "best room" at the beginning of *The Pearl of Orr's Island* briefly mentions "its low studded walls, white dimity window-curtains, rag carpet, and polished wood chairs," suggesting Mrs. Pennel's cleanliness, efficiency, and economy. But this description is quickly overshadowed by mention of "the body of James Lincoln" lying "in the centre of the room."[20] The novel's first chapter describes Naomi, pregnant with Mara, and Mara's grandfather, Zephaniah Pennel, as they witness the wreck of a homebound ship.[21] The shipmaster was Mara's father; his dead body is soon laid out on a table in the Pennel house, his clothing and hair "saturated with sea-water, which trickled from time to time, and struck with a leaden and dropping sound into a sullen pool which lay under the table."[22] From the very beginning, the novel's domestic spaces are characterized by and inseparable from the dangers of the sea. In this case, sea-water itself infuses the home, disrupting the carefully curated space. The sea enters domestic space, as it trickles, drop by drop, from the dead body on the table.

As her father's body lies in the Pennels' best room, Mara is born in the apartment above, a premature birth brought on by the anguish and shock of the shipwreck. Her mother dies in childbirth, but not before naming the small, frail baby by quoting "the sad old words of the Hebrew Scripture,—'Call her not Naomi; call her Mara, for the Almighty hath dealt very bitterly with me.'"[23] In the Bible, Naomi, mother-in-law of Ruth, claims the name "Mara" as an expression of grief after the deaths of her husband and sons.[24] Orphaned by the sea, in *The Pearl of Orr's Island* Mara is an expression of bitterness and grief who becomes the "pearl" of the island, a precious gift from the ocean. She is raised by her grandparents, the type of couple who "never read anything but the Bible, the *Missionary Herald*, and the *Christian Mirror*" and by the broader community of Orr's Island.[25]

The intertwining of the oceanic world with the domestic life of Orr's Island, bringing death, hardship, and also precious riches, is illustrated through these opening scenes in the Pennels' house as well as through descriptions of houses and landscapes more generally. The Pennels' home "stands on a little knoll, about a hundred yards from the open ocean." The surrounding shore is "netted in green and azure by its thousand islands, all glorious with their majestic pines, all musical and silvery with the caresses of the sea-waves."[26] Characters move around the coast on the water, taking boats between islands to visit one another, and Captain Kittridge, Sally, and Mara make chowder on the beach, where the girls collect shells and other treasures to bring indoors. Domestic, coastal, and oceanic spaces merge in a way that is dramatized during the storm that washes Moses and the dead woman up on the beach. "You never can seem to remember that houses don't run aground or strike on rocks in storms," Mrs. Kittridge tells the nervous Captain Kittridge as the storm's winds pick up. This conversation prompts one of the novel's female characters, Aunt Ruey, to tell the story of an old captain who built a house "jist like a ship . . . the closet-shelves had holes for the tumblers and dishes, and he had all his tables and chairs battened down, and so when it came a gale, they say the old Cap'n used to sit in his chair and hold on to hear the wind blow." The men who have gone to sea on long voyages to China, Ceylon, Canton, India, and the West Indies have different experiences from "lands-people." They "hears the wind with different ears," as Captain Kittridge reminds his wife, and they bring those different perspectives home in ways that transform home spaces, sometimes quite literally.[27]

These different perspectives are exemplified by Captain Kittridge's tales of life beneath the ocean's surface. While the Orr's Island community at large mythologizes objects that have washed ashore, crafting family legends about "a silver cream-pitcher" found on the beach and a haunted cradle that would rock itself and that cried like a baby after it was broken apart, Captain Kittridge's tall tales often bring his listeners' perspectives underwater. When Sally reflects on how many ships must lie at the bottom of the sea and wonders why people do not go down to retrieve the riches abandoned there, her father says that they do and spins a tale that anticipates later nineteenth-century science fiction. People "have diving-bells, and men go down in 'em with caps over their faces, and long tubes to get the air through, and they walk about on the bottom of the ocean . . . There you could see great big sea critters, with ever so many eyes and long arms, swimming right up to catch you." When asked what the bottom of the ocean looks like, he replies that "trees and bushes grow there, just as they do on land; and great plants,—blue and purple and green and yellow, and lots of great pearls lie round."[28] He claims to have gathered pearls as "big as robins' eggs" and to have traded them for shawls and silks that he brought home to sell. Kittridge articulates unconventional perspectives about the world, crafting playful visions in which people and objects move not just across the surface of the oceans but also above and below the surface. He takes the intertwined nature of land and sea life to extremes through his stories, crafting an uncanny underwater world with the features of a landed one.[29]

Kittridge also encourages Mara's tendency to indulge in these fantasies. As a young girl, Mara spends much of her time imagining the sea, lost in tangles of fact and fancy. This is exemplified by her obsession with a copy of *The Tempest* torn from an old edition of Shakespeare that she finds among her grandparents' things while Moses is away on his first fishing expedition with her grandfather, Captain Pennel. She lies on the beach for hours poring over the "poem," sure that its contents are "authentic fact." The "sea nymphs" of *The Tempest* who hourly ring a knell must be the same as the mermaids of Captain Kittridge's tales: "Had [Kittridge] not said that the bell rung for church of a Sunday morning down under the waters?" When asked, Kittridge confirms that sea nymphs and mermaids are "pretty much" the same thing. And when Mara asks "when people are drowned, how long does it take for their bones to turn into coral, and their eyes into pearl?" he responds, "Well, that depends upon circumstances" rather than denying the basis of her question.[30] Kittridge does eventually tell Mara that the story she has found is what they "call a play, and I've seen 'em act it at a theatre, when I was to Liverpool once." He acknowledges that its events did not exactly happen. When Mara asks if it is "like the Bible and Roman history?" he replies, "Why, no . . . not exactly; but things jist like it, you know. Mermaids and sich is common in foreign parts, and they has funerals for drowned sailors. 'Member once when we was sailing near the Bermudas by a reef, where the *Lively Fanny* went down, and I heard a kind o' ding-dongin',—and the waters there is clear as the sky,—and I looked down and see the coral all a-growin', and the sea-plants a-wavin' as handsome as a pictur', and the mermaids they was a-singin'. It was beautiful; they sung kind o' mournful; and Jack Hubbard, he would have it they was a-singin' for the poor fellows that was a-lyin' there round under the sea-weed."[31] According to Kittridge, the events depicted in the play did not actually occur, but they are like other events that did occur. For him, there is not a firm distinction between his sea stories and life. As the narrator reflects, "When left alone with children, [Kittridge's] mind ran such riot, that the bounds between the real and unreal became foggier than the banks of Newfoundland."[32] His stories provide a way to make sense of life, as well as to escape its boundaries. They are sailors' yarns cultivated at home that fuel Mara's own childhood speculations.

Mrs. Kittridge dismisses her husband's tales as nonsense at odds with religious piety, but Stowe's narrator takes care to remind readers that, "In all real, matter-of-fact transactions, [Kittridge's] word was as good as another's, and he was held to be honest and just in his dealings."[33] His tendency to embellishment is not a danger or failure. It is limited to tales of foreign travel that he spins out with children, and Kittridge is the character who takes creative, firm action when necessary, reinforcing the practicality of his knowledge of the world when necessary. When Mara discovers that Moses is at risk of getting involved with smugglers, it is Kittridge she confides in and Kittridge who devises a solution. He romanticizes the sea but also retains what Margaret Cohen would call the "craft" of the mariner, deftly handling a problem when it arises.[34]

Gillian Brown argues that the different responses by Mara, Moses, and Sally to Kittridge's tales of underwater worlds and the ghost stories that appear throughout *The Pearl of Orr's Island* are part of the novel's "exploration of different ways of reading and of the sometimes tragic consequences that follow when people cannot reconcile their different readings of the world," a concern that she claims *Pearl* shares with *Uncle Tom's Cabin*.[35] Mara is, Brown argues, both the "ideal Christian reader" and "the mistaken reader," all too willing to "conflate the earthly with the divine," to construct Moses as a "false idol," and to treat *The Tempest* as both a true story and an analogue to events in her own life.[36] Eventually, according to Brown, Mara learns to value the divine over the earthly as she turns to God and dies a sentimental, Christian death, the novel reminding us to "read rightly" as well as to "feel right," in part through its own conflation of fiction and scripture.[37] Yet before that sentimental conclusion, even Mara's fanciful conflation of fiction with her own world is linked to the depth of sympathetic feeling that makes her the ultimate "angel in the house." In other words, her "mistaken" reading is an indication of an active mind that attempts to anticipate and imagine others' feelings, attributes that the text treats as positive even when they lead to incorrect readings of a situation. For example, Mara does not initially share the story of *The Tempest* with Moses because she is afraid that its references to shipwreck and lost fathers will upset him. When she finally does so as he is working on building a small schooner, Moses "listened with interest, though without any of the extreme feeling which Mara had thought possible, and even interrupted her once in the middle of the celebrated—'Full fathom five thy father lies,' by asking her to hold up the mast a minute, while he drove in a peg to make it rake a little more. He was, evidently, thinking of no drowned father, and dreaming of no possible sea-caves." That night, Mara spends hours thinking about Moses as she lies in bed "and he lay and thought about a new way of disposing a pulley for raising a sail."[38] His reflections are about practical action rather than deep feeling. While Mara should, perhaps, be lying in bed thinking about God rather than Moses, her compassion and awareness that stories can make people feel is part of what ultimately makes her a "Christian reader" as well as a "mistaken" reader. These questions about ways of reading and interpreting are tied to Stowe's religious messages. But they are also tied to the novel's use of imagination and action in the service of its gender critiques.

"WHAT CAN GIRLS DO AT SEA?"

The Pearl of Orr's Island makes clear that Mara turns to island and underwater fantasy worlds partly because of the limitations placed on her active, sympathetic mind by gender restrictions. These worlds are her escape from the confines imposed on her. Here, the novel merges its emphasis on how intertwined land and sea are in the coastal community of Orr's Island—topographically, materially, and imaginatively—with critiques that have prompted one scholar to write that *The Pearl of Orr's Island* is "as close as Stowe came to writing an *Uncle Tom's Cabin* of women's oppression."[39] Mara finds *The Tempest* and dives into fanciful imagined worlds when Captain Pennel takes Moses on a months-long fishing trip, leaving her behind. Mara is portrayed as yearning after the opportunities available to Moses, from adventure to education. She inserts herself into Moses' program of study, shadowing him and quickly outpacing him in his attempts to learn Latin and history. When Moses is given Plutarch's *Lives*, which he is told "has more particular accounts of the men you read about in history," Mara immediately asks, "Are there any lives of women?," making the novel's gender concerns explicit. Yet when her grandfather marvels at her inquisitiveness and love of books, Moses' teacher, the local minister Reverend Sewell, replies, "That child thinks too much, and feels too much, and knows too much for her years! . . . If she were a boy, and you would take her away cod-fishing, as you have Moses, the sea-winds would blow away some of the thinking, and her little body would grow stout, and her mind less delicate and sensitive. But she's a woman . . . and they are all alike. We can't do much for them, but let them come up as they will and make the best of it."[40] Mara is trapped between her desire for knowledge and adventure and the limited mobility available to her, exemplified in Sewell's comments.

The novel's critique of gender restrictions and expectations frequently relies on the gendered divisions of maritime labor and opportunity also suggested in Sewell's comment. Moses can go to sea, whereas Mara must stay at home. The domestically capable and practical Sally, on the other hand, is sometimes imagined as occupying a space between the two. Toward the end of the novel Sally tells Mara: "If I were only a young fellow now, Mara, I'd have you myself, and that would be just the thing; and I'd shoot Moses, if he said a word; and I'd have money, and I'd have honors, and I'd carry you off to Europe, and take you to Paris and Rome, and nobody knows where; and we'd live in peace, as the story-books say."[41] In this queer moment, Sally imagines herself as Mara's swashbuckling rescuer. "Mrs. Eaton, a thrifty energetic widow of a deceased sea-captain," reinforces this vision of Sally's capabilities but reinscribes it within the boundaries of heterosexual marriage.[42] She offers her opinion on Mara and Moses' intended marriage by remembering her own labor at sea and suggesting that Sally would be capable in a similar situation and thus a better partner for Moses. At a quilting bee, Mrs. Eaton tells a story about a time when her husband was ill and she took her young baby and went to sea with him, keeping the crew warm and fed in harsh conditions. Sally, she concludes, would rise to the challenge of being a seafarer's wife in a way that Mara could not. These ideas are even anticipated in the scene where Captain Kittridge, Mara, and Sally find Moses on the beach: Sally untwists coils of seaweed "with the air of an experienced hand in the business," as if she is ready to grab a rope and labor at sea.

Yet while stories like Mrs. Eaton's celebrate active women and make clear that a strong, resourceful woman is as capable at sea as on land, the novel does not consistently posit the mobility of the maritime world as a solution to restrictions placed on women. This is because the mobility and adventure of the maritime world is also associated with violent, imperial ambitions. When Mara wishes she could go on the fishing trip to the Banks with Moses and her grandfather, Moses asks: "'What can girls do at sea? you never like to catch fish—it always makes you cry to see 'em flop.' 'Oh, yes, poor fish!' said Mara, perplexed between her sympathy for the fish and her desire for the glory of her hero, which must be founded on their pain; 'I can't help feeling sorry when they gasp so.'" And when Mara and Moses take a trip to an island where Moses climbs an old hemlock tree and steals eggs from an eagle's nest, he proudly proclaims, in response to Mara's weak protestations: "I beat them just as the Romans used to beat folks,—I played their nest was a city, and I spoiled it."[43] Moses' maritime, imperial ambitions are presented as youthful folly, always harmful to others. They are presented as superficially attractive opportunities to Mara, who is not quite content to stay home and work on embroidery. But they are opportunities framed as harmful and violent, motivated by desires that Moses must get out of his system before he can be fully enfolded into the life of Orr's Island.

That conclusion is only realized with Mara's death. Though Moses and Mara are drawn to each other, Moses is presented as a religious skeptic attracted to the earthly and ultimately incompatible with Mara's goodness. Stowe biographer Joan Hedrick argues that Stowe could not "resolve the intractable gender issues she had engaged" by starting the novel with a dreamy, intellectual girl; a dashing, uncontemplative boy; and a practical, more traditional, yet coquettish girl.[44] She finished the novel, Hedrick concludes, only by letting go of some of its complications through Mara's death and the resolution of the novel's love triangle through Sally and Moses' marriage. But that marriage, as I will argue further below, both sidesteps some of the novel's gender complications and also further highlights the inextricability of maritime empire and the home, not only through the "silks and satins, and flowered India chintz" brought home by Captain Pennel from his voyages, which Mrs.

Pennel keeps "carefully stowed away" while wearing practical homespun every day, but also through Moses himself.[45] Characters and objects move between land and sea in *The Pearl of Orr's Island* in ways that blur boundaries between them. Moses emerges from the sea, while Captain Kittridge and the children spend time wandering the beach and imaginatively submerged below the ocean's surface in a submarine landscape that provides an outlet for Mara's active mind and a reminder of the oceanic worlds that also constitute the home.

OBJECTS FROM ELSEWHERE

The absorption of products of maritime travel and empire into the home in a novel concerned with gender also defines Stowe's earlier novel *The Minister's Wooing*, though that novel emphasizes the types of objects that *The Pearl of Orr's Island*'s practical Maine women hide away for special occasions more than it does bodies that wash ashore or turn into coral and pearls. The familiar plot of the young man who goes to sea for years at a time that structured Mrs. Beckworth's story of patient waiting in *A New Home, Who'll Follow?* and that punctuates *The Pearl of Orr's Island* frames *The Minister's Wooing*. It provides Stowe with the basis for her confrontation with religious beliefs within the text and the narrative space to craft networks of active women. In *The Minister's Wooing*, when James Marvyn is reported lost at sea, his beloved cousin Mary and his mother are wracked with anxiety about the state of his soul at the time of his death. Like Moses in *The Pearl of Orr's Island*, James had expressed religious doubts before he sailed, and according to strict Calvinist doctrine he could not be among the saved if those doubts persisted when he died.[46] Readings of *The Minister's Wooing* have long seen this tension as central to its plot; the novel is often read in terms of Stowe's critiques of the harsh strictures of Calvinism in favor of "experiential piety."[47] This piety, based more in loving faith than in fear, uncertainty, and punishment, is expressed through the novel's network of female characters, most explicitly in a scene where the Marvyn's servant Candace (enslaved at the beginning of the novel and newly freed) comforts Mrs. Marvyn during a crisis of faith brought about by the idea that her lost son is among the damned. Candace comforts Mrs. Marvyn in an emotional and embodied outpouring, "rocking her, as if she had been a babe," and assuring her that Jesus "died for Mass'r Jim,—loved him and *died* for him,—jes' give up his sweet, precious body and soul for him on the cross! Laws, jes' *leave* him in Jesus's hands! Why, honey, dar's de very print o'de nails in his hands now!" The minister, Dr. Hopkins, who boards with Mary and her mother,

Katy Scudder, and who represents more traditional Calvinist theology (the character is based on an actual eighteenth-century theologian), is learned, Candace notes, but he doesn't offer the "strong meat" necessary in such a spiritual crisis.[48] The novel advocates for the "strong meat" of a loving Christ rather than a punitive God.

Although he might not be able to adequately comfort a grieving mother, Dr. Hopkins is respectable and good, and Mrs. Scudder convinces Mary to become engaged to the much older minister. When James suddenly returns a week before the wedding (with appropriate religious convictions), Mary refuses to break her promise to Hopkins, though she loves and is attracted to James. Her promise to marry Hopkins, she reasons, is as binding as marriage itself. Candace and the local dressmaker, Miss Prissy, intervene, telling Hopkins of the love between James and Mary; Hopkins does his duty by releasing Mary from hers. A subplot about a Frenchwoman, Virginie de Frontignac, who grew up in a convent, entered into an arranged marriage, and is tortuously in love with the rakish Aaron Burr, brings the pure and dutiful Mary into contact with ideas about love and happiness that play into the novel's conclusion when she marries James.[49] Though one might expect Mary to sacrifice her earthly happiness to keep her promise to the minister, Stowe's emphasis on the freedoms and benefits of a compatible marriage win the day (as one might argue also occurs in *The Pearl of Orr's Island*).

Despite the novel's conventional ending in marriage, characters such as Virginie, with whom Mary has long conversations about emotion and desire, and Prissy and Candace, who propel the novel toward its happy conclusion, make clear the novel's resistance to patriarchal authority by celebrating female knowledge, independence, and action, sometimes in language that, as in *The Pearl of Orr's Island*, explicitly draws on the text's maritime contexts. While James is away at sea, these women are active at home, facilitating the religious and romantic plotlines that his absence makes possible. "I could take a storm a good deal easier than she could," Prissy quips as she compares herself to a married woman with four children, "'cause I hadn't near so many sails to pull down."[50] When Candace arrives at a quilting gathering bearing baskets of food, she is described as rolling "majestically towards the house, like a heavy-laden Indiaman, coming in after a fast voyage." A minor character, Cerinthy Ann, who resists marriage to a minister because she fears that he would always be underfoot, pronounces: "I like the Nantucketers, that go off on four-years' voyages, and leave their wives a clear field. If ever I get married, I'm going up to have one of those fellows."[51] But by the end of the novel, Cerinthy Ann is happily married to a minister rather than to a "Nantucketer," as the novel weaves its plotlines together in a vision of domestic happiness. The possibilities for female action registered throughout the novel are absorbed into conventional home life.

So, too, are violent, extractive global economies acknowledged and absorbed into the novel's domestic spaces. The Newport setting of *The Minister's Wooing* is not described as vividly as is the Maine coast of *The Pearl of Orr's Island*, but it facilitates maritime plots and also allows Stowe to explicitly conjure histories of the slave trade within what Martha Schoolman calls Stowe's "last antislavery novel."[52] A subplot about Dr. Hopkins's antislavery activism emphasizes that the Newport economy is built on this trade. Mrs. Scudder worries that if Hopkins testifies against slavery he will lose the patronage of the town's most powerful men. Here, the novel pits Katy Scudder's practical concerns against her convictions, a tension that will be repeated through her insistence that Mary become Hopkins's dutiful wife, though Mrs. Scudder herself had married for love and attraction rather than to fulfill any expectations. Like Hopkins, however, the man who the now-widowed Mrs. Scudder married had taken a stance against slavery, refusing to profit from a traffic in humans. Before they were married, readers are told, Katy rejected a splendid India shawl sent to her by a rich sea captain whose money came from the slave trade. Instead, she asked George Scudder "to bring her a spotted shell from the South Sea, like the one on his mother's mantel-piece." Her request for a natural gift picked up from a distant beach is intended to signal her willingness to marry George, despite his lack of wealth. In the novel's logic, choosing the decorative Pacific shell over the shawl also signals a rejection of a life wrapped in the profits of slavery. Katy's choice of one object over the other signifies her choice of a partner and his morals and values. But when she returns home after asking George for a shell, she has a "ring of African gold" on her finger, an object that conjures extractive global economies.[53] Years later, when she worries that Dr. Hopkins will lose the income that supports the Scudder household if he stands up for his convictions and loses the patronage of Newport's wealthy slave traders, the novel emphasizes that her rejection of a life wrapped in the profits of slavery is incomplete. As long as the structures of slavery exist, Mrs. Scudder and the rest of Newport will be dependent on them.

The imbrication of global economies in the domestic sphere signaled at the novel's outset through the false choice between Pacific seashell and India shawl that results in Katy bringing home a "ring of African gold" is reinforced in the novel's depiction of the Scudder home. In the course of the novel's opening chapters, in which Stowe's conversational narrator meanders through characters' backgrounds and accounts of domestic interiors, delaying the preparation of tea with "descriptions and meditations," we are told that Mrs. Scudder's "best room . . . has a polished little mahogany tea-table, and six mahogany chairs, with claw talons grasping balls; the white sanded floor is crinkled in curious little waves, like those on the seabeach; and right across the corner stands the 'buffet,' as it is called, with its transparent glass doors, wherein are displayed the solemn appurtenances of company tea-table. There you may see a set of real China teacups, which George had bought in Canton, and had marked with his and his wife's joint initials,—a small silver cream-pitcher, which has come down as an heirloom from unknown generations,—silver spoons and delicate China cake-plates, which have been all carefully reviewed and wiped on napkins of Mrs. Scudder's own weaving."[54] The best room is comprised of objects from elsewhere—mahogany from the Caribbean and teacups from China—all enfolded within the space of the home, marked with initials and polished with Mrs. Scudder's handiwork.[55] The sanded floor, signaling older everyday routines of cleanliness and care, literally brings the beach and ocean waves into the room, making it at once a curated place of display for eighteenth-century imperial commodities and a place that conjures the spaces those objects crossed. Some of these same objects appear in *The Pearl of Orr's Island*: a "silver cream-pitcher that come ashore in a storm" and Mrs. Kittridge's "china tea-cups, which had been marked with her and her husband's joint initials in Canton."[56] These are the types of objects that signify global travel and trade absorbed into domestic spaces in very particular ways.

Mary's "garret-boudoir," *The Minister's Wooing*'s most intimate and lived-in domestic space, contains "odd comminglings" of items that even further illustrate how artifacts from outside the home and around the world are domesticated and craft domestic spaces within the novel. These objects conjure both family histories and distant places. A "grand easy-chair of stamped-leather . . . had genealogical associations" all the way back to "Old England." On one wall hangs "a dusky picture, in an old tarnished frame, of a woman of whose tragic end strange stories were whispered,—one of the sufferers in the time when witches were unceremoniously helped out of the world." To create her private space, Mary has hung blankets crafted by family members, each with its own story. One is a "Chinese linen" with "quaint patterns" of men "with hands forever raised in act to strike bells, which never are struck and never will be till the end of time . . . brought from the Indies by [Mary's] great-great-grandfather" and made into "her grandmother's wedding-curtains."

Another was spun and woven by a great-aunt, "part of a bridal outfit, prepared in vain, against the return of one from sea, who never came back." The material remnants of female ancestral labors and hopes are intertwined with histories of travel and of war. A blanket used during the American Revolution is "mated" to a bed-quilt made from years of dresses.[57] Supplementing the "dusky picture" of the Salem woman on one wall is "an old engraved head of one of the Madonnas of Leonardo da Vinci, a picture which to Mary had a mysterious interest, from the fact of its having been cast on shore after a furious storm, and found like a waif lying in the seaweed."[58] While this image mysteriously emerged from the sea, Mary essentially frames her own virginal image with natural objects from the sea. In her bedroom, "the small looking-glass was curiously wreathed with corals and foreign shells."[59]

Mary's domestic spaces, her "boudoir" in particular, have been read as highlighting the novel's attention to female networks through the use of female-crafted materials and as exemplifying the novel's appropriation of objects and traditions, including those surrounding Catholicism.[60] For Jenny Franchot, for example, the incorporation of the Madonna found on the beach into Mary's personal space exemplifies how many eighteenth- and nineteenth-century narratives feature "visual encounters with Catholic religious fragments that bespeak loss and ruin in a context of possessive appropriation: the religious past, humbled into the fragmentary, iconic dimension, functions as visual accessory in the development of novelistic character and of the novel's 'inner language.'" Through "stylistic religious appropriation," writes Franchot, "Stowe's heroine can pick up Catholicism entire in an act of ecumenical housewifery."[61] Stowe's "domestic aesthetic," writes Lori Merish, "simultaneously sacralizes everyday life and divests aesthetic objects of the significances and temporal rhythms of collective ritual, reconstituting them as the stuff of personal possessions." Throughout her domestic manuals and novels, Merish argues, Stowe crafts a "discourse of sentimental proprietorship" and "helped establish consumerist domesticity as an instrument of cultural hegemony." This proprietorship is supposedly "consensual" and "compatible with America's democratic ideals," as opposed to other extractive or hierarchical forms of consumption or ownership.[62]

Mary's boudoir exemplifies this "sentimental proprietorship," as she repurposes objects, inherited and found, to craft a space where she works at her spinning wheel and communes with others, where time seems suspended (the bells on the Chinese linen are never struck, the great aunt's love never returns from sea), and in which founding mythologies (Salem women and the American Revolution) are placed alongside of objects from across oceans that represent forms of alterity absorbed into the domestic space. The Madonna, shells, and coral that Mary gathers on her walks along nearby beaches reinforce feminine and nature imagery recurring throughout the book, but they are also part of the novel's "sentimental proprietorship" that invests meaning in objects absorbed into the home, taking the mystery from some and imbuing it in others.[63] Although the Madonna might be made an accessory, removed from religious significance, the wreath of seashells around Mary's mirror takes on a prophetic, mystical function, breaking and shattering on the floor when Mary tells James's mother that she will be happy marrying Dr. Hopkins. "Both women started," Stowe writes, "for the string of shells had been placed there by James; and though neither was superstitious, this was one of those odd coincidences that make hearts throb."[64] Taking care to explain that the string had been eaten by moths so that there is a physical explanation for the occurrence, Stowe nevertheless infuses the shells with a message from the lost-at-sea James.

The sympathetic identification between Mary and James expressed through the string of shells and reiterated when, walking along a cliff over the sea, Mary has a kind of waking dream that fills her with pain just before James reappears is a marker of Stowe's sentimental, domestic fiction. It may also reflect Stowe's interest in spiritualism, especially following personal losses of her own. Spiritualism posits an openness to the outside and to other realms. It posits connections between characters across distance that can be manifest through things. Objects reflect and connect characters in *The Minister's Wooing* as Stowe dabbles in romance and mystery within a novel that critiques slavery without quite imagining its end, critiques Calvinist theology without entirely upending it, and gives space to female networks, knowledge, and desires, while ending in a marriage figured as companionable and thus freeing. Mary and James end up not only happily married but also wealthy. With the profits of his travels, James builds a mansion overlooking the harbor where the "fair poetic maiden, the seeress, the saint, has passed into that appointed shrine for woman, more holy than cloister, more saintly and pure than church or altar,—*a Christian home*."[65] Absorbing the novel's ecumenical and mystical visions into the domestic, the domestic simultaneously absorbs the materials of elsewhere. James has brought white silk back from China, which Prissy fashions into Mary's wedding dress. And among the "strange foreign gifts" that James had brought back from his very first voyage was "a flaming red and yellow turban of Moorish stuff, from Mogadore" for Candace, a turban that she proudly wears to his wedding and for years later as she presides over "a rising race of young Marvyns."[66]

Tess Chakkalakal points out that these "colorful, exotic items situate Candace outside the sober New England household in which she lives," reinforcing the "outsiderly status" that also allows her insight into the novel's white characters.[67] But these items also bring her very much inside the household, one composed of silks and teacups from China and perhaps a seashell or two on the mantel. In *The Minister's Wooing*, Stowe uses the familiar plot of sea-going ventures and the love interest lost at sea to craft a narrative about desire and duty, theology and faith, but it is also one that highlights the appropriation of people and things into the home in ways that leave a remainder. Mary moves from her garret boudoir fashioned from found objects to her own "Christian home," but that home is still crafted from such objects. Returning to *The Pearl of Orr's Island* with this tangle of objects and characters in mind enables us to reconsider Moses and his own absorption into that community.

MOSES, DRAWN OUT OF THE WATER

Though it is easy to forget throughout the middle of *The Pearl of Orr's Island*, when Moses is first found on the beach after the storm that shipwrecks him, he speaks "a language unknown to most present," which Captain Kittridge determines to be Spanish. He must slowly learn English to communicate with his new community. And throughout the novel he is described as an exotic other with a "fervid, tropical richness in his air." He is like a "tropical flower [that] had been washed landward by a monsoon," a being who had "floated ashore . . . like a fragment of tropical sea-weed borne landward by a great gale."[68] Nothing is known about his identity, though the Reverend Sewell's reaction when he first sees the bracelet of hair engraved with the initials "D.M." found with the woman and child on the beach suggests that he has knowledge that he withholds. Later in the novel, when Moses is a twenty-year-old man of the world just returned from lengthy sea voyages, he decides to ask Sewell what he knows about his origins, reasoning that it is time he thought about marrying but that he would not do so until he was rich. He hopes that he may have family somewhere and property coming to him, so he tries to find out about his past. Mr. Sewell gives Moses a letter he had intended for him to read when he turned twenty-one that explains what Sewell suspects about Moses's background.

This letter, spread over two chapters, brings the narrative from Maine to Florida and the Caribbean, revealing that after graduating from Harvard, Sewell had taken a position as tutor for the family of a wealthy man in St. Augustine. Don Jose Mendoza had come to Florida from the Spanish West Indies with one daughter, whose mother had died. Don Jose had then married an American woman with three children, and they had four children of their own, bringing their brood to eight pupils for Sewell to tutor. Sewell describes a tense environment, showing disdain for Don Jose and his "tempestuous" family and revealing his racist attitudes toward the persons enslaved by the family, whose influence he blames for worsening the children's behavior. He presents his training and self-control as qualities that the North can attempt to bring to the "ill-regulated," sprawling southern family.[69] The one exception to this chaos is Dolores, Don Jose's first daughter, who is presented as pure, good, and abused by other family members. Inevitably, Sewell and Dolores fall in love, a fact revealed only when Don Jose arranges a marriage between Dolores and a much older, wealthy, large, and pimply Cuban slaveowner, Senor Don Guzman de Cardona. Sewell does not want to interfere with the marriage because he cannot give Dolores a life of wealth, but in an impassioned moonlight encounter she convinces him that wealth and status are of no concern. Sewell recalls: "What answer I made I cannot say. I only know that every vestige of what is called reason and common sense left me at that moment, and that there followed an hour of delirium in which I—we both were *very* happy—we forgot everything but each other, and we arranged all our plans for flight."[70] Don Jose discovers their plans, however, and Dolores urges Sewell to flee before he is killed. He leaves and later reads of her marriage in the newspaper. Only the bracelet made from the hair of Dolores's mother found with Dolores and Moses on the beach brought all of this back to Sewell. Subsequent inquiries led him to discover that there had been an attempted slave insurrection at Don Guzman's Cuba residence and that he was taking his family to Boston for safety but had not been heard from since embarking. Somehow, Dolores and Moses had ended up on the shore of Orr's Island.

Moses is revealed to be heir to money still in Cuba, which he apparently claims, though the novel moves past this detail so quickly that it is difficult to be sure. One of the novel's female characters, Aunt Ruey, simply says, "How kind o' providential it happened about his getting that property; he'll be a rich man now."[71] Though the novel conjures the specter of slave insurrection in the Caribbean that would evoke such major events as the Haitian Revolution, it stops short of an overt critique of slavery, apparently allowing Moses to inherit wealth linked to Caribbean slave economies. And it stops short of suggesting that one of the reasons Mara cannot marry Moses is because he stands to benefit from the economics of slavery. The novel implies both that love for Mara saves Moses from the extractive violence of global capitalism by bringing him back to Orr's Island to settle down with Sally, united in their sorrow over Mara's death, and also that the earthly world of global capitalism, with its racial and cultural violence and complexities, is always already, inescapably, part of Orr's Island. Sally's marriage to Moses incorporates an "other"—"tropical," Catholic, and ambiguously raced—into the community of Orr's Island.[72] In *The Minister's Wooing*, Mary picks up an image of the Madonna on the beach and hangs it in her garret boudoir, appropriating and demystifying the religious icon. People and objects from elsewhere reconfigure the home. But Sewell's history with the Mendoza family (the novel seems to at least leave open the possibility that he is Moses' father) and the silks and satins stored away for special occasions within women's trunks on Orr's Island serve as reminders that the simple, homespun life of Orr's Island is already built on such appropriations and connections. Sewell, the man who has a role in regulating both the spiritual life on Orr's Island and the formal schooling of Moses and Mara, has knowledge of and links to personal histories in the Caribbean and in Florida that are connected to broader histories of enslavement and racial violence. But he seems to have forgotten all of this until physical reminders wash up on the beach in the form of haunting bodies and objects. Mara's interest in *The Tempest* and in imagining underwater worlds has a parallel in this Caribbean backstory of forced marriage and revolution, one that brings Cuba and Florida into contact with Maine islands covered in pine trees.

COASTAL GOTHIC

We are now used to recognizing how traces of oceanic worlds within domestic fictions conjure the exploitative global structures that dress women in rich gowns and seat them in well-appointed best rooms. We recognize, for example, that British naval characters and men who go to the Caribbean on urgent business in Jane Austen's novels conjure histories of colonialism and slavery. And we read gothic bildungsromane such as Charlotte Brontë's *Jane Eyre*, published in London in 1847, for how a character haunting a house conjures the same. That novel's Bertha Mason has become the paradigmatic "madwoman in the attic" and, especially following the Caribbean backstory imagined for Brontë's novel in Jean Rhys's *Wide Sargasso Sea* (1966), a signifier for violent, gendered global histories hidden within the home. Though it is quiet, filled with quilting and embroidery, and devout, always keeping an eye on heaven, *The Pearl of Orr's Island* evokes aspects of Brontë's novel through its focus on gender restrictions and religion in a female bildungsroman-esque plot punctuated by death, ghosts, and a tension-filled romantic triangle. The narrative that Sewell offers in his letter to Moses also echoes aspects of that novel through its ambiguously raced, abused young woman who ends up on a Maine beach, "inwreathed in sand and shells." According to Stowe biographer Hedrick, Stowe read *Jane Eyre* while writing *The Pearl of Orr's Island*.[73] Certainly Brontë's tale of the orphaned Jane's moral and spiritual growth was a significant cultural and literary influence on both sides of the Atlantic in the decades after its publication. On the American side, its influence has been identified in the popular female bildungsromane of the 1850s such as Susan Warner's *The Wide, Wide World* (1850) and in the recovered manuscript *The Bondswoman's Narrative*, written sometime in the mid-nineteenth century by a formerly enslaved woman, Hannah Crafts.[74]

Stowe's coastal New England novels raise similar issues about how people and objects haunt domestic worlds constructed on racialized violence, but part of what is distinct about them is the extent to which their settings allow Stowe to thematize and depict the oceanic spaces elided in other such fictions. Despite the seemingly peripheral nature of actual maritime action, the maritime world is everywhere in these novels, circulating in objects from the Caribbean and Pacific and linked to mystical events. Others have noted how *The Pearl of Orr's Island* imbues "local color with mysticism" and the supernatural in a way linked to Stowe's religious and spiritual interests.[75] These elements often inhere in connections to the sea, in Captain Kittridge's sailor yarns about life on the ocean floor brought into the kitchen and shared with children, and in shells that mysteriously clatter to the floor when Mary says that she will marry Dr. Hopkins in *The Minister's Wooing*. Though these novels end relatively conservatively in visions of happy Christian marriages and homes, the unsettling tone created by images like Mara's dripping, dead shipmaster father and Moses' kelp-wrapped, sand- and shell-encrusted mother, along with fanciful stories of underwater worlds and island spirits, linger.

Furthermore, the coastal settings of these novels open the home out to islands and peninsulas, such as Florida, whose histories can be traced within Stowe's fictional Maine in *The Pearl of Orr's Island* and whose topographies would, as Michele Navakas argues, eventually challenge Stowe's own ideologies. Florida would become an important part of Stowe's life beginning in 1866, just a few years after publication of *The Pearl of Orr's Island*, when Stowe leased a plantation not far from St. Augustine for her son Frederick and his family after his return from the

Civil War. In 1867 she purchased a plot of land just across the St. Johns River. She would build a house and winter there from 1868 to 1884, and she published various writings about the state. Navakas posits that "Stowe's experience of domesticating postbellum Florida challenged her own imperial ideology at times by prompting her to value locally specific forms of root-taking, even when they thwarted the 'forms of civilized life' she elsewhere idealized in classic expressions of 'manifest domesticity.'"[76] While some of her Florida writings show "evidence that Stowe fashioned herself as one of the South's 'new masters,'" as various scholars have argued, Navakas claims that a deeper look at Stowe's Florida writings shows her negotiating complex histories and landscapes that resist easy domestication in ways that recognize the need for incorporation into the nation to "take a variety of forms."[77]

Florida's resistant topographies are very different from the New England spaces of *The Minister's Wooing* and *The Pearl of Orr's Island*. And yet the beaches, bays, and grottos of these novels, as well as the people and objects that cross and inhabit them, emphasize how New England domestic worlds contain and open out to other spaces. Though they resolve themselves in visions of Christian domesticity, the tensions surrounding gender restrictions and empire infused throughout these novels, often by means of maritime references and characters and objects that circulate globally, leave a remainder that destabilizes those homes in ways that other contemporary authors take to different extremes. In the next chapter I show how Harriet Prescott Spofford and Elizabeth Stoddard work with very similar material—objects of global circulation, familial tensions, romantic triangles, and haunting histories—in literary styles that often separate them from the more conservative Stowe. But the terraqueous realms of *The Pearl of Orr's Island*, with its religious visions, wailing cradles, and corpses with pearl eyes, enable us to rethink literary relationships between the slightly older, established Stowe and the emerging, "modern" Spofford and Stoddard, whose writing careers were just taking off in the early 1860s, relationships that can be configured around their deployment of the oceanic to destabilize gender and empire through a coastal gothic. Ideas about gender and empire that are ultimately enveloped within Stowe's Christian domestic visions in her novels erupt in Stoddard's and Spofford's texts, in part through literary style and form.

CHAPTER SIX
Elizabeth Stoddard and Harriet Prescott Spofford
Amphibious Style and Archipelagic Forms

"A habit grew upon me of consulting the sea as soon as I rose in the morning," explains Cassandra, the central character of Elizabeth Stoddard's 1862 novel *The Morgesons*. "Its aspect decided how my day would be spent . . . I went there by day unobserved, except by our people, for I never walked toward the village. Mother descried me, as she would a distant sail, or Aunt Merce, who had a vacant habit of looking from all the windows a moment at a time, as if she were forever expecting the arrival of somebody who never came. Arthur, too, saw me, as he played among the rocks, waded, caught crabs and little fish, like all boys whose hereditary associations are amphibious."[1] Only Cassandra's sister, Veronica, stays away from the windows facing the ocean, unless a ship is returning from sea. Cassandra's daily, individual act of communion with the sea is also described as a familial one. Her own habit intersects with those of her "people." The novel's concern with family connections, which for the Morgesons consist of vague histories and a tension-filled present, is momentarily figured through networks of shore walkers, seaward gazes, and "hereditary associations [that] are amphibious."

While this particular phrase is associated with Cassandra's younger brother, Arthur, the notion that "associations are amphibious" is one that underlies much of the novel. To be amphibious is to be able to exist on or to be connected to both land and water. It was a term sometimes used in travel narratives to describe Indigenous Pacific Islanders or Pacific island "beachcombers," emphasizing comfort and proficiency on both land and water and suggesting a sense of the exotic absent from its use in *The Morgesons*.[2] In the context of this scene of shore wandering, the term conjures the Morgeson family's history that straddles both land and sea. And individual characters such as Cassandra seem defined by their interactions with coastal spaces; the sea's aspect decides how Cassandra's day is spent. More generally, the concept of amphibiousness suggests a type of relationship that permeates the novel, from its setting to its sentences, a relationship that might be characterized by the phrase "and also." Arthur's "hereditary associations" involve land and also water. Stoddard's prose is marked by suggestive associations of doubleness and possibility that give the novel a feeling of disconnection and unease. This chapter reads the amphibious stylistic associations of Stoddard's gothic female bildungsroman alongside of the archipelagic forms of Harriet Prescott Spofford's long short story "The Amber Gods" (1860). It argues that in these texts, recognized for their critiques of gender restrictions and their twisted plots and haunting prose, family histories of hidden traumas that stretch across land and sea become a matter of both setting and style.

Published nearly contemporaneously with Stowe's novels discussed in the previous chapter, both "The Amber Gods" and *The Morgesons* have been linked to *Jane Eyre* "fever." Both contain unsettling familial relationships and love triangles within female-centered, coming-of-age stories.[3] In her account of *The Morgesons*'s literary recovery, Amanda Claybaugh notes that "to argue for its literary value . . . the critics who rediscovered *The Morgesons* in the 1980s, Sandra Zagarell and Lawrence Buell, needed to find an alternate literary context in which it could be placed. They found such a context in the British novel. Observing Stoddard's personal affinity for the Brontës and the many intertextualities between *The Morgesons* and *Jane Eyre* (1848), Zagarell and Buell argued that *The Morgesons* revises the female bildungsroman in the largely British mode of the female gothic. As a consequence," Claybaugh concludes, "*The Morgesons* is one of the few novels to have entered the canon under transatlantic auspices."[4]

While the recovery of many nineteenth-century American texts by women writers initially required positioning them in relation to canonical British texts like *Jane Eyre*, making their recovery inherently embedded in conversations about transatlantic circulations of texts and influences, this focus obscures the extent to which the texts discussed in this chapter are also products of more global circulations. Within these texts we see the accrual of decades of U.S. interest in the Pacific and the global circulation of tales and ideas like those reflected within the children's stories about the Pacific written by Child: about contact, captivity, and possession across oceans. These engagements with the Pacific were, as we have seen, pedagogical, economic, affective, and narrative. In *The Morgesons* and "The Amber Gods," they result in narratives indebted to British literary traditions, certainly, but whose deployment of oceanic imagery and movement is also linked to other histories. These texts look westward to the Pacific as well as eastward toward Britain as they challenge ideas about gender conventions while making the local, and local family histories, inseparable from oceanic transactions and relationships rendered stylistically.

"WE MAY ALL BE TATTOOED"

Elizabeth Stoddard was no stranger to the sea. She was born Elizabeth Drew Barstow in the small Massachusetts coastal town of Mattapoisett in 1823. Her father was a shipbuilder whose firm constructed the whaler on which Melville traveled to the Pacific, and the Barstow family existed "in a position of precarious gentility" owing to the risks inherent in the maritime and shipbuilding industry.[5] This small-town coastal life and the maritime economies that undergird it are interwoven throughout much of Stoddard's fiction.[6] Stoddard's three novels, *The Morgesons*, *Two Men*, and *Temple House*, all published in the 1860s, are invested in the sea and in seafaring communities to various degrees.[7] Although Stoddard was born as New England maritime activity expanded, these novels were all published during a decade that saw significant changes to the nature of that activity: commercial whaling was beginning its downward trajectory following the discovery of petroleum in Pennsylvania in 1859; the development of steamships would start to change the types of vessels being built; and a Civil War battle between the *Monitor* and *Merrimack* would mark the introduction of new naval technology in the form of ironclad warships. In other words, these texts were published at a moment when exploration, sealing, whaling, and trade in the Pacific and elsewhere had been going on for decades and just as these economies were starting to shift. These texts are both the product of American maritime culture and a reflection of its changing nature.[8]

In *The Morgesons*, Cassandra, like Stowe's Mara, struggles with the restrictions of nineteenth-century New England. The novel progresses from Cassandra's childhood through her marriage, following a plot of female development, but along the way it pushes the bounds of propriety. It meanders through illicit incestuous attraction and dark desires in prose often identified as dissociative and elliptical. And though the novel ends with marriage, it is not the happy ending of the traditional nineteenth-century marriage plot. The novel's conclusion does not leave readers with Stowe's vision of a happy Christian home; instead, it is shadowed by illness and death. Cassandra and Veronica have married brothers, Desmond and Ben Somers, both of whom have histories of alcoholism. Veronica's husband, Ben, dies, leaving her with a "year-old baby. It smiles continually, but never cries, never moves, except when it is moved."[9] Ben's death, it is vaguely suggested, is precipitated by alcoholism, and the baby, it seems, has been affected by the disease. Inheritance of all kinds is fraught within the novel.

From the very beginning of the novel, Morgeson family ancestors and issues of inheritance are described in terms of water and land. The family has lived in the Massachusetts coastal town of Surrey for generations, but unlike other families, they cannot trace their lineage back to a founding event like the *Mayflower* arrival. Theirs is a vague history of names on gravestones. An ancestor must have "moved from an earlier settlement, and, appropriating a few acres in what was now its center, lived long enough upon them to see his sons and daughters married to the sons and daughters of similar settlers."[10] Tracing an origin story is impossible. This opaque settler past is conjured not by a few cultivated acres, however, but by the gray rock just visible at the foot of the cellar stairs in the home of Cassandra's grandfather. As a child, Cassandra opens the door and stares down into the "black gulf": "The foundation of the house was on the spurs of a great granite bed, which rose from the Surrey shores, dipped and cropped out in the Center of Barmouth. It came through the ground again in the woodhouse, smooth and round . . . and in the border of the garden it burst through in narrow ridges full of seams."[11] A mystery that cannot be illuminated by learning geology in school, the rock places murky family histories at the furthest edges of land, where it rises up from the ocean.

Cassandra's great-grandfather Locke Morgeson begins the family's present-day story. He was, it seemed to her, "born under the influence of the sea, while the rest of the tribe inherited the character of the landscape."[12] Generations later, Arthur, a product of these unions, is "amphibious," a word associated not only with activities along the seashore that he and Cassandra wander but also, in the novel's early pages, with their village, Surrey: "From the observatory of our house we could see how the inlet was pinched by the long claws of the land, which nearly enclosed it. Opposite the village, some ten miles across, a range of islands shut out the main waters of the bay. For miles on the outer side of the curving prongs of land stretched a rugged, desolate coast, indented with coves and creeks, lined with bowlders of granite half sunken in the sea, and edged by seaweed. Nothing alive, except the gulls, abode in these solitary shores. No lighthouse stood on any point, to shake its long, warning light across the mariner's wake. Now and then a drowned man floated in among the sedge, or a small craft went to pieces on the rocks."[13] The geography of home is a stark landscape of half submerged boulders, seabirds, and the occasional corpse. Grandfather Locke laid out plans and possibilities in this space, plans only later brought to fruition by Cassandra's father, who became "a rich Morgeson . . . a new feature in the family annals," through his shipping ventures, creating new circuits involving the space of Surrey, the family home, and the world beyond. "As his business extended," Cassandra reflects, "our visiting list extended. The captains of his ships whose homes were elsewhere brought their wives to be inconsolable with us after their departure on their voyages. We had ministers often . . . there was but small opportunity to cultivate family affinities; they were forever disturbed. Somebody was always sitting in the laps of our Lares and Penates."[14] Conjuring Roman gods associated with the household and household objects, Stoddard emphasizes how the intimacies of family and home life are disrupted by Mr. Morgeson's commercial enterprises. In the novel's present, the circulations of the maritime world move uncomfortably alongside and atop of family life and family histories.

Cassandra's domestic and imaginative worlds, as well as her resistance to convention and propriety, are inextricable from these circulations. At the very beginning of the novel, which opens in the 1820s, readers find young Cassandra Morgeson "climbing a chest of drawers, by its knobs, in order to reach the book-shelves above it, where," she tells the reader, "my favorite work 'The Northern Regions,' was kept, together with 'Baxter's Saints' Rest,' and other volumes of that sort, belonging to my mother . . . To this day," she continues, "Sheridan's Comedies, Sterne's Sentimental Journey, and Captain Cook's Voyages are so mixed up in my remembrance that I am still uncertain whether it was Sterne who ate baked dog with Maria, or Sheridan who wept over a dead ass in the Sandwich Islands." Perched on the edge of a chest of drawers in this opening scene, Cassandra is soon "lost in an Esquimaux hut" while her mother pores over an article in the *Boston Recorder*, a weekly Congregationalist newspaper.[15] Cassandra's reading preferences are grounded in global adventure—in the type of travel narratives that Lydia Maria Child would incorporate into the *Juvenile Miscellany*, a periodical that Stoddard certainly might have had access to as a child. But Cassandra explicitly rejects the type of "good," profitable morals that appear on the surface of many of the *Juvenile Miscellany*'s stories. When her own reading is interrupted, Cassandra's mother asks her daughter, "Why will you waste so much time on unprofitable stories?" Cassandra replies, "Mother, I hate good stories," explicitly contrasting her mother's "profitable" religious reading with exotic travel narratives and adventure stories.[16] Instead of such "profitable," instructive reading, Cassandra's reading produces hybrid global adventures—Sterne eating baked dog, Sheridan weeping over a dead ass—that reinforce her status as a character who pushes the boundaries of propriety in various ways.

Cassandra's reading practices emphasize her precocious nature and the circulation of narratives about distant places—Europe, the polar regions, and the Pacific—that are linked to the profits of empire if not to profitable religious edification and personal industriousness. Her reading practices emphasize the circulation of such narratives into home spaces represented by the image of the chest of drawers that Cassandra must climb to reach the bookshelves above. Those symbols of domestic organization might very well be filled with the stuff of global exchange facilitated by and recorded in the travel narratives that Cassandra consumes. As in Stowe's novels, *The Morgesons* is filled with the objects of global trade brought into the home through the shipping ventures that also bring ship captains' wives and minsters into the house. Domestic spaces contain "speckled Pacific sea-shells," a whale's tooth with a drawing of a ship on its surface, an ostrich egg hanging from a ceiling, sandalwood, green tea, and a "large green parrot . . . from foreign parts."[17] The wealthy girls at young Cassandra's school are unaware that their own family money and their pink calico dresses come from West India rum, the slave trade, whaling, or insurance scams involving wrecked ships. The economics that govern the home in *The Morgesons* are inseparable from violent economies imposed elsewhere.

Even the novel's most vivid image of resistance to the norms that structure traditional New England life is linked to global circulation. Later in the book we are told that Cassandra's friend Helen plans to marry a cousin who is a sailor; she has a tattoo of his initials on her arm. When Cassandra's face is scarred in a carriage accident that kills Charles, her married cousin with whom she has an illicit, passionate relationship, Cassandra claims the scars as tattoos. As Jennifer Putzi describes, Stoddard's decision to tattoo these female characters—Helen's arm and Cassandra's cheek—aligns their bodies with a tradition of tattooing that began circulating in such travel narratives as those of Captain James Cook and that was associated with indigeneity, an outsider status, or incorporation into another way of life.[18] Part of what is at stake in these images of marked female bodies in the novel, Putzi notes, is the ability of women to "claim their own bodies and the experiences they represent." When Cassandra claims her scars as tattoos, she reappropriates the marks as part of the novel's "uneasy compromise between Cassandra's sexual, economic, and moral freedom, and the bleak future that seems to be in store for her and her family."[19] Even bodies in *The Morgesons*, like that of Child's "Mary Howard" discussed in chapter 2, are marked by oceanic associations. These marks might signal female agency, as Putzi suggests, but they also link these characters to distant encounters and forms of bodily violence inseparable from pasts and presents of global empire. "We may all be tattooed," Ben Somers remarks when he and Cassandra first see Helen's marks, suggesting the universal nature of claims on the self and others, of scarring life experiences, and of global circulations.[20] Cassandra and the Morgeson family more generally benefit from the networks suggested here. Goods, people, and money come ashore, though they are sometimes lost to the sea. As Shirley Samuels notes, the novel presents "conjunctions of commerce and desire" that hum with violence and loss.[21] The family that has settled on a bed of granite and that lives, sometimes precariously, off of the products of maritime ventures is also marked by these associations.

MINGLED ESSENCE

Sometimes these intersections between family relations, global economics, and female agency are conveyed through representations of the sea itself. Toward the end of *The Morgesons*, Cassandra goes to walk by the seashore. It is the first time she has done so since her return home to Surrey after a stay with the Somers family in Belem, a town abandoned by the sea, one whose "wooden suburbs" are "bordered by an ancient marsh, from which the sea had long retired."[22] This walk by the seashore is thus a kind of homecoming, to Surrey and to the sea. It also takes place weeks after the death of Cassandra's mother, and that loss, with its "aching, aimless melancholy," infuses the scene, which begins with attention to the physical experience of being on the shore:

> Picking my way over the beach, left bare by the tide, with my eyes fixed downward till I could see, I reached the point between our house and the lighthouse and turned toward the sea, inhaling its cool freshness. I climbed out to a flat, low rock, on the point; it was dry in the sun, and the weeds hanging from its sides were black and crisp; I put my woolen shawl on it, and stretched myself along its edge. Little pools meshed from the sea by the numberless rocks round me engrossed my attention. How white and pellucid was the shallow near me—no shadow but the shadow of my face bending over it—nothing to ripple its surface, but my imperceptible breath! By and by a bunch of knotted wrack floated in from the outside and lodged in a crevice; a minute creature with fringed feet darted from

> it and swam across it. After the knotted wrack came the fragment of a green and silky substance, delicate enough to have been the remnant of a web, woven in the palace of Circe. "There must be a current," I thought, "which sends them here." And I watched the inlet for other waifs; but nothing more came. Eye-like bubbles rose from among the fronds of the knotted wrack, and, sailing on uncertain voyages, broke one by one and were wrecked to nothingness. The last vanished; the pool showed me the motionless shadow of my face again, on which I pondered, till I suddenly became aware of a slow, internal oscillation, which increased till I felt in a strange tumult. I put my hand in the pool and troubled its surface.
>
> "Hail, Cassandra! Hail!"[23]

This passage begins with vivid language that emphasizes the appearance and materiality of Cassandra's surroundings: "a flat, low rock," "dry in the sun," "weeds" that are "black and crisp." Her body is depicted as separate from the rock and the dry weeds, breathing in the sea's "cool freshness." In the next sentences, however, as Cassandra's attention shifts to the "little pools meshed from the sea," her body begins to merge with and to impact the water. The only shadow on the pool's surface is "the shadow of my face bending over" the shallow. Her "imperceptible breath" is the only force that ripples the surface of the water. This intimate moment is disrupted with the arrival of a "bunch of knotted wrack," "a minute creature," "the fragment of a green and silky substance," and the subsequent realization that "there must be a current." There is a world outside these pools and outside Cassandra, after all. But that world recedes again, and the pool returns to stillness. No longer able to feel still herself, Cassandra must trouble the pool's surface so that it matches her internal "tumult." The pools and Cassandra's self exist in an intimate relationship even as other material enters and disappears, "wrecked to nothingness."

As Cassandra's internal "strange tumult" erupts and manifests itself in a disturbance of the surface of the pool, the exclamation "Hail, Cassandra! Hail!"—an imperial exclamation of uncertain origin soon attributed to a "flying Spirit"—marks a shift in focus in the passage from attention to the minuscule ("eye-like bubbles") to the broader scale of the sea:

> I sprang up the highest rock on the point, and looked seaward, to catch a glimpse of the flying Spirit who had touched me. My soul was brought in poise and quickened with the beauty before me! The wide, shimmering plain of sea—its aerial blue, stretching beyond the limits of my vision in one direction, upbearing transverse,

> cloud-like islands in another, varied and shadowed by shore and sky—mingled its essence with mine.
>
> The wind was coming; under the far horizon the mass of waters began to undulate. Dark, spear-like clouds rose above it and menaced the east. The speedy wind tossed and teased the sea nearer and nearer, till I was surrounded by a gulf of milky green foam. As the tide rolled in I retreated, stepping back from rock to rock, round which the waves curled and hissed, baffled in their attempt to climb over me. I stopped on the verge of the tide-mark; the sea was seeking me and I must wait. It gave tongue as its lips touched my feet, roaring in the caves, falling on the level beaches with a mad, boundless joy![24]

These paragraphs, while marking a shift in focus and scale from the minute detail to the expanse of the sea, continue to pursue the idea of a relationship between the "shimmering plain of sea" and Cassandra herself—the sea "mingled its essence with mine." Yet Cassandra backs away from the sea's pursuit, which is figured in sensuous language. The sea will have to wait. Cassandra "turned and walked swiftly homeward, treading the ridges of white sand, the black drifts of sea-weed, as if they had been a smooth floor."[25]

In many ways, the sea is an abstract force in this scene. As Ayşe Çelikkol observes, Cassandra's account of her experience at the seashore "is fraught with the language of the sublime," an "embodiment of infinity" whose "limitlessness" is accompanied by a "feeling akin to terror."[26] Yet Çelikkol also notes that Cassandra's self is not completely at odds with or overwhelmed by the sublimity of the sea, which "mingled its essence" with hers. This scene, where Cassandra's confrontation with the sea's sublimity is also a confrontation with her own self, is part of rather than separate from the many financial and material aspects of oceanic circulations within the novel, from Helen's and Cassandra's tattoos to the sperm oil and shells that sometimes find their way into the harbor on one of Mr. Morgeson's ships. Indeed, the way that these passages emphasize interaction—of the pool with "knotted wrack," "a minute creature," and a "green and silky substance," and of the sea itself with Cassandra—makes clear that the sea in *The Morgesons* is not simply an abstract idea or a sublime force but also a physical space of exchange. In Çelikkol's formulation, this seashore episode suggests "that the experience of the sublime is analogous to economic activity in so far as both involve the self's recognition of its own inherent dependence on its outside. Cassandra's desire to let herself be nurtured by the sea embodies the fundamental premise underlying all economic activity: the self—or, analogously, a community—recognizes itself as an entity that is neither self-sufficient nor detached from its outside."[27] The sea in *The Morgesons* is at once a kind of sublime other, a reflection of individual characters' emotions, and an influence on individual characters within the novel, as it is also the space that is traversed to facilitate economic exchange. Materially and symbolically, the sea in this novel emphasizes the mutually constitutive relationship between exteriors and interiors of spaces and of selves, intertwined relationships that are also depicted through familial ties. As with the seashore pools that Cassandra contemplates, where a current brings a minute creature and knotted wrack into the pool, the maritime economies that Cassandra's father engages and creates bring bodies and things into the space of the home, disturbing "family affinities."

AMPHIBIOUS STYLE

These associations are reinforced stylistically in the novel in a way that is related to, though not exclusive to, the sea's relationship to individual characters and to familial bonds or ruptures. *The Morgesons* is often noted to feel surprisingly "modern" in its tone and style, picking up aspects of Hawthorne's New England and throwing them ahead toward types of psychological realism and fragmentation that we generally associate with late nineteenth- or early twentieth-century fiction. Exchanges between characters often seem loaded, yet opaque. For example, at one point Cassandra notes that her cousin Charles, seemingly apropos of nothing, "asked me if I knew whether the sea had any influence upon me; I replied that I had not thought of it. 'There are so many things you have not thought of,' he answered, 'that this is not strange.'" Just a few paragraphs later, during a conversation about whether Cassandra should stay with Charles and his wife and attend school in their town, Cassandra's mother defers to her husband in an exchange that prompts Cassandra to tap her mother's "shoulder till she turned round and smiled. I whispered, 'Mother, your eyes are as blue as the sea yonder, and I love you.' She glanced toward it; it was murmuring softly, creeping along the shore, licking the rocks and sand as if recognizing a master. And I saw and felt its steady, resistless heaving, insidious and terrible."[28] Like the scene of Cassandra's interaction with the pools and the sea, this passage makes the sea at once powerful and terrible and also subordinate. It also contributes to an unsettled sense of relationality that emerges throughout the novel in its treatment of relationships between land and sea, characters, and family members, as well as on the sentence level. The sentence "Mother, your eyes are as blue as the sea yonder, and I love you" is one that exemplifies *The Morgesons*'s often remarked-upon fragmented, dissociative style. There is a sense of cause and effect here (because your eyes are as blue as the sea, I love you), but ultimately the sentence denies that reading—it does not move forward, arrow-like. Rather, the sentence turns back on itself; it presents associated, but separate, ideas. Cassandra's mother's eyes are as blue as the sea. And, also, Cassandra loves her mother. Placed side by side within the same sentence in a paratactic construction only loosely connected with the word "and," these ideas, like the doubleness of amphibiousness, are distinct yet overlapping. The sentence's components function as adjacent pools or as wave and shore, floating into or moving over each other in variable relationships.

At a later moment in the novel while visiting another family's home, Cassandra notes: "The table reminded me of our table at Surrey, it was so covered with vast viands; but the dishes were alike, and handsome. I wondered whether mother had bought the new china in Boston, and, buttering my second hot biscuit, I thought of Veronica; then, of the sea. How did it look? Hark! Its voice was in my ear! Could I climb the housetop? Might I not see the mist which hung over our low-lying sea by Surrey?"[29] As Cassandra's thoughts wander from dishes to her sister and to the sea, all become connected in a web of domesticity—dishes, sisters—that is also connected to a wider world—new china purchased in Boston, the sea. But it is not entirely clear how these elements are connected, just as it is not clear why Charles asks about the sea's influence on Cassandra or how the color of Cassandra's mother's eyes being like the sea is related to Cassandra's love for her mother. These are not quite non sequiturs. They are sentences that exemplify the associations and movements of a text attuned to "vague spaces of sea and land—the motion of the one—the stillness of the other" in both physical and figurative senses.[30] In *The Morgesons*, terrestrial and oceanic spaces, domestic and global economies, and characters are put in "vague" relations in general and also at the sentence level.

Certainly, syntactically unsettling sentences and associations appear throughout *The Morgesons*, and not only in relation to content about the sea. They are part of the "textual experiments" that Dorri Beam identifies in the writing of nineteenth-century female authors, including Margaret Fuller, Ann Stephens, and Pauline Hopkins. Such authors, Beam shows, engaged in a "sensuous and extravagant style of writing" that allowed them to "reformulate residual and unaccommodated feminine doubt, ambition, anger, longing, and pleasure as essential, substantial, and palpable."[31] "Highly wrought" style, according to Beam, "allowed women writers to generate alternative models of gendered self and desire" in a way that engaged "a variety of debates at the crux of romantic literary production." Beam admits that "Elizabeth Stoddard's style seems more condensed and taut than elaborately wrought."[32] It does not quite feature "the voluptuously turned language, the textured layering of sensual detail and image, and a syntax of endless accrual" that the authors featured in her book demonstrate. But, Beam continues, Stoddard's "concern in *The Morgesons* with undercutting the woman's plot of self-cultivation and acculturation in favor of indulgences in a sensual style that renders the world opaque and strange rather than assimilable and interpretable, is another version of the experiments [that Beam describes]. Through different techniques, Stoddard achieves similar effects . . . forcing the reader to pause and savor her language."[33]

One of the ways we can think about Stoddard's style in *The Morgesons*, especially in relation to the ornate style of Harriet Prescott Spofford, whom Beam does treat at length, is that it is characterized by associations that force the reader to pause, to review, to return. Stoddard's style "that renders the world opaque and strange" is often one of loose connection that places ideas side by side while also allowing them to blend together and merge. This sentence-level style of relationality reinforces *The Morgesons*'s attention to the movements of global circuits and to the familial associations that are inseparable from and enable those global circuits. In a novel pervaded by the oceanic and by relationships between the "out there" and the "here," relationships also between generations and family members that are never, perhaps can never be, fully acknowledged or articulated, attending to sentence-level associations or dissociations can help us recognize the undercurrents that constitute and unsettle home spaces within the novel. To say that style is like land and water in this novel is to say that the relationships suggested by Stoddard's stylistic choices reinforce and reflect the "amphibious associations" that *The Morgesons* emphasizes.

ARCHIPELAGIC RELATIONS

Harriet Prescott Spofford's "The Amber Gods" extends this style of lateral and mobile relationality into its archipelagic associations. This story, published in the *Atlantic Monthly* in January and February 1860 and as the title story of an 1863 collection, is dominated by the confident, sensual, self-absorbed voice of its narrator, Yone (short for Giorgione).

In the story's first, longer section, Yone recounts her life story on the morning of the day she will marry Vaughn Rose. In its second, shorter section, set ten years later, she recounts her unhappy marriage and defies convention, and even death itself, by speaking to the reader from the beyond. The story raises questions surrounding female agency similar to those presented by Cassandra's scars claimed as tattoos, but it does so even more boldly. "'The Amber Gods' does not simply register its critique [of female constraint within expected norms]," writes Beam, "it performs its resistance through voice and style."[34] Like Cassandra in *The Morgesons*, Yone claims herself, her body, and her sexuality. "I seem to myself like the complete incarnation of light, full, bounteous, overflowing," she thinks at the beginning of the story as she describes herself to the reader, "and I wonder at and adore anything so beautiful; and the reflection grows finer and deeper while I gaze, till I dare not do so any longer."[35] Yone is anything but a demure woman. She is as "overflowing" as the words used to describe her.

Early recovery work on this text focused on these questions of gendered agency—on the tension between Yone's self-realization and self-celebration and the restrictions of her eventual marriage and death, as well as the gothic nature of her voice's persistence even in death. More recent scholarship has extended analysis of gender and agency into the narrative's depiction of global histories of gendered, imperial violence.[36] These histories are exemplified within the text through the character of the "Asian imp" brought into the Willoughby family—enslaved and abused—by Yone's great-grandfather, a sea captain involved in the slave trade. Although the coastal geography of the home space is less clearly articulated in "The Amber Gods" than it is in *The Morgesons*, it is still presented as a permeable, amphibious space connected to and constituted by the intimacies and violence of colonial exploitation across oceans.

Like *The Morgesons*, "The Amber Gods" is interested in family lineage and inheritance. Even more so than the Morgeson family, the Willoughbys are presented as a New England family tainted and haunted by the past as it relates to their present: "I am the last of the Willoughbys, a decayed race," Yone reflects toward the end of the story. The Willoughby home where much of the action of the story is set is proximal to the coast, near to a tidal river. "If I were at home by the river," Yone thinks on her death bed, "the tide would be turning down, down, and out to the broad, broad sea." In happier times, Yone and Vaughn Rose, the boy who grows up with Yone and her orphan cousin, Lu, and who is Lu's childhood love until Yone wrests him away into an unhappy marriage, "almost lived upon the river . . . floating seaward, swimming slowly up with late tides, reaching home drenched with dew."[37] The water, the sea, seems to give life to the land. Even mayflowers, which Rose playfully depicts as colonial settlers—"fair little Puritans"—"need our sea," or at least Rose claims to like it best when they do. Their fragrance, according to Rose, is "the very quintessence of those regions all whose sweetness exudes in sun-saturated balsams,—the very breath of pine woods and salt sea winds." What are they "but an expression of New England character?" Rose queries, joining sea and land through the little flowers that he imagines binding the coast with a "network of flower and root."[38]

The sea is a vague presence within the physical home space of the story, but it is much more explicitly present as a space of exchange and a marker of the effects of global exchanges of goods and peoples. As noted above, Yone's great-grandfather brought "home cargoes of slaves" and once "fetched to his wife a little islander, an Asian imp, six years old, and wilder than the wind." In Willoughby family legend, the "imp" is remembered as a witchlike creature, uncontrollable and incomprehensible, with no accounting for the fact of her violent displacement from her home and the sexual abuse hinted at in the story. The captain's wife eventually "packed the sprite off with him,—to cut, rip, and tear in New Holland, if she liked, but not in New England." The "imp" was rescued from a shipwreck off the "Cape de Verdes" and then taken to Italy, where, years later, Yone's father encountered her in a church with an Italian girl. When he came across this girl saying "devout prayers on an amber rosary, with a demure black slave so tiny and so old behind her," the legend of the "Asian sprite . . . flashed back on him." He was momentarily distracted, however, and the pair disappeared. He returned to America, but then went back to Italy, determined to find the girl in the church. That girl became Yone's mother, against the wishes of the "little Asian," who was "livid" when she realized that the man was linked to the Willoughby family who enslaved her. "The dwarf," Yone narrates, "seemed always after haunted by a dreadful fear" of Yone's father. She "pursued him with a rancorous hate, but could not hinder his marriage . . . Her only revenge was to take away the amber beads, which had long before been blessed by the pope" for the girl who became Yone's mother. The old woman refused to return to New England with the couple, "declaring that neither should her charms ever cross the water."[39]

Those charms, the beads that originate somewhere in the Pacific with the "imp" and are then transformed into a rosary in Italy, become central to "The Amber Gods," not only through family legend but also because they reappear in Yone's life when her aunt sends them to Yone after both Yone's mother and the enslaved woman have died. The beads become linked to Yone's sexuality and self as she claims the amber's earthiness, leaving her cousin Lu with the alternative offered by Yone's father: aqua-marina.[40] The amber and the aqua-marina are presented as being in opposition with each other, one an earthy accretion of past times and the other a cool replica of seawater: "If you know aqua-marina, you know something that's before every other stone in the world. Why, it is as clear as light, white, limpid, dawn light; sparkles slightly and seldom; looks like pure drops of water, sea-water, scooped up and falling down again; just a thought of its parent beryl-green hovers round the edges; and it grows more lucent and sweet to the centre, and there you lose yourself in some dream of vast seas, a glory of unimagined oceans."[41] But while aqua-marina is figured as like or in terms of the oceans, the earthy amber necklace is a product of oceanic travel and exchange and also the object in the story that figures the role of narrative in yoking disparate domains of oceanic, imperial violence.[42] The necklace gives the story its title and symbolizes the tangled relationship between Yone and her cousin Lu. Yone claims the beads, but both women wear them at points in the story. Both get them tangled in their hair, and in those instances Vaughn Rose helps the women disentangle themselves; the beads release their "pungent smell," their "penetrating incense."[43] But the beads do more than envelope Yone, Lu, and Rose in their perfume, highlighting the web of desire and jealousy that unites them. The beads also serve as a constant physical reminder of the tangled relationships of colonial exploitation through their connection to the "Asian imp," whose story links the Atlantic world space of Protestant New England to Catholic Italy and to the Pacific through enslaved labor.[44]

By making it clear that the "Asian imp" is "a little islander," Spofford brings the Pacific into a global account of enslavement often focused around the Atlantic. This might conjure the coerced movements of Indigenous bodies associated with missionary work and exploratory and economic movement into Pacific spaces in earlier decades of the nineteenth century, discussed in this book's first chapters on Child's use of stories about Māori travelers. But a traffic in Pacific bodies was also a reality in the 1860s. These decades saw the rise of indentured servitude and forms of slavery in the Pacific sometimes known as "blackbirding." Ships traveled around the Pacific kidnapping Pacific Islanders, transporting them to places like Peru to mine guano deposits or to Australia or Fiji to work on plantations. The same thing had been happening in South Asia and China for decades: people were transported to labor in places as far-flung as Singapore, Jamaica, and Cuba. With the abolition of the slave trade in the British Empire in 1807 and in the United States in 1808, the search for forced labor turned to the Pacific and took other forms—forms still dependent on the racialization and fundamental violation of others.[45] The fact that the beads in "The Amber Gods" accompany a "little islander" to New England, then to an Atlantic archipelago associated with the Atlantic slave trade where she is shipwrecked, and then to Italy, before eventually being returned to New England, make clear that the Pacific is part of the global networks of exploitation that allow Yone to exist and to flourish in the first place.[46]

Indeed, the Willoughby family lives off of the legacies of the global trade of enslaved persons represented by the "Asian imp" and the amber beads, and Yone herself explicitly thrives in spaces usually associated with practices of enslavement and coerced labor. Right after telling the story of the enslaved woman and how the beads came into her possession, Yone proclaims: "I was born upon the sea, in a calm, far out of sight of land, under sweltering suns; so, you know, I'm a cosmopolite, and have a right to all my fantasies. Not that they are fantasies, at all; on the contrary, they are parts of my nature, and I couldn't be what I am without them, or have one and not have all."[47] Though she is elsewhere associated with the earthiness of amber, here Yone claims the sea as her place of origin, figuring herself as a Venus-like character seemingly more associated with aqua-marina than with amber. But this apparent contradiction is negotiated through her claim that "on the contrary," any contraries are not contrary at all: they are all parts of her nature. Her contradictions "are harmonious; in my veins; I was born with them. Not that I was always what I am now. Oh, bless your heart! plums and nectarines and luscious things that ripen and develop all their rare juices, were green once, and so was I. Awkward, tumble-about, near-sighted, till I was twenty, a real raw-head-and-bloody-bones to all society; then mamma, who was never well in our diving-bell atmosphere, was ordered to the West Indies, and papa said it was what I needed, and I went, too,—and oh, how sea-sick! Were you ever? You forget all about who you are, and have a vague notion of being Universal Disease. I have heard of a kind of myopy that is biliousness, and when I reached the islands my sight was as clear as my skin; all that tropical luxuriance snatched me to itself at once, recognized me for kith and kin; and mamma died, and I lived."[48] The list-like sentences of this passage accumulate and accrue like amber ("plums and nectarines and luscious things that ripen and develop all their rare juices, were green once, and so was I. Awkward, tumble-about, near-sighted") rolling along until the abrupt statement "and mamma died, and I lived." Rather than accrual here there is a disturbing sense of exchange of mother for daughter, expressed in a way that makes the life of one contingent on the death of the other, though that is not explicitly stated. But the idea that Yone comes into her own and is recognized "for kith and kin" by the "tropical luxuriance" of the West Indies while her own mother dies links Yone specifically and even more explicitly to networks of global exchange. Her life is, in essence, exchanged for her mother's in a space marked by histories of violence and ruptured kinship.

Though the sentences of this passage accumulate, they are also marked by associative tendencies not entirely unlike those within Stoddard's *The Morgesons*. Because she was born on the sea, Yone claims, she has a right to all her fantasies. Mamma died, and so "I lived." In *The Morgesons*, Cassandra's mother's eyes are blue like the sea, and she loves her mother. Although, as Beam points out, Spofford's prose is different from Stoddard's in its extreme ornateness, both *The Morgesons* and "The Amber Gods" thematize the global networks that constitute the home and complicate familial and maternal relations. And they do so through a prose style that questions forms of relation between words, concepts, entities, people, and spaces of land and sea.

This style of relationality at once highlights particular intimacies—between spaces, bodies, and even narrators and readers—and also might be thought of as not only amphibious but also archipelagic in a way modeled by the string of amber beads. Strings of words, strings of beads, strings of islands like the ten that make up Cape Verde or those that are home to the enslaved "sprite" are all connected associatively, whether through syntax, geography, economic circulation, or the movement of stories such as the family legends involving the little islander. Recognizing these forms of relation models the kind of "decontinentalizing" that Brian Russell Roberts and Michelle Ann Stephens discuss as a method for archipelagic studies in our own moment: "a shift toward recognizing the Americas as a set of spaces that has been persistently intertwined with, constituted by, and grounded in the archipelagic."[49] This can involve both acknowledging the many, geographically diverse, insular spaces of U.S. empire such as those brought to light by the movements of the "Asian imp" in "The Amber Gods" as well as "recovering the insular and archipelagic status of spaces that have sometimes been casually perceived as easily continental," as I have done in my chapter on Caroline Kirkland's *A New Home, Who'll Follow?*[50] In that text, I showed how the peninsula of Michigan is shown to itself be watery and also a settler space whose risks and uncertainties are narrated through maritime plots that connect it to distant oceans and islands.

In "The Amber Gods," this decontinentalizing reorientation is furthered through the amphibiousness of stylistic relationality and association brought to extremes in the representation of conversations between characters, which sometimes lack clear attribution of speakers. This is especially true in key conversations between Yone and Vaughn Rose that are sometimes rendered in ways that make it difficult to determine who is speaking when, so that the two voices flow into each other:

> "I can carry on all the dialogue? Then let *me* say how you liked the Islands."
>
> "I shall do no such thing. I liked the West Indies because there is life there; because the air is a firmament of balm, and you grow in it like a flower in the sun; because the fierce heat and panting winds wake and kindle all latent color and fertilize every germ of delight that might sleep here forever. That's why I liked them; and you knew it just as well before as now."
>
> "Yes; but I wanted to see if you knew it."[51]

> "But a mere animal or vegetable life is not much. What was ever done in the tropics?"
>
> "Almost all the world's history,—wasn't it?"
>
> "No, indeed; only the first, most trifling, and barbarian movements."
>
> "At all events, you are full of blessedness in those climates, and that is the end and aim of all action; and if Nature will do it for you, there is no need of your interference. It is much better to be than to do;—one is strife, the other is possession."[52]

This type of dialogue, unattributed to the individual speakers, continues for pages, eventually turning to the topic of the amber beads themselves and to amber itself; meaning develops through slow and indirect accretion, mimicking the way that the amber itself was formed. But while meaning accumulates, the form of such dialogue also stretches out archipelagically—long strands of conversation cover pages, islands of thought lead to associations that move the wandering conversation ahead. Communication is diffuse and associative in a way that occasionally renders the distinction between characters unclear, even though, as Dana Luciano illustrates, these particular conversations articulate fundamental differences in the characters' worldviews, revealing Rose's commitment to teleological master narratives and Yone's to the recurrent, deep times of earthy amber.[53] As they play out, these conversations hover between advancing and recurring.

Yone's own recurrent and associative thought extends beyond this dialogue into the story's second, "last" section, a structure that emphasizes the narrative's play with the relationships between entities. Though a story with two sections suggests a diptych, the section titles of "The Amber Gods"—"Story First" and "Story Last"—draw attention to seemingly absent middles or to narratives cut short. In "Story Last," the reader realizes belatedly, along with Yone, that she is dead: "What was this thing I had become? I had done with time. Not for me the hands moved on their recurrent circle any more. I must have died at ten minutes past one."[54] This haunting ending has often been read as a continuation of Yone's agency. She cannot be captured in marriage, or even in death. But at what seems to be the moment of her death, Yone is herself haunted: She is haunted by the image of Rose and Lu looking at each other as they looked at each other on the day when Yone received the amber beads. She is haunted by a look that seems to foretell a future for the pair. She seems to reach for the fragrant amber: "These costly liqueurs, these precious perfumes beside me here . . . There the thread breaks again! the little cruel gods go tumbling down the floor! Come, lay my head on your breast! kiss my life off my lips! I am your Yone! I forgot a little while,—but I love you, Rose! Rose!"[55] In this moment, Yone's desire for Rose and for the beads become linked, and as she moves into death she remains linked, through the beads, to the haunting image of the "Asian imp." Female desire and agency, realized and denied, are linked to a textual figure of global capitalism's inhumanity, racialized violence, and injustice.

In her reading of "The Amber Gods," Luciano emphasizes that the story's "lush extravagance . . . makes possible a quasi-palimpsestic layering of two forms of nonlinear time . . . the deep geological time Yone associates with amber's prehistoric generation and the spectral resurfacing of erased histories of dehumanization."[56] The first is associated with the material of the amber beads themselves, the second with the history of the "Asian imp" to which they are tied. The geographic reach and archipelagic form of the story might seem to counter these recursive temporalities through the linearity of strands of islands, beads, or phrases. But as so many theorists of islands and archipelagoes have pointed out, archipelagic thought involves openness, multiplicity, and repetition. Though emanating from the Caribbean-based thinking of someone like Martinican theorist Édouard Glissant, this recognition of the multiplicity of archipelagic forms has implications for reading the temporal and spatial multiplicities of "The Amber Gods," for recognizing how the multiple and, as Luciano notes, "unproductive" temporalities of the story draw together disparate spaces in "a relative obliteration of geographical distance and a problematization of conventional binary oppositions between center and margin, near and far" that Paul Giles finds in the "archipelagic turn."[57] The "entanglements of world-wide relation" that Glissant proclaims his "real subject" in the *Poetics of Relation* and the "reality of archipelagos in the Caribbean or the Pacific" that become figures for his poetics intersect with the Americas, in Glissant's returns to William Faulkner and the haunting racial histories of his texts, for example.[58] In "The Amber Gods," Spofford conjures these histories through archipelagic movements.

"The Amber Gods" itself models a practice of "spatial and temporal accretion" that Giles finds in an archipelagic method, in opposition to an outright rejection of previous critical practices.[59] Like the texts discussed in previous chapters, "The Amber Gods" makes clear that U.S. homes and families and the violence they are built upon are inseparable from oceanic circulations of peoples and goods, but the story goes further as it makes this a matter of style and form. Associations at the sentence and paragraph level reinforce other forms of association within "The Amber Gods," depicting a world in which relationships are implied, multiple, and archipelagic. The "Asian imp" who brings the "cruel little gods" of the amber beads into the Willoughby family and its legend is herself coercively brought into the family and its lore, a reminder of racialized and gendered violence that sits alongside of Yone's claims of self-actualization within the story. The "conjunctions of commerce and desire" that Shirley Samuels finds in *The Morgesons* are even more explicit in "The Amber Gods," where Yone's overflowing, pleasuring sense of self, of blonde brilliance, is explicitly linked to the consumption, enjoyment, or erasure of others.[60]

In "The Amber Gods" and *The Morgesons*, Spofford and Stoddard craft narratives of female development that pool and eddy in tangles of desire, violence, and harm, ending not with happy homes but with death and with questionable futures. And they unmoor New England family histories from settler pasts suggested by the rock beneath the Morgeson home and the mayflowers that are "little Puritans" binding the "coast with [a] network of flower and root" in "The Amber Gods."[61] They show those histories to be constituted by the networks of the maritime world in ways that emphasize disruptions to home spaces. Recognizing this idea enables us to revise the broad tradition of mid- to late nineteenth-century "women's seashore literature" that Melody Graulich argues "explores the tidal boundaries of female identity and of the female body."[62] These particular texts highlight gender restrictions in ways that link them to traditions of female gothic as they make claims for female agency through their deployment of coastal settings. But they also situate these concerns within histories of global circulation and violence, showing the self to always be contingent on others, elsewhere. Acknowledging how the stylistic choices deployed within *The Morgesons* and "The Amber Gods" are linked to the thought experiments of these texts also allows us to reread an author like Stowe. Stoddard's and Spofford's texts make claims for the agency of particular female characters while also diffusing agency stylistically, emphasizing interconnections between land and sea, geographies, and characters. The critical practices modeled by these texts provide ways to focus on the multiple relations within Stowe's novels, even as those novels end in more conservative, future-oriented, domestic conclusions. And this understanding of the texts of Stowe, Stoddard, and Spofford enables us to look back to Child's children's stories, to the circulation of information about events like the mutiny on the *Bounty*, as well as to the use of popular maritime plots within texts set nowhere near the sea, to recognize these as part of the cultural and literary contexts that infuse midcentury coastal gothic. Narratives do not need to be set at sea for authors to use the maritime world to probe gender restrictions or histories of global exploitation. Recognizing diverse engagements with the maritime world reveals uses of the oceanic across the first half of the nineteenth century that lie between the abstraction of metaphor and the experience of seagoing ventures.

CODA

For a brief moment in the spring of 2017, conversations about gender and the maritime world entered popular news reports. This occurred in relation to discoveries about the Franklin Expedition. In 1845 the British expedition set out to find the Northwest Passage, a route said to exist between the Atlantic and the Pacific. This search was recommended to Mr. Beckworth by Job in Caroline Kirkland's 1839 *A New Home, Who'll Follow?* as a way to "to take the nonsense out of him."[1] The expedition's ships, HMS *Erebus* and HMS *Terror*, went missing in 1848, and their disappearance remained a mystery. They were finally located in 2014 and 2016, respectively (though Inuit communities pointed out they had knowledge and stories about the expedition all along, stories that were devalued or ignored). Skeletal remains from expedition members had been discovered in the nineteenth and twentieth centuries at sites along the southern shore of Erebus Bay in the Canadian Arctic and had already been studied. But the Parks Canada search that led to the discovery of the ships had also involved the recovery of additional remains. Results of DNA analyses of fragments were published in 2017. The analysis of the remains of twenty-four sailors from the Franklin Expedition showed that four of those individuals may have been female and that those individuals were not Inuit. Researchers were quick to point out that these were likely false female readings caused by degraded DNA taken from remains that had been exposed to harsh conditions for well over one hundred years. Nevertheless, the authors of the study published in an archaeology journal note "that women are known to have served in disguise in the Royal Navy in the 17th and 18th centuries." They briefly recount the stories of some of those women before writing: "Despite these well documented instances of women serving secretly in the Royal Navy, we conclude that the amelogenin findings in these four instances are almost certainly incorrect, not least because of the improbability of so many women serving secretly on this expedition."[2] The recognition of these seemingly romantic, adventurous histories of cross-dressing, gender-bending heroines, prompted by the hard data of DNA analysis, momentarily captured the popular imagination, even as it seemed clear that in this case the data were inspiring just that: imagination.[3]

The pleasures, and importance, of thinking about women at sea, historical and fictional, will continue to motivate work that investigates ideas about gender, innovations in genre, and work that helps break down stereotypes persistent in the present. But in this book I have suggested that we would do well to focus on Kirkland's brief reference to the Northwest Passage in her fictional travelogue rather than solely on imagining the possibilities of women at sea participating in that enigmatic search. This shift in focus enables us to expand our archive of texts associated with the maritime world and to consider female authors usually excluded from discussions of that world. Female authors are often absent from such conversations altogether because, as one recent monograph that advances an argument about the antebellum Pacific puts it, "accounts [of the Pacific] tended to be written by men who made up the bulk of oceanic travelers on the Pacific."[4] While this is true, always accepting this absence means that scholarship on the nineteenth-century U.S. Pacific continues to limit itself to certain ideas about what U.S. cultural engagement with the Pacific looks like in this period: it is male, and it is largely defined by travel narratives, logbooks, and novels set on the oceans or on islands. This archive limits our understanding of the extent to which the Pacific infused U.S. literature and culture, the ways in which it did so, and how the Pacific was linked to Atlantic world economies and injustices.

But the shift I explore here is not merely additive; it does more than expand an archive. Its effect is to expose different geographic imaginaries that bring distant spaces into conceptual contact with one another. These conceptual reorientations highlight relationships between imperial and settler colonial spaces often elided in more traditional conceptions of terrestrial and maritime locations and activities. Lydia Maria Child stages a conversation between two men who represent New England and New Zealand spaces and histories. Elizabeth Craw's inclusion of the poem "Anxiety" in her diary brings events in the Pacific into the territory that will become Texas, whether intentional or not. Harriet Prescott Spofford's archipelagic vision strings Caribbean and Pacific islands onto the Mediterranean and New England. And when read in conjunction with the review of Melville's *Mardi* that Kirkland may have authored, her vision of Michigan as a peninsula once "covered with water" that became a "porous mass" where water is drawn up from below links the U.S. West to "the vast Continent of Islands that lies outstretched in the great Pacific Ocean."[5] Kirkland's writing creates a vision of a terraqueous America that is part of a terraqueous globe. In so doing, it ruptures the boundaries of home, personal and national, as a coherent nineteenth-century domestic space sometimes envisioned in the domestic manuals and mothers' books written by some of the same authors I discuss here, serving as a reminder of the contested nature of the domestic.

In many ways my readings of these texts extend critical traditions that unsettle narratives of linear providential progress previously thought to have structured nineteenth-century spatial and temporal imaginaries. Nineteenth-century authors, we now recognize, did not unproblematically subscribe to visions of the westward march of Manifest Destiny that would end by "conquering" the Pacific.[6] Discomfort with the violence and racialization inherent to settler colonialism and the legal fictions that sought to mask the tensions inherent in national territorial expansion can sometimes be identified in a geographic and even a topographical uncertainty like that associated with some of the terraqueous landscapes discussed in *Oceans at Home*. By making women writers central to this story of unfixity, I have shown how concerns about the unsettlement of U.S. domestic spaces through recourse to oceanic peoples and stories were also sometimes linked to critiques of gender conventions. But, of course, here my own archive is limited to white, middle-class, female authors. And these authors did not have direct contact with distant regions and peoples. They absorbed information through the circulations of nineteenth-century print. Others have addressed how gender and sexuality were harnessed as forms of resistance to imperialism in Pacific contexts. For example, J. Kēhaulani Kauanui explores "how white American notions of property title, state sovereignty, and normative gender relations and sexuality become intimately imbricated in aspirations for Hawaiian liberation and in mobilizing available categories for acknowledging Kanaka [Maoli] distinctiveness."[7] In making gender and sexuality central to her exploration of the "paradoxes" of "Hawaiian sovereignty," Kauanui helps us see how these ideas operated within a nineteenth-century Pacific settler colonial context and how they move into the present. Although my focus here has been on U.S.-based writers who were embedded in, and beneficiaries of, settler colonial structures, it is my hope that attending to the variety of ways that gender intersected with the Pacific and oceanic more generally in the nineteenth century, as well as how women writers drew on oceanic circulations to explore problems within home spaces, will enable a better understanding of imperial pasts and presents.

Mrs. Clavers's humorous theory about Michigan's watery past in relation to its damp, mudhole-filled present in Kirkland's *A New Home, Who'll Follow?* conjures another relationship of the oceans to home spaces embedded in the title *Oceans at Home*, one that has not been a focus of this book but that presses on our present. Mrs. Clavers imagines the timescales and workings of geologic change rather than our present reality of anthropogenic climate change and rise in sea level when she imagines that when Michigan "was covered with water, as it doubtless was before the Niagara met with such a fall, the porous mass became so thoroughly soaked, that the sun performs the office of rain, by drawing from below to the rich surface, the supplies of moisture which, under ordinary circumstances, are necessarily furnished from aerial reservoirs."[8] Nevertheless, this passage, and *Oceans at Home*'s attention to historical relationships between terrestrial homes and oceans, requires us to acknowledge changes in these relationships over time. Industrialization under way in the period examined within this book contributed to the global warming and rise in sea level that threatens low-lying Pacific atolls and that is projected to affect continental coastlines, including major U.S. cities. As glaciers and ice sheets melt, as warmer temperatures change weather patterns, drenching the U.S. Midwest and South, we experience the effects of complex processes set in motion long ago, processes sometimes resulting in increasingly watery landscapes. In response, some have imagined "seasteading" as a futuristic solution to environmental and political upheaval, effectively envisioning the oceans *as* home. In concluding with this gesture toward environmental connections between oceanic and terrestrial spaces, I turn, finally, to one more writer at the intersection of sea and land.

In 2013, a statue of the environmentalist and writer Rachel Carson was installed in Waterfront Park in Woods Hole, Massachusetts. Carson is best known for her 1962 book *Silent Spring*, which exposed the environmental effects of widely used pesticides, eventually leading to a U.S.-wide ban on agricultural uses of DDT and helping inspire the modern environmental movement. Although *Silent Spring* draws its evidence largely from the effects of aerial spraying on insects, birds, as well as humans, part of its point is the interconnection of ecological systems. But Carson's likeness now sits in a Cape Cod park overlooking the nearby harbor not because of the ecological interconnections between land, air, and water but because of her specific connections to Cape Cod and to Woods Hole, where she was a graduate student and a researcher at the Marine Biological Laboratory and where she worked at the Bureau of Fisheries (later the Fish and Wildlife Service, and now an element of the National Oceanic and Atmospheric Administration). The activist and author best known for her warnings about the bleak future prospects for the natural world as a result of human impacts began her career researching the oceans.

Carson's first essay, "Undersea," appeared in the *Atlantic Monthly* in 1937, seventy-seven years after Spofford's "The Amber Gods" was published in that magazine. The rolling sentences of Carson's prose could almost have been lifted from Spofford's story or from Cassandra's seaward reveries in Stoddard's *The Morgesons*. "Who has known the ocean?" Carson begins. "Neither you nor I, with our earth-bound senses, know the foam and surge of the tide that beats over the crab hiding under the seaweed of his tide-pool home; or the lilt of the long, slow swells of mid-ocean, where shoals of wandering fish prey and are preyed upon, and the dolphin breaks the waves to breathe the upper atmosphere."[9] As Jill Lepore has recently written of this essay: "It left readers swooning, drowning in the riptide of [Carson's] language, a watery jabberwocky of mollusks and gills and tube worms and urchins and plankton and cunners, brine-drenched, rock-girt, sessile, arborescent, abyssal, spine-studded, radiolarian, silicious, and phosphorescent, while, here and there, 'the lobster feels his way with nimble wariness through the perpetual twilight.'" The three books that Carson published before writing *Silent Spring*—*Under the Sea-Wind* (1941); *The Sea around Us* (1951); *The Edge of the Sea* (1955)—all concerned oceans and shorelines, but these are now all overshadowed by the legacy of *Silent Spring*, a "landlubber" of a book, in Lepore's words.[10]

I end by invoking Carson's seaward gaze and her "watery jabberwocky" of prose not so much to suggest that she is the literary heir of Stoddard and Spofford but to emphasize another articulation of interconnection and relation inherent in this prose style and another way in which the oceans come home. Though it is not why Carson's statue is placed on the Massachusetts shore, an effect of Carson's lifework and writing is indeed our understanding that everything is connected—that what happens on inland farms affects fish in the ocean, and what happens in waterways affects life on land. What happens in the Pacific affects what happens in the Atlantic, and vice versa. Understanding of these types of relationships has arrived belatedly for many of us. Kirkland's "cunning magicians," who "set themselves about concocting a new species of gramarye, by means of which the millions of acres of wild land which were left on their hands might be turned into *bonâ fide* cash . . . acres of wood and meadow [transmuted] into splendid metropolitan residences . . . burr-oaks . . . turned into marble tables, tall tamaracks into draperied bedsteads, lakes into looking-glasses, and huge expanses of wet marsh into velvet couches," could not foresee the consequences of their sorcery. Although Kirkland here references the "fraud" of unstable financial schemes, the transformations she conjures were not always purely speculative. They had material, environmental impacts.[11]

My focus in *Oceans at Home* has been on the circulation of print material and plotlines between oceanic and terrestrial realms rather than on chemicals and climate change, but those print materials and plotlines register imperial, extractive histories—of land, of labor—that are part of the story of our ecological present. In *Moby-Dick*, Herman Melville famously used the immense space of the Pacific to probe various types of interconnection, including questions of ecological interconnection and resource extraction. In *Moby-Dick*'s "Chapter 105: Does the Whale's Magnitude Diminish?—Will He Perish?," for example, he offered a comparison between the whale and the buffalo as resources associated with two different frontiers, one aquatic and one terrestrial. As we combat our "hydrophasia," our "forgetting the sea," we need not forget these relationships between sea and land.[12] Attending to the writing of women who did not go to sea at all or go for significant amounts of time, but who engaged with the nineteenth-century's maritime imaginaries and popular narratives about travel and global circulation, is one way to make sure that we do not forget those relationships.

Notes

PREFACE AND ACKNOWLEDGMENTS

1. Paul Gilroy, *The Black Atlantic: Modernity and Double Consciousness* (Cambridge, MA: Harvard University Press, 1993); Epeli Hau'ofa, "Our Sea of Islands," in *A New Oceania: Rediscovering Our Sea of Islands*, ed. Vijay Naidu, Eric Waddell, and Epeli Hau'ofa (Suva, Fiji: School of Social and Economic Development, University of the South Pacific/ Beake House, 1993); Greg Dening, *Beach Crossings: Voyaging across Times, Cultures, and Self* (Philadelphia: University of Pennsylvania Press, 2004).
2. Hester Blum, *The View from the Masthead: Maritime Imagination and Antebellum American Sea Narratives* (Chapel Hill: University of North Carolina Press, 2008).
3. Melody Jue, *Wild Blue Media: Thinking through Seawater* (Durham, NC: Duke University Press, 2020); Tiffany Lethabo King, *The Black Shoals: Offshore Formations of Black and Native Studies* (Durham, NC: Duke University Press, 2019).

INTRODUCTION: TERRAQUEOUS AMERICA

1. Caroline Kirkland, *A New Home, Who'll Follow? or, Glimpses of Western Life*, ed. Sandra A. Zagarell (New Brunswick, NJ: Rutgers University Press, 1990), 88, 98.
2. Kirkland, *A New Home, Who'll Follow?*, 11.
3. Zagarell in Kirkland, xi. Poe quoted by Zagarell in Kirkland, xi.
4. For discussion of Melville and women, see, for example, the essays in Elizabeth Schultz and Haskell Springer, eds., *Melville and Women* (Kent, OH: Kent State University Press, 2006).
5. See Jason Berger, *Antebellum at Sea: Maritime Fantasies in Nineteenth-Century America* (Minneapolis: University of Minnesota Press, 2012). Berger employs a Lacanian psychoanalytic approach to explore the antebellum "maritime world as not only a field of new economic and cultural experiences but also a differentiated scene of desire" (3). He argues "that considering the social function of fantasy" provides a "means to examine how maritime narratives operated in the political landscape of nineteenth-century America" (3–4).
6. Margaret Cohen, *The Novel and the Sea* (Princeton, NJ: Princeton University Press, 2010), 14.
7. Hester Blum, "The Prospect of Oceanic Studies," *PMLA* 125, no. 3 (May 2010): 670. On the role of "craft" in maritime fiction, see Cohen, *Novel and the Sea*.
8. Brian Russell Roberts and Michelle Ann Stephens, "Archipelagic American Studies: Decontinentalizing the Study of American Culture," in *Archipelagic American Studies*, ed. Brian Russell Roberts and Michelle Ann Stephens (Durham, NC: Duke University Press, 2017), 1.
9. Paul Giles, "Afterword: The Archipelagic Accretion," in Roberts and Stephens, *Archipelagic American Studies*, 429.
10. For a history of the whaling industry, see Eric Jay Dolin, *Leviathan: The History of Whaling in America* (New York: Norton, 2007). Dolin terms the period "from the conclusion of the war of 1812 through the twilight of the 1850s" the "golden age" of American whaling (205). See Dolin, *Leviathan*, 309–41, for an account of whaling's

decline toward the end of this period. Though *Oceans at Home* ends with texts published during the Civil War, it does not do so because of the war. I acknowledge this major historical and cultural event, and yet I also want to trouble historical and literary narratives that position the war period as an end or a beginning, in keeping with arguments like those in Christopher Hager and Cody Marrs's essay "Against 1865: Reperiodizing the Nineteenth Century," *J19: The Journal of Nineteenth-Century Americanists* 1, no. 2 (Fall 2013): 259–84.

11. For a focus on early U.S. entanglement with the Pacific, see Michelle Burnham, *Transoceanic America: Risk, Writing, and Revolution in the Global Pacific* (Oxford: Oxford University Press, 2019); Geoffrey Sanborn, *Whipscars and Tattoos: "The Last of the Mohicans," "Moby-Dick," and the Maori* (Oxford: Oxford University Press, 2011); and Paul Lyons, *American Pacificism: Oceania in the U.S. Imagination* (London: Routledge, 2006). A notable scholarly trend has been a turn from the "Black Atlantic" to the "Black Pacific." For a brief survey of uses of the term "Black Pacific," see Heather Smyth, "The Black Atlantic Meets the Black Pacific: Multimodality in Kamau Brathwaite and Wayde Compton," *Callaloo: Journal of African Diaspora Arts and Letters* 37, no. 2 (Spring 2014): 389–403. See also Etsuko Taketani, *The Black Pacific Narrative: Geographic Imaginings of Race and Empire between the World Wars* (Hanover, NH: Dartmouth College Press, 2014), and Robbie Shilliam, *The Black Pacific: Anti-Colonial Struggles and Oceanic Connections* (London: Bloomsbury Academic, 2015). Much transpacific scholarship has focused on the twentieth and the twenty-first centuries and on issues related to the militarization of the Pacific region, economics, and the environment, among other concerns. Many transpacific discussions address U.S. engagement with Asia, highlighting the geographic breadth of the transpacific. See, for example, Yunte Huang, *Transpacific Imaginations: History, Literature, Counterpoetics* (Cambridge, MA: Harvard University Press, 2008). For a collection of essays about the transpacific, see Janet Hoskins and Viet Thanh Nguyen, eds., *Transpacific Studies: Framing an Emerging Field* (Honolulu: University of Hawai'i Press, 2014).
12. Jennifer L. Morgan, *Laboring Women: Reproduction and Gender in New World Slavery* (Philadelphia: University of Pennsylvania Press, 2004), 50, and Christina Sharpe, *In the Wake: On Blackness and Being* (Durham, NC: Duke University Press, 2016), 17, 40–43.
13. Burnham, *Transoceanic America*, 93.
14. For example, in 1846 Caroline Mayhew supposedly nursed the crew of a whaling ship en route to New Zealand and served as navigator when a smallpox epidemic on board kept her husband, the ship's captain, from his duties. See Joan Druett, *Petticoat Whalers: Whaling Wives at Sea, 1820–1920* (Hanover, NH: University Press of New England, 2001), 107. See Lisa Norling, *Captain Ahab Had a Wife: New England Women and the Whalefishery, 1720–1870* (Chapel Hill: University of North Carolina Press, 2000), 261, for discussion of restrictions on captains' wives at sea.
15. For discussion of "women's work and colonization" in Hawai'i, see Jennifer Thigpen, *Island Queens and Mission Wives: How Gender and Empire Remade Hawai'i's Pacific World* (Chapel Hill: University of North Carolina Press, 2014), 2, where Thigpen argues that "relationships of exchange, originated and successfully maintained by women, determined the contours of the American mission in Hawai'i."
16. See Linda Colley, *The Ordeal of Elizabeth Marsh: A Woman in World History* (New York: Pantheon Books, 2007), for an account of the life of one such global eighteenth-century woman. See also Linda Colley, *Captives: Britain, Empire, and the World,*

1600–1850 (London: Jonathan Cape, 2002). Jeanne Baret was the first woman known to have circumnavigated the globe after disguising herself and signing on as an assistant to the naturalist on Louis-Antoine de Bougainville's 1766 expedition. The tradition of the female Robinsonade also reinforces tensions surrounding global empire and gender.

17. Margaret Fuller, *Woman in the Nineteenth Century*, in *The Essential Margaret Fuller*, ed. Jeffrey Steele (New Brunswick, NJ: Rutgers University Press, 1992), 345–46.
18. See the discussion of Bonny and Read, and of female pirates in general, in Marcus Rediker, *Villains of All Nations: Atlantic Pirates in the Golden Age* (London: Verso, 2004), 103–26, and Jo Stanley, ed., *Bold in her Breeches: Women Pirates across the Ages* (London: Pandora, 1996).
19. These pamphlets were Louisa Baker, *An Affecting Narrative of Louisa Baker, a Native of Massachusetts* (New York: Printed by Luther Wales, Reprinted by Nathaniel Coverly, June 1814); Lucy Brewer, *The Adventures of Lucy Brewer, Alias Louisa Baker. Being a Continuation of Miss Brewer's Adventures* (Boston: Printed by N. Coverly Jr., 1815); Lucy Brewer, *The Awful Beacon to the Rising Generation of Both Sexes, or, A Farewell Address to the Youths of, and Final Adieu to, the State of Massachusetts* (Boston: Printed for N. Coverly Jr., 1816). For a recent edition of these texts, see Daniel A. Cohen, ed., *"The Female Marine" and Related Works: Narratives of Cross-Dressing and Urban Vice in America's Early Republic* (Amherst: University of Massachusetts Press, 1997).
20. Such narratives certainly predate *The Female Marine* pamphlets as well. See, for example, *The Story of Constantius and Pulchera*, first published serially in Boston in Nathaniel Coverly's *The Gentleman and Ladies' Town and Country Magazine* (June 1787–January 1790). This story features a woman who cross-dresses on a privateer ship. See also *The Life and Surprising Adventures of Mary Ann Talbot*, a supposedly autobiographical account of an orphaned girl coerced into service in the British Navy, first published in *Kirby's Wonderful and Scientific Museum; or, Magazine of Remarkable Characters* (London: R. S. Kirby, 1804) and then posthumously by Robert S. Kirby in 1809. See Dolin, *Leviathan*, for an account of what Dolin terms "the best-documented case of . . . gender duplicity . . . the discovery that green hand George Johnson was actually Ann Johnson" (238–40). This is one of numerous such accounts. Dolin cites one estimate that "amazing feats of secrecy did . . . occur on at least one out of every thousand whaling voyages" (238).
21. Fuller, *Woman in the Nineteenth Century*, 310.
22. "No More Separate Spheres!" special issue, ed. Cathy N. Davidson, *American Literature* 70, no. 3 (September 1998), and the edited volume *No More Separate Spheres! A Next Wave American Studies Reader*, ed. Cathy N. Davidson and Jessamyn Hatcher (Durham, NC: Duke University Press, 2002), that followed from that issue consolidated such challenges to the perceived division between "male public" and "female private." The literature on these issues is extensive. For example, see also Lora Romero, *Home Fronts: Domesticity and Its Critics in the Antebellum United States* (Durham, NC: Duke University Press, 1997), and the essays in Mary Chapman and Glenn Hendler, eds., *Sentimental Men: Masculinity and the Politics of Affect in American Culture* (Berkeley: University of California Press, 1999), for related work emerging in the same years. In *Public Sentiments: Structures of Feeling in Nineteenth-Century American Literature* (Chapel Hill: University of North Carolina Press, 2001), 19, Glenn Hendler helpfully cites Linda Kerber and Eve Sedgwick on these divisions: "At least since Linda Kerber's 1988 review essay, 'Separate Spheres, Female Worlds, Women's Place,' literary critics

and historians have been conscious that 'political systems . . . and systems of gender relations . . . are reciprocal social constructions.' And as Eve Sedgwick has concisely put it, 'The immense productiveness of the public/private crux in feminist thought has come, not from the confirmation of an original hypothesized homology that male:female::public:private, but from the wealth of its deconstructive deformations.'"

23. See Anita J. Duneer, "Voyaging Captains' Wives: Feminine Aesthetics and the Uses of Domesticity in the Travel Narratives of Abby Jane Morrell and Mary Wallis," *ESQ: A Journal of the American Renaissance* 56, no. 2 (Spring 2010): 192–230, and Norling, *Captain Ahab Had a Wife*, 46–47.
24. William Apess, "An Indian's Looking-Glass for the White Man," in *On Our Own Ground: The Complete Writings of William Apess, a Pequot*, ed. Barry O'Connell (Amherst: University of Massachusetts Press, 1992), 155.
25. Norling, *Captain Ahab Had a Wife*, 218; see 218–23 for an account of the work of seamen's aid societies and the sailors' home movement. See also Duneer, "Voyaging Captains' Wives," and Bryan Sinche, "Lydia Sigourney's Sailors and the Limits of Sentiment," *Legacy* 29, no. 1 (2012): 62–85.
26. Mary Kathleen Eyring, *Captains of Charity: The Writing and Wages of Postrevolutionary Atlantic Benevolence* (Durham: University of New Hampshire Press, 2017), 15.
27. Amy Kaplan, "Manifest Domesticity," in "No More Separate Spheres!," ed. Cathy N. Davidson, special issue, *American Literature* 70, no. 3 (September 1998): 582. I cite the first publication of this essay here. It was later revised as a chapter of Kaplan's *The Anarchy of Empire in the Making of U.S. Culture* (Cambridge, MA: Harvard University Press, 2002).
28. Kaplan, "Manifest Domesticity," 583.
29. See, for example, Anne McClintock, *Imperial Leather: Race, Gender, and Sexuality in the Colonial Contest* (New York: Routledge, 1995); Ann Laura Stoler, ed., *Haunted by Empire: Geographies of Intimacy in North American History* (Durham, NC: Duke University Press, 2006); and Lisa Lowe, *The Intimacies of Four Continents* (Durham, NC: Duke University Press, 2015). While Lowe's book certainly is not invested in domesticity in the way that separate spheres discourses and associated critiques were, its method of intimate reading brings notions of intimacy associated with domesticity into accounts of global histories.
30. Robin Miskolcze, *Women and Children First: Nineteenth-Century Sea Narratives and American Identity* (Lincoln: University of Nebraska Press, 2007).
31. See Iyko Day, *Alien Capital: Asian Racialization and the Logic of Settler Colonial Capitalism* (Durham, NC: Duke University Press, 2016), 17. See also Maile Arvin, *Possessing Polynesians: The Science of Settler Colonial Whiteness in Hawai'i and Oceania* (Durham, NC: Duke University Press, 2019). Arvin argues that "settler colonialism in Hawai'i and Polynesia more broadly is fueled by a logic of possession through whiteness . . . both Polynesia (the place) and Polynesians (the people) become exotic, feminized possessions of whiteness—possessions that never have the power to claim the property of whiteness for themselves" (3).
32. See Meredith McGill, *American Literature and the Culture of Reprinting, 1834–1853* (Philadelphia: University of Pennsylvania Press, 2003).
33. Ryan Cordell, "Reprinting, Circulation, and the Network Author in Antebellum Newspapers," *American Literary History* 27, no. 3 (Fall 2015): 422.
34. See Ellen Gruber Garvey, *Writing with Scissors: American Scrapbooks from the Civil War to the Harlem Renaissance* (Oxford: Oxford University Press, 2012), for discussion of such practices in a later period.

35. Caroline Wigginton, *In the Neighborhood: Women's Publication in Early America* (Amherst: University of Massachusetts Press, 2016), 7, 12–13, 28–29.
36. Again, see McGill, *American Literature and the Culture of Reprinting.*
37. See Arvin, *Possessing Polynesians*, for a history of nineteenth- and twentieth-century social science and its production of forms of racialized difference across Oceania.
38. Epeli Hau'ofa, "Our Sea of Islands," in *A New Oceania: Rediscovering Our Sea of Islands*, ed. Vijay Naidu, Eric Waddell, and Epeli Hau'ofa (Suva, Fiji: School of Social and Economic Development, University of the South Pacific/Beake House, 1993), 7, 8.
39. See Lyons, *American Pacificism*, for a discussion of the politics of the terms "Oceania" and "Pacific" (201n1). "Australasia" designates the Pacific-adjacent British settler nations of Australia and New Zealand. As Paul Giles notes, this term, too, is a "loaded" one; see his *Antipodean America: Australia and the Constitution of U.S. Literature* (Oxford: Oxford University Press, 2013), 3.
40. Roberts and Stephens, "Archipelagic American Studies," 7.
41. My use of the term "relationality" here and in chapter 6 gestures toward the influence of Caribbean thinkers and writers like Édouard Glissant on archipelagic studies. Glissant's *Poetics of Relation*, trans. Betsy Wing (Ann Arbor: University of Michigan Press, 1997), for example, emphasizes dynamic processes, connections, and entanglements across geographies that are also at stake in my readings. In occasionally drawing, in general terms, on Caribbean and Pacific theorizations and methodologies foundational to island and archipelagic studies, I seek to harness their insights while acknowledging and respecting the specific histories that brought about this work and the present-day specifics that they continue to engage.

CHAPTER ONE: PACIFIC VOICES IN THE *JUVENILE MISCELLANY*

1. *Juvenile Miscellany*, September 1832, 27.
2. James Belich, *Making Peoples: A History of the New Zealanders, from Polynesian Settlement to the End of the Nineteenth Century* (Honolulu: University of Hawai'i Press, 1996), 145.
3. Belich, *Making Peoples*, 143. Of course, Māori were not the only Indigenous peoples engaged in global movement. For accounts of other Indigenous travelers, see Coll Thrush, *Indigenous London: Native Travelers at the Heart of Empire* (New Haven, CT: Yale University Press, 2016); Jace Weaver, *The Red Atlantic: American Indigenes and the Making of the Modern World, 1000–1927* (Chapel Hill: University of North Carolina Press, 2014); Nancy Shoemaker, ed., *Living with Whales: Documents and Oral Histories of Native New England Whaling History* (Amherst: University of Massachusetts Press, 2014); and Nancy Shoemaker, *Native American Whalemen and the World: Indigenous Encounters and the Contingency of Race* (Chapel Hill: University of North Carolina Press, 2015). For a history of particular Pacific and North American Indigenous men brought to a Connecticut missionary school, see John Demos, *The Heathen School: A Story of Hope and Betrayal in the Age of the Early Republic* (New York: Knopf, 2014). For a discussion of indigeneity and migration among Māori and Pacific peoples, see Alice Te Punga Somerville, *Once Were Pacific: Māori Connections to Oceania* (Minneapolis: University of Minnesota Press, 2012). For discussion of indigeneity as transit, see Jodi A. Byrd, *The Transit of Empire: Indigenous Critiques of Colonialism* (Minneapolis: University of Minnesota Press, 2011).
4. Child edited the *Juvenile Miscellany* from 1826 to 1834, when controversy surrounding the publication of *An Appeal in Favor of That Class of Americans Called Africans* (Boston: Allen and Ticknor,1833) forced her to step down from that position. Sarah

Josepha Hale took over the editorial position from 1834 through 1836, when the *Juvenile Miscellany* ceased publication entirely.

5. Patricia Crain, *Reading Children: Literacy, Property, and the Dilemmas of Childhood in Nineteenth-Century America* (Philadelphia: University of Pennsylvania Press, 2016), 8, 12. For discussion of the implicit whiteness of cultural ideas of childhood and attention to writing for Black children, see Katharine Capshaw and Anna Mae Duane, eds., *Who Writes for Black Children? African American Children's Literature before 1900* (Minneapolis: University of Minnesota Press, 2017). See Robin Bernstein, *Racial Innocence: Performing American Childhood from Slavery to Civil Rights* (New York: New York University Press, 2011), and Caroline Levander, *Cradle of Liberty: Race, the Child, and National Belonging from Thomas Jefferson to W. E. B. Du Bois* (Durham, NC: Duke University Press, 2006), for discussion of how children figured in constructions of race and nation across the nineteenth century. See also Brigitte Fielder, "Black Girls, White Girls, American Girls: Slavery and Racialized Perspectives in Abolitionist and Neoabolitionist Children's Literature," *Tulsa Studies in Women's Literature* 36, no. 2 (Fall 2017): 323–52, for discussion of how slavery was presented to free white children and other possibilities that consider Black child readers.
6. Carolyn L. Karcher, *The First Woman in the Republic: A Cultural Biography of Lydia Maria Child* (Durham, NC: Duke University Press, 1994), 67.
7. There are many spellings of these names in the historical record. I follow Alison Jones and Kuni Kaa Jenkins in using Tuai and Tītere as the names of the historical figures, except when quoting a historical document that uses a different spelling or referencing a textual representation like the character Tooi in the *Juvenile Miscellany*'s story. See Alison Jones and Kuni Kaa Jenkins, *Tuai: A Traveller in Two Worlds* (Wellington, New Zealand: Bridget Williams Books, 2017), 244–45, for discussion of various spellings of Tuai's name.
8. Letter from Tooi to the Rev. Samuel Marsden, October 12, 1818, and Letter from Teeterree to the Rev. Samuel Marsden, October 12, 1818, reprinted in *Proceedings of the Church Missionary Society* 19 (1818–19): 348–49; See also Titere to Reverend Samuel Marsden, October 12, 1818, Marsden Online Archive, last modified October 3, 2014, http://www.marsdenarchive.otago.ac.nz/MS_0056_099.
9. Reverend Samuel Marsden to Reverend Josiah Pratt, March 2, 1817, Marsden Online Archive, last modified October 3, 2014, http://www.marsdenarchive.otago.ac.nz/MS_0056_044.
10. Reverend Samuel Marsden to Reverend Josiah Pratt.
11. *A Grammar and Vocabulary of the Language of New Zealand*, was published by the Church Missionary Society in London in 1820 after Lee had worked with other Māori sources. Thomas Kendall's *A Korao no New Zealand, or, the New Zealander's First Book: Being An Attempt to Compose some Lessons for the Instruction of the Natives* was printed in Sydney in 1815 and sent to New Zealand. Jones and Jenkins note that "the little 54-page book was the first printed attempt at full sentences and phrases in the Māori language" (*Tuai*, 69).
12. Jones and Jenkins, *Tuai*, 97. For discussion of the processes through which the Māori language was written, see also Alison Jones and Kuni Jenkins, *Words between Us—He Kōrero: First Māori–Pākehā Conversations on Paper* (Wellington, New Zealand: Huia, 2011).
13. Note by Francis Hall on the back of Thomas Tuai to Josiah Pratt, June 26, 1818, Letters, MS-Papers-0288, Church Missionary Society Archives Relating to the Australian

and New Zealand Missions, Alexander Turnbull Library, Wellington, New Zealand, quoted in Jones and Jenkins, *Tuai*, 96.

14. For the histories of such ideas, see Tim Cassedy, *Figures of Speech: Six Histories of Language and Identity in the Age of Revolutions* (Iowa City: University of Iowa Press, 2018), esp. 17–21.
15. Teeterree to the Rev. Samuel Marsden.
16. See Appendix XXIII, "Some Account of the New Zealand Chiefs, Tooi and Teeterree; with Extracts of Letters from Them," *Proceedings of the Church Missionary Society* 19 (1818–19): 344–51. See George Lillie Craik, *The New Zealanders* (London: C. Knight, 1830), 301–2, for Craik's use of excerpts from the same letters. See "Some Account of Tooi, the Late New-Zealand Chief," *Missionary Register*, 1826, 302–4, for a concise record of previous accounts of Tooi and his death and for the portrait of Tooi reproduced in Craik, *New Zealanders*, 119.
17. Citing an 1831 review, Geoffrey Sanborn notes that *The New Zealanders* sold well in the United States. It was pirated twice by New York publishers (in 1838 and 1846). See his *Whipscars and Tattoos: "The Last of the Mohicans," "Moby-Dick," and the Maori* (Oxford: Oxford University Press, 2011), 10, 137n48.
18. Karcher, *First Woman in the Republic*, 67. The remainder of the *Juvenile Miscellany* was written by contributors who included some of the most popular women writers of the era: Hannah Flagg Gould, Sarah Josepha Hale, Lydia Huntley Sigourney, and others. These contributors are sometimes, but not always, identified by initials, whereas Child's contributions are unsigned. I have not attributed articles and stories from the *Juvenile Miscellany* to Child in citations, even when her authorship can be assumed or confirmed, because that is not how they appear in the *Miscellany*. See Karcher, *First Woman in the Republic*, 757–72, for a partial list of Child's works.
19. *Letters from New-York* grew out of Child's column of the same name in the *National Anti-Slavery Standard*. Child uses a New Zealand figure to critique contemporary life twice in the book. In the May 26, 1842, entry she writes: "Sometimes, it is true, I am tempted to say of the Nineteenth Century, as the exile from New Zealand did of the huge scramble in London streets, 'Me no like London. Shove me about'"; see Lydia Maria Child, *Letters from New-York* (New York: C. S. Francis; Boston: J. Munroe, 1843), 117. The second occurrence is less sympathetic. In a letter critiquing capital punishment, she writes, "Specimens" of contemporary hangings like the "printed circulars" used to gather witnesses "should be kept, as relics of a barbarous age, for succeeding generations to wonder at. They might be hung up in a frame; and the portrait of a New Zealand Chief, picking the bones of an enemy of his tribe, would be an appropriate pendant" (208).
20. See Anna Mae Duane, *Suffering Childhood in Early America: Violence, Race, and the Making of the Child Victim* (Athens: University of Georgia Press, 2010). See also Karen Sánchez-Eppler, *Dependent States: The Child's Part in Nineteenth-Century American Culture* (Chicago: University of Chicago Press, 2005).
21. Lucy Maddox, "American Indians, Civilized Performance and the Question of Rights," *Comparative American Studies: An International Journal* 1, no. 3 (2003): 320.
22. Lydia Maria Child, *An Appeal for the Indians* (1868), in *"Hobomok" and Other Writings on Indians*, ed. Carolyn L. Karcher (New Brunswick, NJ: Rutgers University Press, 1986), 220.
23. Maddox, "American Indians, Civilized Performance," 318.
24. Laura Mielke, *Moving Encounters: Sympathy and the Indian Question in Antebellum Literature* (Amherst: University of Massachusetts Press, 2008), 28, 35.

25. "Adventure in the Woods," *Juvenile Miscellany*, September 1826, 7.
26. "Adventure in the Woods," 13.
27. Mielke, *Moving Encounters*, 21. This story is a revision of the well-known tale "The Children in the Wood" (sometimes known as "Babes in the Wood"), discussed in the next chapter. See Lesley Ginsberg, "Race and Romantic Pedagogies in the Works of Lydia Maria Child," in *Romantic Education in Nineteenth-Century American Literature: National and Transatlantic Contexts*, ed. Monika M. Elbert and Lesley Ginsberg (New York: Routledge, 2015), 143, for discussion of this connection.
28. Karen L. Kilcup, "'Frightful Stories': Captivity, Conquest, and Justice in Lydia Maria Child's Native Narratives," *Children's Literature Association Quarterly* 39, no. 3 (Fall 2014): 323.
29. See Michelle Burnham, *Transoceanic America: Risk, Writing, and Revolution in the Global Pacific* (Oxford: Oxford University Press, 2019), 144, for a brief account of Ledyard's life in these contexts.
30. "The American Traveller," *Juvenile Miscellany*, September 1826, 19–20. Ledyard had published a popular account of his voyage with Cook in 1783. In 1828, two years after "The American Traveller" appeared in the pages of the *Juvenile Miscellany*, Jared Sparks would publish *The Life of John Ledyard, the American Traveller* (Cambridge, MA: Hilliard and Brown, 1828) indicating the consistent contemporary popularity of Ledyard's travels.
31. Goodrich's pamphlet indicates that it is taken "from the Second London Edition." Woodd's "Memoir and Obituary of Mowhee" appeared in the *Missionary Register*, February 1817, 71–79, and was then reprinted in various Church Missionary Society publications, as well as in pamphlet form in London (Ellerton & Henderson for the Church Missionary Society, 1817), Belfast (Belfast Religious Tract Society by Simms and M'Intyre, 1817), and Philadelphia (Sunday and Adult School Union, 1818), before Goodrich's edition. It continued to circulate after 1820 as well.
32. Basil Woodd, *Memoir of Mowhee, a Young New Zealander: Who Died at Paddington, on Saturday, December 28, 1816; In a Letter Addressed to the Rev. Josiah Pratt, B.D. Secretary of the Church Missionary Society* (Hartford, CT: S. G. Goodrich, at the Hartford Sunday School Repository, 1820), 2.
33. Woodd, *Memoir of Mowhee*, 3. Another popular text recounting the travels of a Pacific Islander to England and his subsequent death was *The Interesting History of Prince Lee Boo, Brought to England from the Pelew Islands*. This text appeared in more than twenty English and numerous foreign-language editions between 1789 and 1850.
34. For an extended discussion of relationships between pedagogy and empire in nineteenth-century America, see Sánchez-Eppler, *Dependent States*, 186–220, and Etsuko Taketani, *U.S. Women Writers and the Discourses of Colonialism, 1825–1861* (Knoxville: University of Tennessee Press, 2003).
35. Samuel Griswold Goodrich, *Peter Parley's Tales about the Islands in the Pacific Ocean* (1831; Philadelphia: Thomas, Cowperthwait, 1839), 49–50.
36. Goodrich, *Peter Parley's Tales*, 56–57.
37. Goodrich, 115.
38. Maile Arvin, *Possessing Polynesians: The Science of Settler Colonial Whiteness in Hawai'i and Oceania* (Durham, NC: Duke University Press, 2019), 3.
39. Arvin notes, "While whiteness is commonly the named referent, antiblackness is also always a significant part of the Western construction of the Polynesian race as almost white . . . Ideas about Polynesians being almost white were formed in

distinction to ideas about Melanesians being black" (*Possessing Polynesians*, 3–4). See Sanborn, *Whipscars and Tattoos*, 6–11, for an overview of nineteenth-century favorable accounts of Māori.

40. Goodrich, *Peter Parley's Tales*, 132.
41. "Wonders of the Deep," *Juvenile Miscellany*, January 1827, 80.
42. "Coral Reefs," *Juvenile Miscellany*, November 1826, 69. For discussion of the complex history of ideas about coral in this period, see Michele Currie Navakas, "Antebellum Coral," *American Literature* 91, no. 2 (June 2019): 263–93.
43. "Conchology," *Juvenile Miscellany*, March 1830, 81.
44. For example, "Again, the kingdom of heaven is like unto a merchant man, seeking goodly pearls: Who, when he had found one pearl of great price, went and sold all that he had, and bought it" (Matt. 13:45–46 [King James Version]).
45. See "The Fisherman's Family," *Juvenile Miscellany*, March 1831, 3–13. This story may have been inspired by "The Fisherman" by S. C. Hall, which appeared in *The Amulet, or Christian and Literary Remembrancer*, vol. 4 (London: Frederick Westley and A. H. Davis and Wightman and Co., 1829), 113–22. "The Fisherman" was reprinted in such publications as *The Cabinet of Religion, Education, Literature, Science, and Intelligence*, vol. 4 (New York: H. R. Piercy, 1830), 380–83, and the *Museum of Foreign Literature and Science*, September 1830, 193–95. It later appeared in Mrs. S. C. Hall [Anna Maria Hall], *"Alice Stanley" and Other Stories* (London: T. Nelson and Sons, 1868), 25–34. The *Juvenile Miscellany*'s version is not a reprint but a similar story that is oriented toward child readers in its language and focus on child characters and the family's dog, who is the hero of the story. The *Miscellany* version may have been authored by Child, given the presence of a phrase ("the darling of the whole household") that also appears (as "the darling of the whole house") in Child's story "Mary Howard," discussed in chapter 2. The story also features references to places like the Sandwich Islands that appear in Child's other stories. Versions of the *Juvenile Miscellany* story were reprinted with slight changes in other publications, for example, "The Fisherman's Family" in Henry Wightman, *The Juvenile Polyanthos, or Fireside Companion: Being a Selection of Amusing Stories* (Newark, NJ: Benjamin Olds, 1835), 30–37.
46. "Volney Beckner," *Juvenile Miscellany*, November 1830, 138–44. An account of Volney Beckner appeared in the column "Lives of Celebrated Children" in the *Columbian Star and Christian Index*, June 19, 1830, 393, and in the same column in the *Monthly Repository and Library of Entertaining Knowledge*, June 1830, 21–24. An account appeared as "Volney Beckner and the Shark" in the *Sailor's Magazine, and Naval Journal*, April 1832, 242–43, and in different forms throughout the nineteenth century ranging from Marmaduke Park, *Thrilling Stories of the Ocean* (Philadelphia: C. G. Henderson, 1852), 5–10, to a four-stanza poem titled "Volney Beckner" in *Routledge's Every Boy's Annual*, ed. Edmund Routledge (London: Routledge, Warne, and Routledge, 1865), 320.
47. "William Burton; or, the Boy Who Would Be a Sailor," *Juvenile Miscellany*, September 1831, 46. As Paul Lyons notes, Paulding's narrative was a source for both Edgar Allan Poe's *Narrative of Arthur Gordon Pym of Nantucket* (1838) and Melville's *Typee*; see Lyons, *American Pacificism: Oceania in the U.S. Imagination* (London: Routledge, 2006), 209n9.
48. "William Burton," 3.
49. "William Burton," 7.
50. "William Burton," 14.

51. Hiram Paulding, *Journal of a Cruise of the United States Schooner* Dolphin *among the Islands of the Pacific Ocean* (New York : G. & C. & H. Carvill, 1831), 150. In Paulding's book the name Hussey is spelled "Huzzy."
52. "William Burton," 23, 22.
53. Mielke notes that "William Burton," along with "The Adventures of a Bell," another one of Child's "anticaptivity tales" in the *Miscellany*, features "Anglo-American boys held in captivity far from home [who] find themselves well treated by Natives in accord with a recognizable moral code and briefly appreciate life-changing intimate relationships. The protagonists' travel between these habitations dramatizes the moral action of sympathy but also its link to the ideology of removal: geographic segregation in accord with cultural-racial hierarchy as overseen by benevolent Euro-Americans" (*Moving Encounters*, 21). In other words, such stories join "moral instruction with the dismantling of racial prejudice" as Child's work so often does (21), but as Mielke points out they also reflect and reinforce difference and "what Susan M. Ryan identifies in this period as 'the notion that white benevolence—its narratives, practices, and institutions—would produce better white people in the present and coming generations'" (*Moving Encounters*, 205n14, citing Ryan, *The Grammar of Good Intentions: Race and the Antebellum Culture of Benevolence* [Ithaca, NY: Cornell University Press, 2003], 75).
54. "Productions of the Sandwich Islands," *Juvenile Miscellany*, May 1828, 224–28.
55. Among the others who arrived with Stewart were his wife, child, and Betsey Stockton, who was the first Black missionary to serve with the American Board of Commissioners for Foreign Missions and their first unmarried female missionary.
56. "Lealea-Hoku: The Little Sandwich Island Girl," *Juvenile Miscellany*, May 1828, 207.
57. "Lealea-Hoku," 210. The character "Kaahu-manu" references the historical Ka'ahumanu, a high-ranking Hawaiian woman.
58. "Lealea-Hoku," 214, 217.
59. "William Burton," 28–29.
60. "William Burton," 35.
61. For a study that complicates the perceived binary between literacy and illiteracy in narratives of colonial contact by focusing on Indigenous textual practices, see Birgit Brander Rasmussen, *Queequeg's Coffin: Indigenous Literacies and Early American Literature* (Durham, NC: Duke University Press, 2012). For a consideration of the Pacific in particular, see chapter 4, "Indigenous Literacies, *Moby-Dick*, and the Promise of Queequeg's Coffin." For discussion of language and early nineteenth-century U.S. continental empire, see Robert Gunn, *Ethnology and Empire: Languages, Literature, and the Making of the North American Borderlands* (New York: New York University Press, 2015).
62. See Craik, *New Zealanders*, 135–36, 137 for the passage reproduced in the *Juvenile Miscellany* (which silently omits part of the passage from Craik). See Juniper Ellis, *Tattooing the World: Pacific Designs in Print and Skin* (New York: Columbia University Press, 2008), 156–61, for details of Rutherford's life and consideration of the inclusion of Rutherford's story in Craik's *New Zealanders*. The *Juvenile Miscellany* uses the word "tattoo." Craik takes care to note that "the term tattoo is not known in New Zealand, the name given to the marks, which are elsewhere so called, being in this country Moko" (*New Zealanders*, 142). *Moko* is, as Ngārino Ellis notes, "distinctive from Pacific *tatau* 'tattoo' in that it was literally carved into the skin in grooves up to a depth of 6 mm" ("'Ki tō Ringa ki ngā Rākau ā te Pākehā?' Drawings and Signatures

of 'Moko' by Māori in the Early 19th Century," *Journal of the Polynesian Society* 123, no. 1 [March 2014]: 30).

63. "New Zealanders," *Juvenile Miscellany*, November 1830, 192. See Craik for the source of this reflection, itself inspired by details in texts like Richard Cruise's *Journal of a Ten Months' Residence in New Zealand* (1823), J. L. Nicholas's *Narrative of a Voyage to New Zealand* (1817), Adriano Balbi's *Introduction à l'Atlas Ethnographique* (1826), and the *Missionary Register*, as indicated by footnotes in Craik's text: "When the missionaries purchased a piece of land, from one of the Bay of Islands chiefs, named Gunnah, a copy of the tattooing on the face of the latter, being drawn by a brother chief, was affixed to the grant as his signature; while another native signed as a witness, by adding the amoco [moko] of one of his own cheeks. This is certainly a more perfect substitute for a written name than that said to have been anciently in use in some parts of Europe. In Russia, for example, it is affirmed that in old times, the way in which an individual generally gave his signature to a writing, was by covering the palm of his hand with ink, and then laying it on the paper. M. Balbi, who states this, adds that the Russian language still retains an evidence of the practice in its phrase for *signing* a document, which is *roukou prilojite*, signifying, literally, to put the hand to it. It may be remarked, however, that this is a form of expression even in our own country; although there is certainly no trace of the singular custom in question having ever prevailed among our ancestors" (*New Zealanders*, 145–46).
64. Juniper Ellis notes that "representations of *moko* were used historically as signatures on treaties and deeds" (19–20), and it was also common for non-Pacific peoples to try to make sense of tattoo by imagining the designs as a text that could be read if one knew how to read them (*Tattooing the World*, 1). See also Ngārino Ellis, "'Ki tō Ringa ki ngā Rākau ā te Pākehā?,'" 29–66, for a comprehensive survey of the use of moko as signatures in nineteenth-century New Zealand.
65. "New-Zealand Ideas of Writing," *Juvenile Miscellany*, March 1832, 86.
66. See Craik, *New Zealanders*, 353. For this episode in Mariner, see *An Account of the Natives of the Tonga Islands in the South Pacific Ocean: With an Original Grammar and Vocabulary of Their Language, Compiled and Arranged from the Extensive Communications of William Mariner by John Martin*, 2 vols. (London: J. Martin, 1817), 1:123–26.
67. Craik, *New Zealanders*, 14.
68. Craik, 398.
69. Craik, 351–52.
70. For accounts of histories of the philosophy of language that contextualize the ideas espoused in Craik, see Nicholas Hudson, *Writing and European Thought, 1600–1830* (Cambridge: Cambridge University Press, 1994); Hans Aarsleff, "Philosophy of Language" in *The Cambridge History of Eighteenth-Century Philosophy*, 2 vols., ed. Knud Haakonssen (Cambridge: Cambridge University Press, 2006), 1:451–95; and Cassedy, *Figures of Speech*. It is worth noting that the 1799 *Pantographia*, "a putatively comprehensive catalog of languages," included the "New Zealand" language and other South Pacific languages among the 208 alphabets that it recorded (Cassedy, 145).
71. Child, *Appeal for the Indians*, 220.
72. Craik, *New Zealanders*, 3, 362.
73. Sanborn, *Whipscars and Tattoos*, 83.
74. "Dialogue, between the Shades of Duaterra, a New Zealand Chief, and Philip of Pokanocket. *By a little girl ten years old*," *Juvenile Miscellany*, July 1829, 311. This piece has what appears to be a byline, "LINIE," at its conclusion. Child usually left her

contributions to the *Miscellany* unsigned, while other contributors would use pseudonyms or initials. Nevertheless, the content and format suggest Child's authorship.

75. Belich, *Making Peoples*, 141–44. Ruatara's and Tuai's paths crossed, in the Bay of Islands and with the missionaries in Australia. See Jones and Jenkins, *Tuai*, esp. 40–41, 45–48, 53–54.
76. J. L. Nicholas, *Narrative of a Voyage to New Zealand,* 2 vols. (London, 1817), 1:24, quoted in Belich, *Making Peoples*, 147.
77. Belich, *Making Peoples,* 148. See Anne Salmond, "Maori and Modernity: Ruatara's Dying," in *Signifying Identities: Anthropological Perspectives on Boundaries and Contested Identities,* ed. Anthony P. Cohen (London: Routledge, 2012), 37–58, for discussion of what Ruatara's death signified from both Māori and European perspectives and in the intersection between them.
78. Lydia Maria Child, *The First Settlers of New-England, or, Conquest of the Pequods, Narragansets and Pokanokets: As Related by a Mother to Her Children* (Boston: Munroe and Francis for the author, 1829), iii–iv.
79. Child, *First Settlers,* 170.
80. [Washington Irving], "Philip of Pokanoket: An Indian Memoir," *Analectic Magazine*, June 1814, 515.
81. "Dialogue," 311. The word "Yengeese" means English colonists.
82. "Dialogue," 312.
83. "Dialogue," 312.
84. "Dialogue," 314.
85. Of course, even in the nineteenth century there were questions about how Metacom was remembered. See, for example, William Apess's "Eulogy on King Philip, as Pronounced at the Odeon, in Federal Street, Boston," in *On Our Own Ground: The Complete Writings of William Apess, a Pequot*, ed. Barry O'Connell (1836; Amherst: University of Massachusetts Press, 1992), 277–310. For recent accounts of these histories, see Lisa Brooks, *Our Beloved Kin: A New History of King Philip's War* (New Haven, CT: Yale University Press, 2018), and Christine DeLucia, *Memory Lands: King Philip's War and the Place of Violence in the Northeast* (New Haven, CT: Yale University Press, 2019).
86. Child's use of the dialogue format had precedent in earlier Enlightenment-era writing for children by English authors such as Anna Laetitia Barbauld. Discussing Barbauld's ideas about the novel in relation to her writing for children, Frances Ferguson notes, "Unlike catechisms that represent both questions and answers in the form of a mock dialogue, conversations develop directions of their own"; see "The Novel Comes of Age: When Literature Started Talking with Children," *differences: A Journal of Feminist Cultural Studies* 28, no. 1 (May 2017): 43. See Karcher, *First Woman in the Republic,* 60–65, for discussion of Barbauld's influence on Child and her dialogues for children.

CHAPTER TWO: MARY HOWARD'S MARK

1. "Dialogue, between the Shades of Duaterra, a New Zealand Chief, and Philip of Pokanocket. *By a little girl ten years old," Juvenile Miscellany*, July 1829, 311–14.
2. Ngārino Ellis, "'Ki tō Ringa ki ngā Rākau ā te Pākehā?' Drawings and Signatures of 'Moko' by Māori in the Early 19th Century," *Journal of the Polynesian Society* 123, no. 1 (March 2014): 30. Nineteenth-century Māori "signatures and drawings," Ellis continues, "act as mnemonic devices in that they have the capacity to reveal to contemporary audiences the wider worlds in which our ancestors engaged, not only culturally, but also artistically and politically. Such marks are heralded by Māori as

tohu 'signs', not only physical markings on paper, but also as visionary signs of the future, which would become much more complicated than either group, Māori or Pākehā, could have envisaged" (30).

3. Geoffrey Sanborn, *Whipscars and Tattoos: "The Last of the Mohicans," "Moby-Dick," and the Maori* (Oxford: Oxford University Press, 2011), 82.
4. Herman Melville, *Moby-Dick*, ed. Hershel Parker (New York: Norton, 2018), 80.
5. Paul Lyons, *American Pacificism: Oceania in the U.S. Imagination* (London: Routledge, 2006), 1–2. See Melville, *Moby-Dick*, 244, for this scene.
6. See Nicholas Thomas, *Entangled Objects: Exchange, Material Culture, and Colonialism in the Pacific* (Cambridge, MA: Harvard University Press, 1991).
7. *Juvenile Miscellany*, November 1830, 197.
8. Lydia Maria Child, "Mary Howard," in *The Little Girl's Own Book* (Boston: Carter, Hendee, and Babcock, 1831), 232–33. Later editions, titled *The Girl's Own Book*, are more commonly found. Later versions sometimes include slight alterations in wording or punctuation and in pagination.
9. For relevant advice in contemporary mothers' books, see Lydia Maria Child, *The Mother's Book* (Boston: Carter, Hendee and Babcock, 1831): "Kindness toward animals is of great importance. Children should be encouraged in pitying their distress and if guilty of any violent treatment toward them, they should see that you are grieved and displeased at such conduct" (6–7). See also Lydia Sigourney, *Letters to Mothers* (Hartford: Hudson and Skinner, 1838): "Let the next lesson to your infant pupil, be kindness to all around. The rudiments are best taught by the treatment of animals. If it seizes a kitten by the back, or pulls its hair, show immediately by your own example, how it may be held properly, and soothed into confidence. Draw back the little hand, lifted to strike the dog. Perhaps it may not understand that it thus inflicts pain. But be strenuous in confirming an opposite habit. Do not permit it to kill flies, or to trouble harmless insects" (37–38).
10. See Iona Opie and Peter Opie, eds., *The Oxford Dictionary of Nursery Rhymes* (Oxford: Oxford University Press, 1997), 354, for a brief history of the poem's origins.
11. Child, "Mary Howard," 233.
12. Child, "Mary Howard," 234.
13. See Patricia Crain, *Reading Children: Literacy, Property, and the Dilemmas of Childhood in Nineteenth-Century America* (Philadelphia: University of Pennsylvania Press, 2016), 43–61, for a history of this story across four centuries.
14. Child, "Mary Howard," 234. Other nineteenth-century stories about women and global economies prominently feature amber. See, for example, Spofford's "The Amber Gods," which contrasts amber with "aqua-marina," earth with water. Aquamarine stones also appear in Stoddard's *The Morgesons*. These texts are discussed in chapter 6.
15. Child, "Mary Howard," 235.
16. Child, 237–38.
17. Child, 238.
18. Child, 237, 239.
19. Child, 240.
20. Child, 241.
21. Child, 243.
22. Child, 245, 246.
23. Child, 245–46.
24. Child, 235.

25. See Sanborn, *Whipscars and Tattoos*, 20–25, for his account of these events.
26. See James Belich, *Making Peoples: A History of the New Zealanders, from Polynesian Settlement to the End of the Nineteenth Century* (Honolulu: University of Hawai'i Press, 1996), 141.
27. "New Zealanders," *Juvenile Miscellany*, November 1830, 192.
28. Craik, drawing on Marsden as a source, also recounted shipboard mistreatment of Ruatara (*New Zealanders*, 79–80). This composite figure is similar to the merging of Tuai, Tītere, and their letters in the *Juvenile Miscellany*, discussed in chapter 1.
29. J. L. Nicholas, *Narrative of a Voyage to New Zealand*, 2 vols. (London: Printed for James Black and son, 1817), 1:24, quoted in Belich, *Making Peoples*, 147.
30. Child, "Mary Howard," 237.
31. "New Zealanders," *Juvenile Miscellany*, 193–94; see also Craik, *The New Zealanders*, 71–73.
32. Craik, *The New Zealanders*, 278, quoted in Juniper Ellis, *Tattooing the World: Pacific Designs in Print and Skin* (New York: Columbia University Press, 2008), 159. For discussion of social status and the reception of tattoos, see J. Ellis, *Tattooing the World*, 154–56.
33. See Jennifer Putzi, *Identifying Marks: Race, Gender, and the Marked Body in Nineteenth-Century America* (Athens: University of Georgia Press, 2006), 23.
34. Herman Melville, *Typee: A Peep at Polynesian Life* (1846; New York: Penguin, 1996), 220; Samuel Otter, *Melville's Anatomies* (Berkeley: University of California Press, 1999), 10, 19.
35. Melville, *Typee*, 218, 219.
36. J. Ellis, *Tattooing the World*, 30.
37. See Trevor Bentley, *Captured by Maori: White Female Captives, Sex and Racism on the Nineteenth-Century New Zealand Frontier* (Auckland: Penguin, 2004), for a brief account of Elizabeth Guard's captivity as well as accounts of other New Zealand captivity narratives. See Melissa Gniadek, "The Captivity of Translation: The Legacy of William Barrett Marshall's Personal Narrative," *International Journal of Francophone Studies* 11, no. 4 (December 2008): 581–600, for analysis of the rhetoric surrounding Guard's capture and rescue.
38. See Ian J. McNiven, Lynette Russell, and Kay Schaffer, eds., *Constructions of Colonialism: Perspectives on Eliza Fraser's Shipwreck* (London: Leicester University Press, 1998), and Kay Schaffer, *In the Wake of First Contact: The Eliza Fraser Stories* (Cambridge: Cambridge University Press, 1995), for discussion of the circulation of Eliza Fraser's story.
39. See Edward Markham, *New Zealand or Recollections of It*, ed. E. H. McCormick (1834; Wellington, New Zealand: Government Printer, 1963), 78.
40. "Account of the Crew of the Ship Stirling Castle, and the Conduct of the Savages," *New Hampshire Sentinel* (Keene), October 19, 1837 (see figure 6).
41. For discussion of historical representations of Fraser's body, see Rod Macneil, "'Our Fair Narrator' Down-Under: Mrs Fraser's Body and the Preservation of Empire," in McNiven, Russell, and Schaffer, *Constructions of Colonialism*, 63–76.
42. See Margot Mifflin, *Bodies of Subversion: A Secret History of Women and Tattoo*, 3rd ed. (Brooklyn: PowerHouse, 2013), for a popular history of tattooed women.
43. It is notable, however, that the first European account of Pacific tattooing—in Joseph Banks's *Endeavor* journal—describes "the operation of *Tattowing* the buttocks performd upon a girl of about 12 years old," witnessed in the Marquesas. See Joseph

Banks, *The Endeavour Journal of Joseph Banks, 1768–1771*, ed. J. C. Beaglehole, 2 vols. (Sydney: Angus and Robertson, 1963), 1:309.

44. J. Ellis, *Tattooing the World*, 9.
45. Child, "Mary Howard," 241.
46. See Royal B. Stratton, *Life among the Indians: Being an Interesting Narrative of the Captivity of the Oatman Girls* (San Francisco: Whitton, Towne, 1857).
47. According to Jennifer Putzi, Oatman's story may have influenced Stoddard's novel *The Morgesons*, in which a white female character, Helen Perkins, has a bracelet tattooed on her arm. See *Identifying Marks*, 92. While *The Morgesons* does not explicitly link tattooing to interracial relationships, it situates the education of young women—and tattooing—at the center of global economies and exchanges in a way that intersects with "Mary Howard." See chapter 6.
48. For example, the Missouri Compromise of 1820 regulated slavery in the western states, while the Indian Removal Act of 1830 set the stage for the resettlement of Indigenous populations from the U.S. South. See Shirley Samuels, "Women, Blood, and Contract," *American Literary History* 20, nos. 1–2 (Spring–Summer 2008): 57–75.
49. Samuels, "Women, Blood, and Contract," 61.
50. For consideration of captivity in the context of global empire and transnational studies, see, for example, Linda Colley, *Captives: Britain, Empire and the World, 1600–1850* (London: Jonathan Cape, 2002), and Gordon M. Sayre, "Renegades from Barbary: The Transnational Turn in Captivity Studies," *American Literary History* 22, no. 2 (Summer 2010): 347–59.
51. See Paul Giles, *Antipodean America: Australia and the Constitution of U.S. Literature* (Oxford: Oxford University Press, 2013), 6.
52. Kathryn Tomasek, "'Duaterra's Tattooing': Marking Bodies in Lydia Maria Child's 'Mary Howard,'" *Letterature d'America* (Italy) 25, no. 106 (2005): 25.
53. Tomasek, "'Duaterra's Tattooing,'" 5–6, 27.
54. For discussion of the importance and complexity of ideas of industrious behavior within stories in the *Juvenile Miscellany*, see Carolyn L. Karcher, *The First Woman in the Republic: A Cultural Biography of Lydia Maria Child* (Durham, NC: Duke University Press, 1994), 68–78.
55. As Cathy Davidson notes, books were often printed locally in eighteenth- and nineteenth-century New England, and they circulated locally because of the expense of travel and distribution; see her *Revolution and the Word: The Rise of the Novel in America*, expanded ed. (Oxford: Oxford University Press, 2004), 80. For a more recent account of early U.S. local and regional print publics, see Trish Loughran, *The Republic in Print: Print Culture in the Age of U.S. Nation Building, 1770–1870* (New York: Columbia University Press, 2007).
56. I have located thirteen extant copies of *The Little, but Affecting History of Mary Howard* in addition to the four copies held by the American Antiquarian Society. These copies reside in institutions ranging from the New Hampshire State Historical Society to Columbia University to the Alexander Turnbull Library in Wellington, New Zealand, showing that the chapbook traveled the world in the twentieth century. Of these thirteen copies, two others have presentation inscriptions on the inside cover, and an additional two are inscribed with female names in ink that appears to be from the mid-nineteenth century.
57. Later Sarah Spaulding Fox. Hillsborough Country is in southern New Hampshire and is separated from Belknap County, where Sanbornton is located, by just one other county.

58. Both women appear to have spent their lives in the state, Spaulding dying in 1846 and Colby (whose married name was Woods) in 1914.
59. Patricia Crain, *The Story of A: The Alphabetization of America from "The New England Primer" to "The Scarlet Letter"* (Stanford: Stanford University Press, 2000), 4, 5, 56.
60. For discussion of a later children's story, "The Girl Who Inked Herself," in which the stain of writing ink rather than tattooing becomes inseparable from the threat of a racialized body, see Jonathan Senchyne, *The Intimacy of Paper in Early and Nineteenth-Century American Literature* (Amherst: University of Massachusetts Press, 2020), 131–34.
61. Much of this thinking is, of course, in dialogue in some way with Lee Edelman, *No Future: Queer Theory and the Death Drive* (Durham, NC: Duke University Press, 2004).
62. See Anna Mae Duane, ed., *The Children's Table: Childhood Studies and the Humanities* (Athens: University of Georgia Press, 2013), for a variety of recent approaches to such questions.
63. Laura Soderberg, "Writing the Criminal Child: Antebellum Prison Records, Parenting Manuals, and the Rise of the Incorrigible Child," *J19: The Journal of Nineteenth-Century Americanists* 6, no. 2 (Fall 2018): 308. In the context of my argument here, it is notable that Soderberg's archive of records from antebellum Houses of Refuge reveals that whaling was an outlet for unredeemable, "incorrigible" boys. The ship was seen to offer an alternative "house" of correction, whereas girls tend to slip from the archive, presumably into "hidden economies such as sex work and theft" (330).
64. See Jacqueline Rose, *The Case of Peter Pan, or, The Impossibility of Children's Fiction* (London: Macmillan, 1984).
65. See Robin Bernstein, *Racial Innocence: Performing American Childhood from Slavery to Civil Rights* (New York: New York University Press, 2011), on notions of "childhood innocence" in relation to race in American culture.
66. For a well-known introduction to reading for "symptom" and "surface," see Stephen Best and Sharon Marcus, "Surface Reading: An Introduction," *Representations* 108, no. 1 (Fall 2009): 1–21.

CHAPTER THREE: "DOUBTING, DREADING, FRETFUL GUEST"

1. Elizabeth Craw diary, 1833–1841, MS 386, Woodson Research Center, Fondren Library, Rice University, Houston, TX, October 22, 1835. Earlier in the diary "Mr. and Mrs. M" are identified as "Macky." Throughout this chapter I preserve line breaks when quoting from Craw's diary to maintain the feel of her prose as it appears on the diary's pages.
2. Craw diary, October 25, 1835. The prominent theologian, educator, and reformer (and father of thirteen children, including Harriet Beecher Stowe), Lyman Beecher had moved to Cincinnati from Boston in 1832 to take over as president of Lane Theological Seminary. Harriet Beecher (she would not marry until 1836) moved to Cincinnati to join her father in the same year.
3. Craw diary, October 26 and 27, 1835.
4. Craw diary. This entry, like others throughout the manuscript, is undated. I have opted not to assign numbers to diary pages in lieu of dates. Though this would help identify undated passages, numbering would impose artificial order on a manuscript that resists such order. Pages are not numbered in the manuscript, and blank and cut pages make numbering difficult. When an entry is undated, I cite "Craw diary." For a reading of the Mississippi as a space that "complicated the dominant symbolism

of continental settlement in the nineteenth-century," see Stephanie LeMenager, *Manifest and Other Destinies: Territorial Fictions of the Nineteenth-Century United States* (Lincoln: University of Nebraska Press, 2004), 2. LeMenager's discussion hinges on the river as a passageway that is part of a commercial version of Manifest Destiny involving "apparently landless places like deserts, oceans, and rivers" that she investigates as heterotopias challenging hegemonic spatial representations (2, 4). On the resistance of swamp spaces in the context of the "plantation zone," see Monique Allewaert, *Ariel's Ecology: Plantations, Personhood, and Colonialism in the American Tropics* (Minneapolis: University of Minnesota Press, 2013).

5. Craw diary.
6. Craw diary, October 19, 1835.
7. Craw diary.
8. Craw diary.
9. Craw diary.
10. Craw diary, November 30, 1835.
11. Craw diary, January 7, 1837.
12. Craw diary, March 20, 1836.
13. *Scioto Gazette* (Chillicothe, Ohio), September 2, 1835, 1, Nineteenth Century U.S. Newspapers, https://link-gale-com.myaccess.library.utoronto.ca/apps/doc/GT3009180385/NCNP?u=utoronto_main&sid=NCNP&xid=92cc9c22. Texonians, Texicans, and, more commonly, Texians were among the terms used for the diverse settlers in Texas before and during the Texas Revolution. Tejano was often used for residents of Mexican descent.
14. "War in Texas," *Scioto Gazette* (Chillicothe, OH, reprinted from the *Cincinnati Gazette*), November 4, 1835, 2, Nineteenth Century U.S. Newspapers, https://link-gale-com.myaccess.library.utoronto.ca/apps/doc/GT3009180311/NCNP?u=utoronto_main&sid=NCNP&xid=fcf7355e.
15. Craw diary.
16. Craw diary.
17. See, for example, the guide to the Elizabeth Craw Diary at www.lib.utexas.edu/taro/ricewrc/00204/rice-00204.html. This guide asserts that Samuel Evans grew up in Ohio, which contradicts available information about the Samuel Evans killed at the Alamo.
18. See genealogies such as "Jefferson County, NY Pioneers," Pioneer Samuel Evans Family, http://jefferson.nygenweb.net/evanssp.htm, and Bill Groneman, "Evans, Samuel B. (1812–1836)," Texas State Historical Association, Handbook of Texas Online, http://www.tshaonline.org/handbook/online/articles/fev21.
19. Craw diary.
20. Craw diary. The lines of this poem in the diary do not correspond exactly to Wolfe's poem. As with much of the published material written into the diary, there are slight alterations in spelling and punctuation. Throughout this chapter I have quoted Craw's diary rather than quoting texts as they appear elsewhere.
21. See, for example, Meredith McGill, *American Literature and the Culture of Reprinting, 1834–1853* (Philadelphia: University of Pennsylvania Press, 2003), for discussion of the marketplace of reprinting that characterizes the very years when Craw kept her diary.
22. Craw diary, June 17 [year unknown]; Margaret Roberts, *Duty, a Novel . . . interspersed with poetry and preceded by a character of the author by Mrs. Opie*, 3 vols. (London: Printed for Longman, Hurst, Rees, Orme, and Brown, 1814), 3:149.

23. Craw diary, November 1 [year unknown]. The second line quoted here is crossed out in the original. The word given as "reflect" is difficult to read and may be another word in the original. See also Stephen Glover and Edward Fitz Auburn, "The Dream Is Past" (1839), Digital Commons @ Connecticut College, Historic Sheet Music Collection, 890, http://digitalcommons.conncoll.edu/sheetmusic/890.
24. Craw diary; John Malcolm, *Tales of Field and Flood, with Sketches of Life at Home* (Edinburgh: Oliver & Boyd; London: Simpkin & Marshall, 1829), 153.
25. Craw diary.
26. See, for example, *Ladies' Magazine and Literary Gazette*, September 1, 1830, 405–6; *Godey's Lady's Book*, March 1, 1842, 150, where the stanza Craw quotes appears at the beginning of a story by someone other than Gould. Sarah Josepha Hale edited the Boston-based *Ladies' Magazine* and, later, the Philadelphia-based *Godey's*.
27. Craw diary.
28. For a helpful account of scholarship on women's diaries, including the tension between public and private, see Suzanne L. Bunkers and Cynthia Anne Huff, eds., *Inscribing the Daily: Critical Essays on Women's Diaries* (Amherst: University of Massachusetts Press, 1996). On eighteenth- and nineteenth-century expressions of grief in relation to generic conventions, see Desirée Henderson, *Grief and Genre in American Literature, 1790–1870* (Burlington, VT: Ashgate, 2011). On nineteenth-century expressions of grief in terms of temporality, see Dana Luciano, *Arranging Grief: Sacred Time and the Body in Nineteenth-Century America* (New York: New York University Press, 2007). For discussion of a book of "remembrances" started nearly contemporaneously with Craw's diary, see Mary Louise Kete, *Sentimental Collaborations: Mourning and Middle-Class Identity in Nineteenth-Century America* (Durham, NC: Duke University Press, 2000).
29. For accounts of the *Bounty* mutiny and its aftermath, see Caroline Alexander, *The Bounty: The True Story of the Mutiny on the Bounty* (New York: Viking, 2003), and Greg Dening, *Mr Bligh's Bad Language: Passion, Power and Theatre on the Bounty* (Cambridge: Cambridge University Press, 1992). Dening notably emphasizes the extent to which the *Bounty* story is one about historical narrative, uncertainty, authority, and power. For discussion of the breadfruit project, see Jennifer Newell, *Trading Nature: Tahitians, Europeans, and Ecological Exchange* (Honolulu: University of Hawai'i Press, 2010), 141–70.
30. This poem was reproduced in Sir John Barrow, *The Eventful History of the Mutiny and Piratical Seizure of H.M.S.* Bounty: *Its Cause and Consequences* (London: John Murray, 1831), 247–48, and the U.S. version of this book. The poem, along with other Heywood papers and correspondence, was also reproduced in Edward Tagart, *A Memoir of the Late Captain Peter Heywood, R.N.* (London: Effingham Wilson, 1832), and may have been reprinted elsewhere. Barrow's book went through multiple editions and so seems a likely source. The punctuation of the poem as written in Craw's diary does not appear to exactly follow that of the poem as it appears in Barrow. There are five known versions of a manuscript of letters and poems from the Heywood family. See Christiane Conway, *Letters from the Isle of Man: The* Bounty *Correspondence of Nessy and Peter Heywood* (Onchan, Isle of Man: Manx Experience, 2005), and Peter Heywood and Nessy Heywood, *Innocent on the* Bounty: *The Court-Martial and Pardon of Midshipman Peter Heywood, in Letters*, ed. Donald A. Maxton and Rolf E. Du Rietz (Jefferson, NC: McFarland, 2013).
31. *Milton's Selected Poetry and Prose*, ed. Jason P. Rosenblatt (New York: Norton, 2011), 69, lines 8–14.

32. Barrow, *Eventful History of the Mutiny*, 190–91, 272–73.
33. Barrow, *Eventful History of the Mutiny*, 136, 275–76.
34. Justine Murison, *The Politics of Anxiety in Nineteenth-Century American Literature* (Cambridge: Cambridge University Press, 2011), 7.
35. For a useful history of "hysteria," see Sander L. Gilman, Helen King, Roy Porter, G. S. Rousseau, and Elaine Showalter, *Hysteria beyond Freud* (Berkeley: University of California Press, 1993), esp. Elaine Showalter, "Hysteria, Feminism, and Gender," 286–344.
36. Alexander, *The Bounty*, 48.
37. Michelle Burnham, *Transoceanic America: Risk, Writing, and Revolution in the Global Pacific* (Oxford: Oxford University Press, 2019), 89.
38. Barrow, *Eventful History of the Mutiny*, 143–44. See also Peter Heywood to Mrs. [Elizabeth] Heywood, August 15, 1792, in Heywood and Heywood, *Innocent on the* Bounty, 88.
39. "War in Texas."
40. "War in Texas."
41. "War in Texas."
42. There is a great deal of scholarship on American empire and 1848. See, for example, Shelley Streeby, *American Sensations: Class, Empire, and the Production of Popular Culture* (Berkeley: University of California Press, 2002).
43. As Murison puts it, "Because anxiety accrued both somatic and psychological meaning throughout the centuries, it is well poised to open a conversation about both the history of affects and the affects of critical methods" (*Politics of Anxiety*, 7).
44. I draw here on Maile Arvin's gloss of the key operations of power within settler colonialism. See Arvin, *Possessing Polynesians: The Science of Settler Colonial Whiteness in Hawaiʻi and Oceania* (Durham, NC: Duke University Press, 2019), 15.
45. Lisa Lowe, *The Intimacies of Four Continents* (Durham, NC: Duke University Press, 2015), 18.

CHAPTER FOUR: "OUTRE-MER ADVENTURES"

1. Caroline M. Kirkland, *A New Home, Who'll Follow? or, Glimpses of Western Life*, ed. Sandra A. Zagarell (1839; New Brunswick, NJ: Rutgers University Press, 1990), 3.
2. Rachel Azima, "Promotion, Borrowing, and Caroline Kirkland's Literary Labors," *ESQ: A Journal of the American Renaissance* 57, no. 4 (2011): 413. For discussion of the "culture of reprinting," see Meredith McGill, *American Literature and the Culture of Reprinting, 1834–1853* (Philadelphia: University of Pennsylvania Press, 2003).
3. Kirkland, *A New Home*, 12. Throughout this chapter I refer to the narrator as Mrs. Clavers, despite the antiquated tone of this name, since this is how she is most often named in the text.
4. Kirkland, 160.
5. Kirkland, 112.
6. Thomas Philbrick, *James Fenimore Cooper and the Development of American Sea Fiction* (Cambridge, MA: Harvard University Press, 1961), 66; Francis Parkman, *The Oregon Trail*, ed. David Levin (1849; New York: Penguin, 1982), 245; James Hall, "The New Moon: A Tradition of the Omawhaws," in *The Wilderness and the War Path* (New York: Wiley and Putnam, 1846), 60, and "The Indian Hater," in *Wilderness and the War Path*, 146. See Stephanie LeMenager, *Manifest and Other Destinies: Territorial Fictions of the Nineteenth-Century United States* (Lincoln: University of Nebraska Press, 2004), for an extended discussion of heterotopic spaces like the "landless West" and the

oceans as counternarratives to Manifest Destiny. See especially 113–14 for discussion of how "the sea and West exist in charged, dialectical tension in nineteenth-century U.S. literature."

7. Philbrick, *James Fenimore Cooper*, vii.
8. Jason Berger, *Antebellum at Sea: Maritime Fantasies in Nineteenth-Century America* (Minneapolis: University of Minnesota Press, 2012), 4.
9. Berger, *Antebellum at Sea*, 3, 4.
10. While Berger does consider the question of gender—in readings of Melville's renderings of Pacific islands, for example, and in a brief survey of gender-bending female maritime characters—his analysis remains primarily focused on male writing, realms, and characters. See Berger, 123–72.
11. Kirkland, *A New Home*, 177; Philbrick, *James Fenimore Cooper*, vii.
12. Amy Kaplan, *The Anarchy of Empire in the Making of U.S. Culture* (Cambridge, MA: Harvard University Press, 2002), 26, 42.
13. Kirkland, *A New Home*, 87.
14. Kirkland, 87–88.
15. See Lisa Norling, *Captain Ahab Had a Wife: New England Women and the Whalefishery, 1720–1870* (Chapel Hill: University of North Carolina Press, 2000), esp. 165–213, for discussion of the tempos and timing of courtship and marriage in relation to the New England whaling industry in particular.
16. Kirkland, *A New Home*, 92, 97.
17. Kirkland, 87.
18. Kirkland, 94.
19. Kirkland, 97.
20. Kirkland, 88.
21. Kirkland, 94.
22. Kirkland, 88–89, 98.
23. Kirkland, 88, 97.
24. Kirkland, 87.
25. Kirkland, 97.
26. Eric Jay Dolin, *Leviathan: The History of Whaling in America* (New York: Norton, 2007), 270–71. See Michelle Burnham, *Transoceanic America: Risk, Writing, and Revolution in the Global Pacific* (Oxford: Oxford University Press, 2019), 23–46, for discussion of Pacific voyaging and exploration in terms of risk. See also Norling, *Captain Ahab Had a Wife*, 135, for a description of whaling's system of "lays" and its financial consequences and 35–36 for discussion of some of the risks and effects of tying up "capital and labor" for the long duration of whaling voyages.
27. Kirkland, *A New Home*, 97; Dolin, *Leviathan*, 253–54.
28. Kirkland, *A New Home*, 97.
29. Kirkland, 97. Zagarell, *A New Home*'s editor, notes that "Captain Symmes" "may refer to Colonel John Symmes (1742–1814), pioneer and colonizer of the Northwest Territory" (Kirkland, 215), but his nephew, John Cleves Symmes Jr. (1779–1829) is a more likely reference. For a more recent discussion of Symmes Jr. in the context of planetarity and resources, see Hester Blum, "John Cleves Symmes and the Planetary Reach of Polar Exploration," *American Literature* 84, no. 2 (June 2012): 243–71. The elder John Symmes was involved in early versions of the kind of controversial land development projects that Kirkland discusses.

30. See Aaron Sachs, *The Humboldt Current: Nineteenth-Century Exploration and the Roots of American Environmentalism* (New York: Penguin, 2006), 121–28, for discussion of the relationship between Symmes and Reynolds.
31. *Symzonia: A Voyage of Discovery* was published under the pseudonym "Captain Adam Seaborn" and has sometimes (no doubt inaccurately) been attributed to Symmes himself. A case has been made for Nathaniel Ames as author of the work (see Hans-Joachim Land and Benjamin Lease, "The Authorship of *Symzonia*: The Case for Nathaniel Ames," *New England Quarterly* 48, no. 2 [June 1975]: 241–52), but its authorship remains uncertain.
32. See Teresa A. Goddu, *Gothic America: Narrative, History, and Nation* (New York: Columbia University Press, 1997), 81–82, for a brief survey of this tradition of reading *Pym* as an allegory of racial difference in the U.S. South. Goddu's argument exemplifies readings that focus on race and representation in the novel. See also Dana D. Nelson, *The Word in Black and White: Reading "Race" in American Literature, 1638–1867* (Oxford: Oxford University Press, 1992), 90–108, for a reading of how Poe's "narrative itself questions and undermines [a] biological/metaphysical reading [of race] by revealing race as a strategic interpretive construct governed by political motives" (98).
33. Kirkland, *A New Home*, 97.
34. Kirkland, 152.
35. Kirkland, 157.
36. Kirkland, 161, 163–64.
37. Kirkland, 164.
38. Kirkland, 160.
39. See Shawn Thomson, *The Fortress of American Solitude: Robinson Crusoe and Antebellum Culture* (Madison, NJ: Fairleigh Dickinson University Press, 2009), 20.
40. See Michelle Burnham and James Freitas, introduction to *The Female American; or, The Adventures of Unca Eliza Winkfield*, 2nd ed. (1767; New York: Broadview, 2014), esp. 11–16; Michelle J. Smith, "Nineteenth-Century Female Crusoes: Rewriting the Robinsonade for Girls," in *Victorian Settler Narratives*, ed. Tamara S. Wagner (London: Pickering & Chatto, 2011), 165–75; and Thomson, *Fortress of American Solitude*, 173–200, for discussion of female Robinsonades in British, American, and transatlantic contexts, respectively. See Thomson, *Fortress of American Solitude*, 180–92, for discussion of the 1859 article "A Female Robinson Crusoe."
41. Kirkland, *A New Home*, 65, 64.
42. Margaret Cohen, *The Novel and the Sea* (Princeton, NJ: Princeton University Press, 2010), 63.
43. Kirkland, *A New Home*, 26, 25.
44. Kirkland, 52.
45. Caroline M. Kirkland, *Forest Life*, vol. 1 (New York: C. S. Francis, 1842), 136–37.
46. Kirkland, *A New Home*, 5, 7.
47. Kirkland, 31, 11.
48. Kirkland, 30, 28.
49. Kirkland, 112.
50. Jordy Rosenberg, "The Terrestrial Transatlantic," in *Teaching the Transatlantic Eighteenth Century*, ed. Jennifer Frangos and Cristobal Silva (Newcastle upon Tyne: Cambridge Scholars, 2010), 24. Rosenberg instead offers a pedagogical model of the "*terrestrial* or *dry* transatlantic." This is "a materialist approach [to transatlantic

paradigms] grounded in the history of capital accumulation" (25). Philip E. Steinberg usefully summarizes trends in oceanic scholarship, arguing, "All too often, the ocean that binds the societies of the ocean region is undertheorized . . . [it] comes to be seen as a series of (terrestrial) points linked *by* connections, not the actual (oceanic) space *of* connections," or it is "overtheorized" by poststructuralist theorists for whom "the ocean is an ideal medium for rethinking modernist notions of identity and subjectivity." See Steinberg, "Of Other Seas: Metaphors and Materialities in Maritime Regions," *Atlantic Studies* 10, no. 2 (June 2013): 157–58.

51. For discussion of associations between the narrative and spatial conception of "plot," see, for example, Peter Brooks, *Reading for the Plot: Design and Intention in Narrative* (New York: Vintage, 1984), 12: "Common to the original sense of the word [plot] is the idea of boundedness, demarcation, the drawing of lines to mark off and order. This easily extends to the chart or diagram of the demarcated area, which in turn modulates to the outline of the literary work. From the organized space, plot becomes the organizing line, demarcating and diagramming that which was previously undifferentiated. We might think here of the geometrical expression, plotting points, or curves, on a graph by means of coordinates, as a way of locating something, perhaps oneself."
52. Kirkland, *A New Home*, 5, 10, 36. See Michele Currie Navakas, *Liquid Landscape: Geography and Settlement at the Edge of Early America* (Philadelphia: University of Pennsylvania Press, 2018), for discussion of another terraqueous geography—Florida—and how its "indeterminate, shifting ground contributed to the complex history of U.S. founding by raising large conceptual questions about root-taking that had wide-ranging political and cultural implications for a country seeking to expand over and beyond the continent" (3).
53. See William S. Osborne, *Caroline M. Kirkland* (New York: Twayne, 1972), 110–11, for mention of these reviews, which he attributes to Kirkland.
54. Review of *Mardi and a Voyage Thither*, Editorial, *Sartain's Union Magazine of Literature and Art*, August 1849, 126.
55. Kirkland, *A New Home*, 87, 97.
56. Epeli Hau'ofa, "Our Sea of Islands," in *A New Oceania: Rediscovering Our Sea of Islands*, ed. Vijay Naidu, Eric Waddell, and Epeli Hau'ofa (Suva, Fiji: School of Social and Economic Development, University of the South Pacific/Beake House, 1993), 7.
57. Brian Russell Roberts and Michelle Ann Stephens, "Archipelagic American Studies: Decontinentalizing the Study of American Culture," in *Archipelagic American Studies*, ed. Brian Russell Roberts and Michelle Ann Stephens (Durham, NC: Duke University Press, 2017), 7, 11, 14.
58. See Bryan Sinche, "Lydia Sigourney's Sailors and the Limits of Sentiment," *Legacy* 29, no. 1 (2012): 65.
59. Sinche, "Lydia Sigourney's Sailors," 64, 67–68.
60. Kirkland, *A New Home*, 121.
61. Azima, "Caroline Kirkland's Literary Labors," 406.

CHAPTER FIVE: "INWREATHED IN SAND AND SHELLS"

1. Harriet Beecher Stowe, *The Pearl of Orr's Island: A Story of the Coast of Maine* (Boston: Ticknor and Fields, 1862), 56. Page references for this novel are from this edition.
2. Stowe, *The Pearl of Orr's Island*, 57, 102. See Dana Luciano, *Arranging Grief: Sacred Time and the Body in Nineteenth-Century America* (New York: New York University

Press, 2007), for discussion of the temporal dimensions of "memorial relics" like the "commemorative samplers and handwoven hair jewelry" that became "increasingly regular features of the home space" in the nineteenth century (35).

3. Stowe, *The Pearl of Orr's Island*, 57, 58.
4. Stowe, 57.
5. Stowe, 426.
6. See Sandra M. Gilbert and Susan Gubar, *The Madwoman in the Attic: The Woman Writer and the Nineteenth-Century Literary Imagination* (New Haven, CT: Yale University Press, 1979), 533–35, for their reading of Cassy.
7. Jewett herself articulated Stowe's influence on her, writing in the 1893 preface to *Deephaven*, "It was, happily, in the writer's childhood that Mrs. Stowe had written of those who dwelt along the wooded seacoast and by the decaying, shipless harbors of Maine. The first chapters of 'The Pearl of Orr's Island' gave the young author of 'Deephaven' to see with new eyes, and to follow eagerly the old shore-paths from one gray, weather-beaten house to another, Where Genius pointed her the way." See Sarah Orne Jewett, preface to *Deephaven* (1877: Boston: Houghton, Mifflin, 1893), 3–4. An 1889 letter to Annie Fields also captures Jewett's appreciation for and critique of *The Pearl of Orr's Island*: "I have been reading the beginning of 'The Pearl of Orr's Island' and finding it just as clear and perfectly original and strong as it seemed to me in my thirteenth or fourteenth year, when I read it first. I never shall forget the exquisite flavor and reality of delight that it gave me . . . Alas, that she couldn't finish it in the same noble key of simplicity and harmony; but a poor writer is at the mercy of much unconscious opposition. You must throw everything and everybody aside at times, but a woman made like Mrs. Stowe cannot bring herself to that cold selfishness of the moment for one's work's sake, and the recompense for her loss is a divine touch here and there in an incomplete piece of work," in Annie Fields, ed., *Letters of Sarah Orne Jewett* (Boston: Houghton Mifflin, 1911), 46–47. See also Sarah Way Sherman, *Sarah Orne Jewett, an American Persephone* (Hanover, NH: University Press of New England, 1989), 41–45, for discussion of the influence of *The Pearl of Orr's Island* on Jewett and her work.
8. H. B. Stowe to Calvin Stowe, quoted in E. Bruce Kirkham, "The Writing of Harriet Beecher Stowe's *The Pearl of Orr's Island*," *Colby Quarterly* 16, no. 3 (September 1980): 158.
9. Stowe, *The Pearl of Orr's Island*, 205.
10. See Cynthia Alicia Smith, "Uncle Tom's (Ship) Cabin," *ESQ: A Journal of Nineteenth-Century American Literature and Culture* 66, no. 1 (2020): 47–88.
11. Smith, "Uncle Tom's (Ship) Cabin," 75–76.
12. Joan D. Hedrick, *Harriet Beecher Stowe: A Life* (New York: Oxford University Press, 1994), 308. This is a paraphrase of Acts 27:29: "Then fearing lest we should have fallen upon rocks, they cast four anchors out of the stern, and wished for the day" (King James Version [KJV]).
13. As Martha Schoolman notes, "*Uncle Tom's Cabin* . . . revolves around domestic questions that emerge *within* households . . . *Dred*, on the other hand, focuses on relations between households"; see her *Abolitionist Geographies* (Minneapolis: University of Minnesota Press, 2014), 164–65.
14. Carolyn L. Karcher, "Stowe and the Literature of Social Change," in *The Cambridge Companion to Harriet Beecher Stowe*, ed. Cindy Weinstein (Cambridge: Cambridge University Press, 2004), 203–4.

15. See, for example, Monika Mueller, "New England *Tempests*? Harriet Beecher Stowe's *The Minister's Wooing* and *The Pearl of Orr's Island*," in *Beyond "Uncle Tom's Cabin": Essays on the Writing of Harriet Beecher Stowe*, ed. Sylvia Mayer and Monika Mueller (Madison, NJ: Fairleigh Dickinson University Press, 2011), 125–44. Christopher P. Wilson examines the brief allusion to *The Tempest* in *The Minister's Wooing* in "Tempests and Teapots: Harriet Beecher Stowe's *The Minister's Wooing*," *New England Quarterly* 58, no. 4 (December 1985): 554–77.
16. For discussion of Stowe's and other women writers' attraction to the character of Miranda in *The Tempest*, see Elaine Showalter, *Sister's Choice: Tradition and Change in American Women's Writing* (Oxford: Clarendon Press; New York: Oxford University Press, 1991), 22–41. Showalter writes: "*The Tempest* has long been used by American women writers as a metaphorical account of the woman artist or feminist intellectual. Instead of looking to Caliban, American women writers from [Margaret] Fuller to Harriet Beecher Stowe, Louisa May Alcott, Katherine Anne Porter, Sylvia Plath, and Gloria Naylor have appropriated and revised the figure of Miranda in thinking about their relationship to patriarchal power, language, female sexuality, and creativity" (27–28). See also Mueller, "New England *Tempests*?"
17. Dorothy Z. Baker considers the novel's shipwreck imagery in relation to its theological and religious messages, grounding these images in Stowe's use of Puritan providence tales "as generic models for her fiction," in *America's Gothic Fiction: The Legacy of "Magnalia Christi Americana"* (Columbus: Ohio State University Press, 2007), 65–86; quotation is on 66. Judith Fetterley considers the theological context of shipwreck in relation to gender within the novel in "'Only a Story, Not a Romance': Harriet Beecher Stowe's *The Pearl of Orr's Island*," in *The (Other) American Traditions: Nineteenth-Century Women Writers*, ed. Joyce W. Warren (New Brunswick, NJ: Rutgers University Press, 1993), 121–22.
18. Baker, *America's Gothic Fiction*, 65–86.
19. Lori Merish, *Sentimental Materialism: Gender, Commodity Culture, and Nineteenth-Century American Literature* (Durham, NC: Duke University Press, 2000), 137, 138.
20. Stowe, *The Pearl of Orr's Island*, 5, 6.
21. See E. Bruce Kirkham, "The Source of the Shipwreck in *The Pearl of Orr's Island*," *American Transcendental Quarterly* 40 (Fall 1978): 365–66, for discussion of the November 1849 wreck of the *Hanover* at the mouth of the Kennebec River. Kirkham established that this wreck, which left bodies washing up on the Maine coast, was the source of Stowe's opening scene. More recently, Susan F. Beegel has extended this work, considering Stowe's own harrowing experience entering the mouth of the Kennebec and the ongoing local memorialization of the shipwreck in Maine. See Beegel, "Harriet Beecher Stowe and the Loss of the *Hanover*: Transforming a Maine Shipwreck in *The Pearl of Orr's Island*," *American Literary Realism* 50, no. 2 (Winter 2018): 123–44.
22. Stowe, *The Pearl of Orr's Island*, 6.
23. Stowe, *The Pearl of Orr's Island*, 8.
24. Ruth 1:20: "And she said unto them, Call me not Naomi, call me Mara: for the Almighty hath dealt very bitterly with me" (KJV).
25. Stowe, *The Pearl of Orr's Island*, 10.
26. Stowe, 32–33, 81.
27. Stowe, 43.
28. Stowe, 47, 66–67.

29. On our persistent tendency to envision underwater spaces in terms of terrestrial ones, see Melody Jue, *Wild Blue Media: Thinking through Seawater* (Durham, NC: Duke University Press, 2020), esp. 122–30.
30. Stowe, *The Pearl of Orr's Island*, 145–46, 150.
31. Stowe, 151–52.
32. Stowe, 72.
33. Stowe, 72.
34. See Margaret Cohen, *The Novel and the Sea* (Princeton, NJ: Princeton University Press, 2010).
35. Gillian Brown, "Reading and Children: *Uncle Tom's Cabin* and *The Pearl of Orr's Island*," in *The Cambridge Companion to Harriet Beecher Stowe*, ed. Cindy Weinstein (Cambridge: Cambridge University Press, 2004), 78.
36. Brown, "Reading and Children," 89, 91.
37. Brown, 78–79.
38. Stowe, *The Pearl of Orr's Island*, 188. The well-known line quoted here is from "Ariel's song" in Act 1, scene 2, of *The Tempest*, also a source for key images of Kittridge's tales of underwater worlds.
39. Hedrick, *Harriet Beecher Stowe*, 455n53. Here Hedrick glosses Judith Fetterley's reading of *The Pearl of Orr's Island* in the introduction to *Provisions: A Reader from 19th-Century American Women*, ed. Judith Fetterley (Bloomington: Indiana University Press, 1985), 13, 12.
40. Stowe, *The Pearl of Orr's Island*, 165, 167.
41. Stowe, 362–63.
42. Stowe, 352.
43. Stowe, 136, 176. The parallels between this episode of *The Pearl of Orr's Island* and Sarah Orne Jewett's short story "A White Heron" have been well established. See, for example, Katherine T. Jobes, "From Stowe's Eagle Island to Jewett's 'A White Heron,'" *Colby Library Quarterly* 10 (December 1974): 515–21.
44. Joan D. Hedrick, forward to *The Pearl of Orr's Island* (Boston: Houghton Mifflin, 2001), xiii.
45. Stowe, *The Pearl of Orr's Island*, 132.
46. Many have noted the biographical resonances of these concerns. In 1857, the year before she began writing *The Minister's Wooing*, Stowe's son Henry had drowned while swimming with friends. Her sister's fiancé had drowned at sea in 1822. "These deaths were especially painful for Stowe and her Calvinist family," writes Susan K. Harris, "because none of the victims had indicated signs of 'saving grace,' redemption from sin, before they died, and the survivors were haunted by the fear that their loved ones had gone to hell." See Harris, introduction to Stowe, *The Minister's Wooing* (New York: Penguin Books, 1999), vii.
47. Susan K. Harris, "The Female Imaginary in Harriet Beecher Stowe's *The Minister's Wooing*," *New England Quarterly* 66, no. 2 (June 1993): 180. See also Hedrick, *Harriet Beecher Stowe*, 276–84, for discussion of these concerns within the context of *The Minister's Wooing*.
48. Harriet Beecher Stowe, *The Minister's Wooing* (New York: Derby and Jackson, 1859), 347, 348. Page references are to this edition.
49. As the grandson of Jonathan Edwards, the historical figure of Aaron Burr highlights tensions between traditional Protestant theology and individualistic, impulsive behavior within the text. The Burr conspiracy and Burr's presence as a fictional character in

texts such as Leonora Sansay's *Secret History* (1808), set in early nineteenth-century Haiti, serve as reminders that this character is also a link to hemispheric, imperial histories.

50. Stowe, *The Minister's Wooing*, 256.
51. Stowe, 444, 455.
52. Schoolman, *Abolitionist Geographies*, 19.
53. Stowe, *The Minister's Wooing*, 9, 10.
54. Stowe, 27, 18.
55. For discussion of white, middle-class American households as "contact zones" where the domestic is inflected by "international connections" in a slightly later period, see Kristin L. Hoganson, *Consumers' Imperium: The Global Production of American Domesticity, 1865–1920* (Chapel Hill: University of North Carolina Press, 2007), 8.
56. Stowe, *The Pearl of Orr's Island*, 47, 93.
57. Stowe, *The Minister's Wooing*, 247–49.
58. Stowe, 250.
59. Stowe, 29.
60. Mary herself is associated with Catholic and Marian imagery throughout the novel. See John Gatta, *American Madonna: Images of the Divine Woman in Literary Culture* (Oxford: Oxford University Press, 1997), 62–67; Dorothy Z. Baker, "French Women, Italian Art, and Other 'Advocates of the Body' in Harriet Beecher Stowe's *The Minister's Wooing*," *New England Quarterly* 83, no. 1 (March 2010): 47–72; Joseph Helminski, "Harriet Beecher Stowe's Marianettes: Reconstruction of Womanhood in *The Minister's Wooing* and *Agnes of Sorrento*," in Mayer and Mueller, *Beyond "Uncle Tom's Cabin,"* 169–87; and Merish, *Sentimental Materialism*, 135–37. Much of this work, along with scholarship such as Neil Meyer's "'One Language in Prayer': Evangelicalism, Anti-Catholicism, and Harriet Beecher Stowe's *The Minister's Wooing*," *New England Quarterly* 85, no. 3 (September 2012): 468–90, takes up broader contexts of U.S. nineteenth-century attractions and aversions to Catholicism. For that context, see also Jenny Franchot, *Roads to Rome: The Antebellum Protestant Encounter with Catholicism* (Berkeley: University of California Press, 1994), and Elizabeth Fenton, *Religious Liberties: Anti-Catholicism and Liberal Democracy in Nineteenth-Century U.S. Literature and Culture* (New York: Oxford University Press, 2011).
61. Jenny Franchot, "Unseemly Commemoration: Religion, Fragments, and the Icon," *American Literary History* 9, no. 3 (Fall 1997): 506.
62. Merish, *Sentimental Materialism*, 137–38.
63. See Harris, "Female Imaginary," for discussion of the intersection of Marian and nature imagery in the novel, including imagery involving the sea.
64. Stowe, *The Minister's Wooing*, 458–59.
65. Stowe, 567.
66. Stowe, 116, 568.
67. Tess Chakkalakal, "'Whimsical Contrasts': Love and Marriage in *The Minister's Wooing* and *Our Nig*," *New England Quarterly* 84, no. 1 (March 2011): 165.
68. Stowe, *The Pearl of Orr's Island*, 60, 112, 119, 252–53.
69. Stowe, 267, 268.
70. Stowe, 282.
71. Stowe, 370.
72. It is worth noting that Sally, too, is often described as having a "Spanish complexion" and "Spanish eyes" (Stowe, 196, 305).

73. Hedrick, *Harriet Beecher Stowe*, 297.
74. See John Seelye, *Jane Eyre's American Daughters: From "The Wide, Wide World" to "Anne of Green Gables": A Study of Marginalized Maidens and What They Mean* (Newark: University of Delaware Press, 2005), for an account of some of these influences. Scholars, including Henry Louis Gates Jr., Hollis Robbins, and Catherine Keyser, have documented passages or echoes of passages from a number of English and American texts, including *Jane Eyre*, within Hannah Crafts's *The Bondswoman's Narrative*.
75. Monika Elbert, "Nature, Magic, and History in Stowe and Scott," in *Transatlantic Stowe: Harriet Beecher Stowe and European Culture*, ed. Denise Kohn, Sarah Meer, and Emily B. Todd (Iowa City: University of Iowa Press, 2006), 47. While *The Pearl of Orr's Island* might seem relatively conservative in its ending and its religious message of Christian devotion and faith, Elbert notes that it is nevertheless "less dogmatic and doctrinaire than Stowe's other New England historical novels," which can be in part attributed to its supernatural qualities (61). In *Scare Tactics: Supernatural Fiction by American Women* (New York: Fordham University Press, 2008), 37, Jeffrey Andrew Weinstock reads *The Pearl of Orr's Island* and a short story from Stowe's later *Sam Lawson's Oldtown Fireside Stories* (1872) alongside Spofford's *Sir Rohan's Ghost* and stories by Anna M. Hoyt and Edith Wharton, arguing that "the ostensibly anomalous presence of supernatural themes in local color realism, and the presentation of occult experience in such fiction as an extension of reality rather than an interruption of it, can be interpreted to a significant extent as the reflection of Spiritualist understandings of a continuum of being connecting natural to supernatural."
76. Michele Currie Navakas, *Liquid Landscape: Geography and Settlement at the Edge of Early America* (Philadelphia: University of Pennsylvania Press, 2018), 127.
77. Navakas, *Liquid Landscape*, 142, 153.

CHAPTER SIX: ELIZABETH STODDARD AND HARRIET PRESCOTT SPOFFORD

1. Elizabeth Stoddard, *The Morgesons*, ed. Lawrence Buell and Sandra A. Zagarell (New York: Penguin Books, 1997), 142–43.
2. As an example, in William Shaw's *Golden Dreams and Waking Realities; Being the Adventures of a Gold-Seeker in California and the Pacific Islands* (London: Smith, Elder, 1851), he describes "'beach comers' [*sic*]; comprising expired convicts from Sydney and Tasmania, Peruvians, Chilians [*sic*], Mexicans, and others, half sailors and half landsmen, who picked up a living in a somewhat questionable manner" as an "amphibious class" (165). He also refers to Samoans as "almost amphibious" (279) and on arriving at "Apea" (Apia, Samoa) notes: "Both sexes were excellent swimmers, playing about in the water quite at their ease, as if they were amphibious" (290). Melville used the term a few times in *Typee*. For example, "The amphibious young creatures swarmed about me like a shoal of dolphins" ([1846; New York: Penguin, 1996], 132). Laurent Dubois mentions that Médéric-Louis-Élie Moreau de Saint-Méry, in his 1797–98 *Description topographique, physique, civile, politique et historique de la partie française de l'isle Saint-Domingue*, referred to a group of white settlers left behind by the rise of sugar plantations in eighteenth-century Saint-Domingue as "'amphibious beings' whose lives as farmers and sailors recalled those of the colony's earlier settlers" (Dubois, *Avengers of the New World: The Story of the Haitian Revolution* [Cambridge, MA: Belknap Press of Harvard University Press, 2004], 20). The term emerges in both Pacific and Caribbean contexts, then, for Indigenous peoples, travelers, and settlers carving out an existence in island spaces.

3. R. J. Ellis writes that "it is reasonable to suggest" that Spofford's "The Amber Gods," "owes some structural debts to *Jane Eyre*," in "'Latent Color' and 'Exaggerated Snow': Whiteness and Race in Harriet Prescott Spofford's 'The Amber Gods,' *Journal of American Studies* 40, no. 2 (August 2006): 263n15. Spofford would later write a biographical and critical essay on Charlotte Brontë published as the introduction to an 1898 edition of *Jane Eyre*.
4. Amanda Claybaugh, *The Novel of Purpose: Literature and Social Reform in the Anglo-American World* (Ithaca, NY: Cornell University Press, 2007), 85.
5. Lawrence Buell and Sandra A. Zagarell, introduction to Stoddard, *The Morgesons*, ix.
6. Stoddard's "literary imagination is rooted," as Buell and Zagarell put it, "in the contemplation of the kind of small, ancient, ingrown New England seaport town in which she grew up" (introduction, xiii).
7. *Two Men* was published in 1865, and *Temple House* was published in 1867.
8. At the beginning of the second chapter of *Temple House* (New York: G.W. Carleton, 1867), 13, Stoddard writes that the town of Kent was "once a great seaport" but that "Commerce has gone elsewhere . . . A hundred younger towns on the Atlantic coast now surpass Kent; her sails are passing sails, her hulls wrecked hulls rotting in the sand."
9. Stoddard, *The Morgesons*, 252.
10. Stoddard, 8.
11. Stoddard, 32.
12. Stoddard, 9.
13. Stoddard, 7–8.
14. Stoddard, 22.
15. Stoddard, 5.
16. Stoddard, 6.
17. Stoddard, 33, 96, 152, 153.
18. See Jennifer Putzi, *Identifying Marks: Race, Gender, and the Marked Body in Nineteenth-Century America* (Athens: University of Georgia Press, 2006), 87: "With an understanding of the history of tattooing and the radical textual potential of tattoos, Stoddard's depiction of the marked female body emerges as a complex representation of one woman's 'battles' with her society's expectations for female behavior (*Morgesons* 173). Although forced to negotiate, even to compromise, her freedom, she remains an agent rather than a victim or an object, defining herself and her body as much as is possible in the society in which she lives."
19. Putzi, *Identifying Marks*, 98, 97.
20. Stoddard, *The Morgesons*, 97.
21. Shirley Samuels, *Reading the American Novel, 1780–1865* (Chichester, West Sussex, UK: Wiley-Blackwell, 2012), 33.
22. Stoddard, *The Morgesons*, 162.
23. Stoddard, 213–14.
24. Stoddard, 214.
25. Stoddard, 215.
26. Ayşe Çelikkol, "*The Morgesons*, Aesthetic Predicaments, and the Competitive Logic of the Market Economy," *American Literature* 78, no. 1 (March 2006): 50.
27. Çelikkol, "*The Morgesons*, Aesthetic Predicaments," 51–52.
28. Stoddard, *The Morgesons*, 62, 63.
29. Stoddard, 96.

30. Stoddard, 160.
31. Dorri Beam, *Style, Gender, and Fantasy in Nineteenth-Century American Women's Writing* (Cambridge: Cambridge University Press, 2010), 1, 5.
32. Beam, *Style, Gender, and Fantasy*, 2, 6.
33. Beam, 2, 6–7.
34. Beam, 139. "No one had *more* style than Spofford, quantitatively speaking," writes Beam earlier in her chapter on Spofford (133).
35. Harriet Prescott Spofford, "The Amber Gods," in *The Amber Gods, and Other Stories*, ed. Alfred Bendixon (New Brunswick, NJ: Rutgers University Press, 1989), 38.
36. See Dana Luciano, "Geological Fantasies, Haunting Anachronies: Eros, Time, and History in Harriet Prescott Spofford's 'The Amber Gods,'" *ESQ: A Journal of the American Renaissance* 55, nos. 3–4 (2009), esp. 289–92.
37. Spofford, "The Amber Gods," 77, 82, 76.
38. Spofford, 59, 60.
39. Spofford, 43–45.
40. See Luciano, "Geological Fantasies, Haunting Anachronies," for an extended discussion of these beads and of amber in relation to the narrative's queer temporalities.
41. Spofford, "The Amber Gods," 42.
42. I am indebted to Hilary Emmett for helping me work through these connections and ideas.
43. Spofford, "The Amber Gods," 48, 68.
44. The amber "rosary" with its "incense" is part of the broader nineteenth-century American interest in and aversion to Catholicism. See, for example, Jenny Franchot, *Roads to Rome: The Antebellum Protestant Encounter with Catholicism* (Berkeley: University of California Press, 1994), and Elizabeth Fenton, *Religious Liberties: Anti-Catholicism and Liberal Democracy in Nineteenth-Century U.S. Literature and Culture* (New York: Oxford University Press, 2011).
45. For histories of this exploitation in the Asia-Pacific region, see *Many Middle Passages: Forced Migration and the Making of the Modern World*, ed. Emma Christopher, Cassandra Pybus, and Marcus Rediker (Berkeley: University of California Press, 2007); Gerald Horne, *The White Pacific: U.S. Imperialism and Black Slavery in the South Seas after the Civil War* (Honolulu: University of Hawai'i Press, 2007); and H. E. Maude, *Slavers in Paradise: The Peruvian Slave Trade in Polynesia, 1862–1864* (Canberra: Australian National University Press, 1981).
46. See Lisa Lowe, *The Intimacies of Four Continents* (Durham, NC: Duke University Press, 2015), for discussion of how "the abolition of slavery and the importing of Chinese and South Asian indentured labor" are linked together and conjoined with "settler colonialism in North American and the West Indies and the African slave trade" and how "the differentially situated histories of indigeneity, slavery, industry, trade, and immigration give rise to linked, but not identical, genealogies of liberalism" (5, 11). Lowe's argument that "social relations in the colonized Americas, Asia, and Africa were the condition of possibility for Western liberalism to think the universality of human freedom, however much freedoms for slaves, colonized, and Indigenous peoples were precisely exempted by that philosophy," seems exemplified in "The Amber Gods" as Yone's radical claims of independence and freedom are predicated on the subordination of others and based in spaces associated with that subordination (16).
47. Spofford, "The Amber Gods," 45–46.
48. Spofford, 45–46.

49. Brian Russell Roberts and Michelle Ann Stephens, "Archipelagic American Studies: Decontinentalizing the Study of American Culture, in *Archipelagic American Studies*, ed. Brian Russell Roberts and Michelle Ann Stephens (Durham, NC: Duke University Press, 2017), 17.
50. Roberts and Stephens, "Archipelagic American Studies," 14.
51. Spofford, "The Amber Gods," 52.
52. Spofford, 53.
53. See Luciano, "Geological Fantasies, Haunting Anachronies," 273–79.
54. Spofford, "The Amber Gods," 83.
55. Spofford, 82.
56. Luciano, "Geological Fantasies, Haunting Anachronies," 297.
57. Luciano, 271; Paul Giles, "Afterword: The Archipelagic Accretion," in Roberts and Stephens, *Archipelagic American Studies*, 429.
58. Édouard Glissant, *Poetics of Relation*, trans. Betsy Wing (Ann Arbor: University of Michigan Press, 1997), 31, 34. On Faulkner, see 21 and 57, for example. Luciano, too, references Glissant's attention to the "'confusion of time'" in which the "'American novelist'" struggles ("Geological Fantasies, Haunting Anachronies," 298).
59. Giles, "Afterword," 430.
60. Samuels, *Reading the American Novel*, 33.
61. Spofford, "The Amber Gods," 59.
62. Melody Graulich, "Opening Windows toward the Sea: Harmony and Reconciliation in American Women's Sea Literature," in *Iron Men, Wooden Women: Gender and Seafaring in the Atlantic World, 1700–1920*, ed. Margaret S. Creighton and Lisa Norling (Baltimore, MD: Johns Hopkins University Press, 1996), 209. In this essay, Graulich surveys texts by a number of women, among them Stowe, Louisa May Alcott, Sarah Orne Jewett, Emily Dickinson, and Kate Chopin.

CODA

1. Caroline M. Kirkland, *A New Home, Who'll Follow? or, Glimpses of Western Life*, ed. Sandra A. Zagarell (1839; New Brunswick, NJ: Rutgers University Press, 1990), 97.
2. D. Stenton, A. Keenleyside, S. Fratpietro, and R. Park, "DNA Analysis of Human Skeletal Remains from the 1845 Franklin Expedition," *Journal of Archaeological Science: Reports* 16 (December 2017): 415.
3. See popular news reports of these findings, such as Jason Daley, "DNA Could Identify the Sailors (including Women) of the Doomed Franklin Expedition," Smithsonian .com, April 26, 2017, www.smithsonianmag.com/smart-news/dna-extracted-doomed -franklin-expedition-sailors-180963031/#IqfSZ7A5JJv5L5uG.99.
4. Edward Sugden, *Emergent Worlds: Alternative States in Nineteenth-Century American Culture* (New York: New York University Press, 2018), 45.
5. Kirkland, *A New Home*, 112; Review of *Mardi and a Voyage Thither*, Editorial, *Sartain's Union Magazine of Literature and Art*, August 1849, 126.
6. There is a great deal of work in this vein, especially surrounding the spatial turn in American literary studies. See, for example, Anne Baker, *Heartless Immensity: Literature, Culture, and Geography in Antebellum America* (Ann Arbor: University of Michigan Press, 2006), 1, for discussion of the "complicated, multifaceted impact on American culture" that the growth of the United States and "the geographical uncertainty it engendered" had during this period. See Stephanie LeMenager, *Manifest and Other Destinies: Territorial Fictions of the Nineteenth-Century United*

States (Lincoln: University of Nebraska Press, 2004), for discussion of heterotopic spaces that challenge national histories. Much of the work on settler colonialism and indigeneity in U.S. contexts that postdates Baker's and LeMenager's books also importantly contributes to our understanding of the historical unfixity of geographies once thought to be more stable within nineteenth-century texts and imaginaries.

7. J. Kēhaulani Kauanui, *Paradoxes of Hawaiian Sovereignty: Land, Sex, and the Colonial Politics of State Nationalism* (Durham, NC: Duke University Press, 2018), 3. Kanaka Maoli refers to Native Hawaiian peoples.
8. Kirkland, *A New Home*, 112.
9. R. L. Carson, "Undersea," *Atlantic Monthly*, September 1937, 322.
10. Jill Lepore, "The Shorebird: Rachel Carson and the Rising of the Seas," *New Yorker*, March 26, 2018, 64.
11. Kirkland, *A New Home*, 121.
12. Margaret Cohen, *The Novel and the Sea* (Princeton, NJ: Princeton University Press, 2010), 14. Cohen quotes the phrase "forgetting the sea" from photographer, writer, and theorist Allan Sekula.

Index

Page references in *italics* refer to figures. Titles including "attr." are presumed to be written by Lydia Maria Child.

An Account of the Natives of the Tonga Islands (Mariner), 41
Acts 27:29, 193n12
"Adventure in the Woods" (Child), 29, 30, 55
"The Adventures of a Bell" (Child), 180n53
Agnes of Sorrento (Stowe), 124
Alamo, Battle of the, 83, 84, 92, 98
"The Amber Gods" (Spofford): amphibious associations and archipelagic connections, overview, 15; Carson and, 166; *Jane Eyre* "fever" and, 145; plot and female agency in, 155–64
American Antiquarian Society, 67, *69*, *70*
"The American Traveller" (Child), 29–30
Ames, Nathaniel, 191n31
amphibious associations and archipelagic connections, 144–64; amphibiousness concept, 144–46; archipelagic relations concept, 3, 155–64; New England life and link to global circulation, 146–50; overview, 15; scale of sea and, 150–53; writing style and characters' relationship to sea, 153–55
The Amulet, or Christian and Literary Remembrancer, 36
Amundsen, Roald, 107
animals, in "Mary Howard" (Child), 53–54, 183n9
antebellum literature, printing, and publishing: culture of reprinting, 11, 13, 100–101; links between frontier and maritime world in, 101–3; print networks, overview, 11–12; Stowe's writing as literature of social change, 125. *See also* "The Amber Gods"; "Anxiety"; *Juvenile Miscellany;* language and writing; "Mary Howard"; *The Minister's Wooing*; *The Morgesons*; *A New Home, Who'll Follow?*; *The Pearl of Orr's Island*
"Anxiety" (Heywood), 77–78, 80–81, 88–94, 97–99, 101, 117, 166
Apess, William, 8
An Appeal for the Indians (Child), 27
An Appeal in Favor of That Class of Americans Called Africans (Child), 23
archipelagic American studies field, 16–17
archipelagic relations concept, 3, 155–64. *See also* amphibious associations and archipelagic connections
Arvin, Maile, 34, 178–79n39
Atlantic Monthly: "The Amber Gods" in, 155; *The Minister's Wooing* in, 124; "Undersea" in, 169
Austen, Jane, 141
Azima, Rachel, 100, 116

"The Babes in the Wood." *See* "The Children in the Wood"
Baker, Dorothy Z., 126, 194n17
Banks, Joseph, 29, 88, 94, 184–85n43
Barbauld, Anna Laetitia, 182n86
Barrow, John, 91–92, 93, 188n30
Beam, Dorri, 154–55, 156, 160
Beckner, Volney, 179n46
Beecher, Lyman, 79, 123, 124, 186n2
Belich, James, 21, 45
Benito Cereno (Melville), 2
Berger, Jason, 2, 102–3, 171n5, 190n10
Black Pacific, terminology for, 172n11
Bligh, William, 89, 94
Blum, Hester, 2
The Bondswoman's Narrative (Crafts), 142

Bonny, Anne, 6
Boston Recorder, in *The Morgesons,* 148
Boyd, attack on (1809), 58–60
A Brief Narrative of the Remarkable History of Barnet Burns (Burns), 61
Brontë, Charlotte, 141–42, 145, 198n3
Brooks, Peter, 192n51
Brown, Gillian, 129–30
Buell, Lawrence, 145, 198n6
Burnham, Michelle, 6, 94–95
Burns, Barnet, 61
Burr, Aaron, 195–96n49

calenture, 103–4
Captains of Charity (Eyring), 8–9
Carson, Rachel: *The Edge of the Sea,* 169; *The Sea around Us,* 169; *Silent Spring,* 168–69; "Undersea," 169; *Under the Sea-Wind,* 169
Cather, Willa, 110
Çelikkol, Ayşe, 152
Child, David Lee, 23
Child, Lydia Maria: "Adventure in the Woods," 29, 30, 55; "The Adventures of a Bell," 180n53; "The American Traveller," 29–30; *An Appeal for the Indians,* 27; *An Appeal in Favor of That Class of Americans Called Africans,* 23; attribution to, 26, 177n18, 179n45, 181–82n74; children's literature and sentimental domesticity, 9–10; "Dialogue, between the Shades of Duaterra, a New Zealand Chief, and Philip of Pokanocket" (attr.), 28, 44–48, 50, 58, 65, 166; *The First Settlers of New-England, or, Conquest of the Pequods, Narragansets and Pokanokets,* 45, 48, 50; global circulation in writing by, 145, 150, 158, 164; *Hobomok,* 23, 47–48, *48,* 49, 65; inspiration for stories by, 10, 12–14, 41, 100; as *Juvenile Miscellany* editor, 175–76n4; "Lealea-Hoku," 38–39, 44; *Letters from New-York,* 26, 177n19; *The Little, but Affecting History of Mary Howard,* 53, 67–71, *69, 70,* 185n56; *The Little Girl's Own Book,* 13, 26, 50–53, 68; "New Books" (attr.), 41–42, 52; "New Zealanders," 42, 52, 59–60; "New-Zealand Ideas of Writing" (attr.), 41–44; "Productions of the Sandwich Islands" (attr.), 38, 39, 44; "Tooi" (attr.), 21–24, *22,* 41, 44; "William Burton; or, the Boy Who Would Be a Sailor," 36–38, 40, 52, 180n53. See also *Juvenile Miscellany;* "Mary Howard"
"The Children in the Wood" ("The Babes in the Wood"), 54–56, 58, 71
children's literature. *See* Child, Lydia Maria; *Juvenile Miscellany;* "Mary Howard"
Christian, Fletcher, 89
Church Missionary Society, 24–26, 30
Claybaugh, Amanda, 145
coastal gothic, 121–43; antislavery messages by Stowe, 123–25, 135–36, 138, 140–42; domestic spaces and religion in Stowe's novels, 126–30, 133–39; gender roles and women at sea, 130–33, 142; shore as otherworldly place and, 121–23; Stowe in Florida and, 142–43; Stowe in Maine and, 123–26
Cohen, Margaret, 2, 111, 129
Colby, Belinda, 68, *70*
Cook, James, 4, 29, 60, 94, 149
Cooper, James Fenimore, 2, 13, 65, 101–3, 106, 112, 125
Cordell, Ryan, 11
The Country of the Pointed Firs (Jewett), 5, 123
Coverly, Nathaniel, Jr., 7
Crafts, Hannah, 142
Craik, George Lillie, 12–13, 26–27, 41–44, 47, 49, *51,* 58–61, 68, 73
Crain, Patricia, 23, 68
Craw, Elizabeth: "Anxiety" within Craw's diary, 14, 77–78, 80–81, 88–94, 97–99, 100, 101, 117, 166; diary structure of, 79, 81, 86–87, 186n1, 186–87n4, 187n20; travels from Ohio to Texas by, 10, 12, 78–88, *82, 85;* unpublished status of diary, 2

Crawford, Mrs. (poet), 87
culture of reprinting, 11, 13, 100–101

Davidson, Cathy, 185n55
Day, Iyko, 10
Deephaven (Jewett), 193n7
Defoe, Daniel, 34, 36, 40, 101, 110–11
Dening, Greg, 188n29
A Description of Pitcairn's Island and Its Inhabitants (Barrow), 92, 93
"Dialogue, between the Shades of Duaterra, a New Zealand Chief, and Philip of Pokanocket" (Child, attr.), 28, 44–48, 50, 58, 65, 166
Dolin, Eric Jay, 106–7
Dolphin (U.S. schooner), 36
"The Dream Is Past" (song), 86, 188n23
Dred (Stowe), 124, 193n13
Duane, Anna Mae, 26
Dubois, Laurent, 197n2
Duneer, Anita, 8
Duty (M. Roberts), 87

The Edge of the Sea (Carson), 169
Ellis, Juniper, 62, 63, 181n64
Ellis, Ngārino, 49, 180–81n62, 182–83n2
Ellis, R. J., 198n3
Endeavor journal, on tattooing, 184–85n43
enslaved people and slave economies: the Atlantic world and, 5; gendered agency and, 156–60; Missouri Compromise of 1820 and, 185n48; Stowe's antislavery messages and, 123–25, 135–36, 138, 140–42
Evans, Samuel, 83, 84, 86, 187n17
The Eventful History of the Mutiny and Piratical Seizure of H.M.S. Bounty (Barrow), 91–92, 93, 188n30
Eyring, Mary, 8–9

Faulkner, William, 163
The Female American; or, the Adventures of Unca Eliza Winkfield, 110
The Female Marine (Coverly), 7
"A Female Robinson Crusoe" (*New York Times*), 110–11
Ferguson, Frances, 182n86
Fetterley, Judith, 194n17
The First Settlers of New-England, or, Conquest of the Pequods, Narragansets and Pokanokets (Child), 45, 48, 50
"The Fisherman's Family," 36
Florida, Stowe's life in, 142–43
Foote, Samuel, 123
Forest Life (Kirkland), 112
Franchot, Jenny, 137
Franklin, John, 107
Franklin Expedition, 107, 165–66
Fraser, Eliza, 63, 64, 65
frontier and maritime world, 100–117; antebellum literature and links between, 101–3; cautions to settlers about, 100–101, 111–13; female travelers and, 110–11, 165–66; fluidity and mobility metaphors in oceanic and maritime scholarship, 113–17; hollow earth theory and, 107–10; *A New Home, Who'll Follow?* as cautionary tale for settlers, 100–101, 111–13; *A New Home, Who'll Follow?* plot, 1, 103–9
Fuller, Margaret, 6, 7, 154

gender and gender roles: expectations of racial purity and, 12, 62–65; female agency, 146–50, 155–64, 198n18; female hysteria concept and, 93–94; female travelers and, 110–11, 165–66; male public and female private concepts, 7–8, 173–74n22; in "Mary Howard," 50–52, 62–73; oceanic and domestic spheres, overview, 5–11, 172n14; *Robinson Crusoe* and plots about female adventurers, 110–11; Stowe on gender roles and women at sea, 130–33, 142; tattoos and, 62–65, 72, 149, 184n43, 185n47, 198n18
Giles, Paul, 3, 65, 162
Glissant, Édouard, 162–63, 175n41
Globe, mutiny on, 36, 37
Godey's Lady's Book: Kirkland and, 1; "Recollections" in, 88
Golden Dreams and Waking Realities (Shaw), 197n2

Goodrich, Samuel Griswold, 31–34, *32*, 39
Gould, Hannah Flagg, 88
Graulich, Melody, 163
Guard, Elizabeth, 62–63, 64, 65

Hale, Sarah Josepha, 8–9, 54
Hall, Francis, 24–25
Hall, James, 100, 102, 103, 112
Hanover, shipwreck of, 194n21
Hardy, R. W. H., 35
Harris, Susan K., 195n46
Hau'ofa, Epeli, 16, 115
Hawthorne, Nathaniel, 126
Hedrick, Joan, 132, 142
Hendler, Glenn, 173–74n22
Henry, Patrick, 96
Heywood, Nessy: "Anxiety" (poem) and Craw, 14, 77–78, 80–81, 88–94, 97–99, 100, 101, 117, 166; death of, 92–94
Heywood, Peter, 77, 89–92, 95, 97
The History of Mary Prince (Prince), 5
HMS *Bounty:* Heywood family and, 77–78, 88–95; historical narrative and, 188n29; *Peter Parley's Tales about the Islands in the Pacific Ocean* and, 31; settler colonialism and, 97–99
HMS *Erebus*, 165
HMS *Hector*, 77, 91
HMS *Pandora*, 89, 95
HMS *Terror*, 165
Hobomok (Child), 23, 47–48, *48*, 49, 65
Hoffman, Charles Fenno, 100
hollow earth theory, 107–10
Hope Leslie (Sedgwick), 65
Hopkins, Pauline, 154
Houston, Sam, 83, 95–96
Hussey, Cyrus, 37
hydrophasia, 2, 170

Incidents in the Life of a Slave Girl (Jacobs), 8
"incorrigible children," 72, 186n63
Independent (Congregationalist weekly), 122, 124
"The Indian Hater" (J. Hall), 102
Indian Removal Act of 1830, 65, 185n48
The Intimacies of Four Continents (Lowe), 199n46
Irving, Washington, 45–46

Jackson, Andrew, 23
Jacobs, Harriet, 8
Jane Eyre (Brontë), 141–42, 145, 198n3
Jemison, Mary, 64–65
Jenkins, Kuni Kaa, 25, 176n11
Jewett, Sarah Orne, 5, 123, 193n7
Jones, Alison, 25, 176n11
Journal of a Cruise (Paulding), 36, 37–38, 49
Journal of a Residence in the Sandwich Islands (Stewart), 38
Juvenile Miscellany, 21–48; articles about oceanic voyaging in, 34–39; Child as editor of, 175–76n4; Child's sources for written works in, 12–14, 21–28, *22*, 41, 44–48, *48*; *The Little Girl's Own Book* and, 52; moral instruction in, 40–44; *The Morgesons* and, 148; pedagogically oriented literature in, 28–35, *32*, 40, 43

Kaplan, Amy, 9, 103
Karcher, Carolyn, 24, 125
Kauanui, J. Kēhaulani, 167
Kendall, Thomas, 25
Kerber, Linda, 173–74n22
A Key to Uncle Tom's Cabin (Stowe), 124
Kilcup, Karen, 29
King, Edward, 91
King Philip/Metacom, 45, 46
King Philip's War, 44–48
Kirkham, E. Bruce, 194n21
Kirkland, Caroline: *Forest Life*, 112; as *Sartain's Union Magazine of Literature and Art* editor, 114. See also *A New Home, Who'll Follow?*

Ladies' Magazine, "Recollections" in, 88
language and writing: Māori language recorded in English, 24–28, 176n11; in "Mary Howard," 50, 55–57, 68, *69*, *70*, 73; in *The Pearl of Orr's Island*, 139–41; in relation to Māori signatures and drawings, 49, 181nn63–64, 182–83n2; of Tahitians, 95; tattooing, selfhood, and, 40–43
The Last of the Mohicans (Cooper), 65
Lay, William, 37
"Lealea-Hoku" (Child), 38–39, 44

Ledyard, John, 29–30, 35
Lee, Samuel, 25
LeMenager, Stephanie, 186–87n4
Lepore, Jill, 169
Letters from New-York (Child), 26, 177n19
Library of Entertaining Knowledge, 26
Life among the Indians ("as told by" Oatman), 64, 185n47
Light Gives Light, to Light Discover—"Ad Infinitum" (Symmes), 107–10, 190n29
The Little, but Affecting History of Mary Howard, 53, 67–71, *69*, *70*, 185n56
The Little Girl's Own Book (Child), 13, 26, 50–53, 68. *See also* "Mary Howard"
Lowe, Lisa, 9, 98, 199n46
Luciano, Dana, 161, 162–63
"Lycidas" (Milton), 90–91

Maddox, Lucy, 26–27
Maine, Stowe's life in, 123–26. See also *The Pearl of Orr's Island*
Malcolm, John, 87
"Manifest Domesticity" (Kaplan), 9, 103
Māori people: Burns's life with, 61; Child's sources for *Juvenile Literacy* references to, 21–28, *22*, 41, 43–48; Child's sources for "Mary Howard" references to, 13–14, 49–53, 58–60; first British troops in New Zealand and, 62; Pākehā, defined, 24, 56. *See also* "Mary Howard"
Mardi (Melville), 114–15, 166
Mariner, William, 41
Marsden, Samuel, 24–25, 26, 45
"Mary Had a Little Lamb" (Hale), 54
"Mary Howard" (Child), 49–73; authorship of, 26; Craw's writing and, 87; gender roles in, 50–52, 62–73; inspiration for, 13–14, 49–53, *51*; Kirkland's writing and, 106; morality lessons of, 57–60, 71–73; New Zealand depiction in, overview, 28; oceanic associations and marks on bodies, 150; plot of, 53–57; tattoos and importance to, 49, 56–57, 59–67, *64*, *66*, 68, 71, 72
Mayhew, Caroline, 172n14
McClintock, Anne, 9
McGill, Meredith, 11, 13, 100–101
Melville, Herman: *Benito Cereno*, 2; inspiration for stories by, 13, 197n2; *Mardi*, 115–16, 166; *Moby-Dick*, 2, 24, 49–50, *51*, 73, 170; *Omoo*, 2; *Redburn*, 114; *Typee*, 2, 4, 24, 33, 36, 61, 114, 197n2
Memoir of Mowhee, a Young New Zealander (Woodd), 30–31
Merish, Lori, 126, 137
Mexico, U.S.-Mexican War, 78, 83–84, 96–99
Michigan, settlers in. *See* frontier and maritime world
Mielke, Laura, 27, 29, 180n53
Milton, John, 90–91
The Minister's Wooing (Stowe), 14–15, 122–26, 133–39, 141–43
Miskolcze, Robin, 9
Missouri Compromise of 1820, 185n48
Moby-Dick (Melville), 2, 24, 49–50, *51*, 73, 170
moko (Māori tattoo), 41, 43, 49, 61, 72. *See also* tattoos
Moreau de Saint-Méry, Médéric-Louis-Élie, 197n2
Morgan, Jennifer L., 5
The Morgesons (Stoddard): amphibious associations and archipelagic connections, overview, 15; "associations are amphibious" in, 144–46; Carson and, 169; gender and agency in, 146–50, 160, 163–64, 198n18; plot of, 146–53, 156; on tattoos, 185n47; writing style in, 153–55
Murison, Justine, 93
Musket Wars, 46
My Ántonia (Cather), 110

Naomi (biblical character), 127
The Narrative of Arthur Gordon Pym of Nantucket (Poe), 108, 191n32
A Narrative of the Life and Travels of Mrs. Nancy Prince (Prince), 5
Narrative of the Shipwreck, Captivity and Sufferings of Horace Holden and Benj. H. Nute, 61
Navakas, Michele, 142–43
"New Books" (Child, attr.), 41–42, 52

New England, stories about. See *The Minister's Wooing*; *The Morgesons*; *The Pearl of Orr's Island*
A New Home, Who'll Follow? (Kirkland): as cautionary tale for settlers, 100–101, 111–13; female travelers and, 110–11, 165–66; fluidity and mobility metaphors, 113–17, 160; frontier and maritime world in popular antebellum literature, 10, 12, 14, 101–3; Northwest Passage reference in, 107, 165–66; plot of, 1, 103–9; Stowe's writing and, 125, 133
"The New Moon" (Hall), 102
Newport, Rhode Island. See *The Minister's Wooing*
New York Times, "A Female Robinson Crusoe," 110–11
New Zealand, Māori characters and Child's sources, 21–28, *22*, 41, 43–48, *48*
"New Zealanders" (Child), 42, 52, 59–61
The New Zealanders (Craik), 12–13, 26–27, 41–43, 47, 49, *51*, 58–61, 68, 73
"New-Zealand Ideas of Writing" (Child, attr.), 41–44
Norling, Lisa, 8
Northwest Passage, 107, 165–66

Oatman, Olive, 64–65, *66*, 185n47
oceanic and maritime scholarship: Black Pacific, terminology, 172n11; fluidity and mobility metaphors in, 113–17; *Juvenile Miscellany* articles about oceanic voyaging, 34–39; Steinberg on trends in, 191–92n50; terminology for, 15–17; whaling industry and, 4, 171–20n10. *See also* amphibious associations and archipelagic connections; coastal gothic; frontier and maritime world; settler colonialism, indigeneity, and race; transoceanic anxiety
O'Connell, James F., 61, 63
Ohio, travel from. *See* Craw, Elizabeth; transoceanic anxiety
Omoo (Melville), 2
The Oregon Trail (Parkman), 102
Otter, Samuel, 61

Pacific Ocean (map) in *Peter Parley's Tales about the Islands in the Pacific Ocean*, *32*
Pākehā, defined, 24, 56
Parkman, Francis, 102, 103, 112
Paulding, Hiram, 36, 37–38, 40, 49
The Pearl of Orr's Island (Stowe): antislavery messages in, 123–25, 135–36, 138, 140–42; coastal gothic, overview, 14–15; domestic space and religion in Stowe's novels, 126–30, 133–39; gender roles and women at sea, 130–33, 142; shore as otherworldly place and, 121–23; Stowe's connection to coastal living and, 123–26, 142–43
Peter Parley's Tales about the Islands in the Pacific Ocean (Goodrich), 31–34, *32*, 39, 71
Philbrick, Thomas, 101–2, 103
Philip of Pokanoket (King Philip), 44–48
Philosophy of Natural History (Smellie), 35
Poe, Edgar Allan, 1, 4, 108, 191n32
Pratt, Josiah, 24
Prince, Mary, 5
Prince, Nancy, 5
Proceedings of the Church Missionary Society, 26
"Productions of the Sandwich Islands" (Child, attr.), 38, 39, 44
Putzi, Jennifer, 149–50

Read, Mary, 6
Reading for the Plot (Brooks), 192n51
"Recollections" (Gould), 88
Redburn (Melville), 114
Red River Herald (Natchitoches, Louisiana), 83
religion: domestic space and religion in Stowe's novels, 126–30, 133–39; missionaries in New Zealand, 21, 24–28, 30–34, 40, 44, 46; missionaries in Sandwich Islands (Hawaii), 38–39; morality instruction in *Juvenile Miscellany* and, 40–44; morality instruction in "Mary Howard" and, 57–60, 71–73; rosary reference in "The Amber Gods," 158, 199n44

A Residence of Eleven Years in New Holland and the Caroline Islands (O'Connell), 61
Reynolds, Jeremiah, 108
Rhys, Jean, 141
Rice University, 79
Roberts, Brian Russell, 3, 17, 160
Roberts, Margaret, 87
Robinson Crusoe (Defoe), 34, 36, 40, 101, 110–11, 190n10
Rose, Jacqueline, 72
Rosenberg, Jordy, 113, 191–92n50
Rowlandson, Mary, 58
Ruatara, 44, 46, 50, 59
Rutherford, John, 41, 61

Samuels, Shirley, 65, 150, 163
Sanborn, Geoffrey, 43, 49
Sanbornton Press (New Hampshire), 67, *69*, *70*, 185n55
Sartain's Union Magazine of Literature and Art, Kirkland as editor of, 114
Schoolman, Martha, 135, 193n13
Scioto Gazette (Chillicothe, Ohio), on Texas-Mexico tensions, 83, 95–97, 187n13
The Sea around Us (Carson), 169
Sedgwick, Catharine Maria, 65
Sedgwick, Eve, 173–74n22
Selkirk, Alexander, 31
Seminole Wars, 23
settler colonialism, indigeneity, and race: captivity in "Adventure in the Woods," 29; Child's sources for related stories, 21–28, *22*, 41, 43–48, *48*; conceptual contact of distant spaces, 166–68, 200–201n6; expectations of racial purity, 11–12; facial tattooing and, 64; HMS *Bounty* and, 97–99; imperial relationships of early nineteenth century, overview, 10–11; Indian Removal Act of 1830, 65, 185n48; King Philip's War and, 44–48; *The Narrative of Arthur Gordon Pym of Nantucket*, 191n32; Seminole Wars and, 23; U.S.-Mexican War and, 95–97; Western construction of Polynesian race, 178–79n39; white benevolence concept, 180n53. *See also* enslaved people and slave economies; gender and gender roles; Māori people; tattoos; transoceanic anxiety
Shakespeare, William, 125, 128–30, 141, 194n16, 195n38
Sharpe, Christina, 5
Shaw, William, 197n2
Showalter, Elaine, 194n16
Sigourney, Lydia Huntley, 8, 9, 116
Silent Spring (Carson), 169
Sinche, Bryan, 115–16
Sketchbook (Irving), 45–46
slavery. *See* enslaved people and slave economies
Smellie, William, 35
Smith, Cynthia Alicia, 123
Society for the Diffusion of Useful Knowledge, 26
Soderberg, Laura, 72, 186n63
Spaulding, Sarah, 68
Spofford, Harriet Prescott: "The Amber Gods," 15, 117, 143, 145, 155–64, 166, 169; on gender restrictions, overview, 10, 12
Steinberg, Philip E., 192n50
Stephens, Ann, 154
Stephens, Michelle Ann, 3, 17, 160
Stewart, Charles Samuel, 38, 39
Stoddard, Elizabeth: *The Morgesons*, 2, 10, 12, 15, 117, 122, 143, 144–56, 160, 163–64, 169, 185n47; *Temple House*, 146, 198n8; *Two Men*, 146
Stoler, Ann Laura, 9
Stowe, Charles "Charley," 124
Stowe, Frederick, 142
Stowe, Harriet Beecher: *Agnes of Sorrento*, 124; coastal gothic, overview, 10, 12, 117; *Dred*, 124, 193n13; family of, 79, 186n2; *A Key to Uncle Tom's Cabin*, 124; *The Minister's Wooing*, 14–15, 122–26, 133–39, 141–43; *The Pearl of Orr's Island*, 14–15, 121–36, 139–42; *Uncle Tom's Cabin*, 79, 122–25, 130, 193n13. *See also* coastal gothic
Stowe, Henry, 124, 195n46
The Swiss Family Robinson, 110
Symmes, John Cleves, Jr., 107–10, 190n29, 191n31

Symmes, John (uncle), 190n29
Symzonia, 108, 109, 191n31

Tahiti: HMS *Bounty* in, 31, 77–78, 88–95, 97–99; language and writing of, 95
Tales of Field and Flood, with Sketches of Life at Home (Malcolm), 87
"Tattooing on the face of Tupai Cupa, from a drawing by himself" (in *The New Zealanders*), *51*
tattoos: in *Endeavor* journal, 184–85n43; Māori signatures and drawings and, 49, 181nn63–64, 182–83n2; "Mary Howard" and importance of, 49, *51,* 56–57, 59–67, *64, 66,* 68, 71, 72; *moko,* 41, 43, 49, 61, 72; *The Morgesons* and female agency, 146–50, 198n18; of Tahitians, 95; terminology for, 180–81n62
Te Ara, 58–59
The Tempest (Shakespeare), 125, 128–30, 141, 194n16, 195n38
Temple House (Stoddard), 146, 198n8
Te Pahi, 58–59
Te Pehi Kupe/Tupai Cupa, 49, 50, *51*
terraqueous globe: Black Pacific, terminology, 172n11; fluidity and mobility metaphors in oceanic and maritime scholarship, 113–17. *See also* oceanic and maritime scholarship; transoceanic anxiety
Texas, settlers in. *See* transoceanic anxiety
Texas Revolution, 78, 83–84, 95–99, 187n13
Thomas, Nicholas, 50
Tītere/Teeterree (Māori man), 24–26, 30, 50, 176n7
"To Mary" (Wolfe), 86
Tomasek, Kathryn, 67
"Tooi" (Child, attr.), 21–24, *22,* 41, 43
"Traits of Indian Character" (Irving), 45
transoceanic anxiety, 77–99; "Anxiety" within Craw's diary, 14, 77–78, 80–81, 88–94, 97–99, 100, 101, 117, 166; Craw's diary of travels from Ohio to Texas and, 78–88, *82, 85;* Craw's diary structure and, 79, 81, 86–87, 186n1, 186–87n4, 187n20; empire and revolution as causes of anxiety, 93–99
Travels (Hardy), 35
Tuai/Tooi (Māori man), 24–26, 30, 50, 176n7
Two Men (Stoddard), 146
Typee (Melville), 2, 4, 24, 33, 36, 61, 114, 197n2

Uncle Tom's Cabin (Stowe), 79, 122–25, 130, 193n13
"Undersea" (Carson), 169
Under the Sea-Wind (Carson), 169
United States Exploring Expedition (U.S. Ex. Ex.), 108–10, 115
U.S.-Mexican War, 78, 83–84, 95–99

"Volney Beckner" (*Juvenile Miscellany*), 36, 179n46

"The Wanderer Come Home" (Crawford), 87
"War in Texas" (*Scioto Gazette*), 83, 95–97, 187n13
Warner, Susan, 142
westward settlement in United States. *See* frontier and maritime world; transoceanic anxiety
whaling industry, 4, 171–72n10
Wheatley, Phillis, 5
Whittemore, D., 68, *70*
The Wide, Wide World (Warner), 142
Wide Sargasso Sea (Rhys), 141
Wigginton, Caroline, 11–12
"William Burton; or, the Boy Who Would Be a Sailor" (Child), 36–38, 40, 52, 180n53
Wolfe, Charles, 86
Woman in the Nineteenth Century (Fuller), 6, 7
Woodd, Basil, 30–31

Zagarell, Sandra, 145, 198n6